Rethinking Assessment in Higher Education

Assessment is a value-laden activity surrounded by debates about academic standards, preparing students for employment, measuring quality and providing incentives. There is substantial evidence that assessment, rather than teaching, has the major influence on students' learning. It directs attention to what is important, acts as an incentive for study, and has a powerful effect on students' approaches to their work.

Rethinking Assessment in Higher Education revisits assessment in higher education and examines it from the point of view of what assessment does and can do. Challenging the overwhelming dominance of marks and grades, expert contributors from a range of countries suggest that we need to think differently about assessment if it is to make a useful contribution to the educational purposes of higher education. Key topics covered include:

- The link between assessment, teaching and learning
- The role of assessment for certification
- The contradictions that occur in assessment today
- The operation of feedback in assessment processes
- The place of self- and peer assessment
- The link between assessment and emotions

Rethinking Assessment in Higher Education argues that assessment should be seen as an act of informing judgement and proposes a way of integrating teaching, learning and assessment to prepare students better for a lifetime of learning. It is essential reading for practitioners and policy-makers in higher education institutions in different countries, as well as for educational development and institutional research practitioners.

David Boud is Professor of Adult Education at the University of Technology, Sydney, and was formerly President of the Higher Education Research and Development Society of Australasia.

Nancy Falchikov, a psychologist by training, is a Research Fellow at the University of Edinburgh. She has taught in higher education for many years, and conducts research into student involvement in assessment and peer learning.

Rethinking Assessment in Higher Education

Learning for the longer term

Edited by David Boud and Nancy Falchikov

Routledge
Taylor & Francis Group

LONDON AND NEW YORK

First published 2007
by Routledge
2 Park Square, Milton Park, Abingdon, Oxon OX14 4RN

Simultaneously published in the USA and Canada
by Routledge
270 Madison Ave, New York, NY 10016

Transferred to Digital Printing 2008

Routledge is an imprint of the Taylor & Francis Group, an informa business

© 2007 selection and editorial matter, David Boud and Nancy Falchikov;
individual chapters, the contributors

Typeset in TimesNewRoman by
Keystroke, 28 High Street, Tettenhall, Wolverhampton
Printed and bound in Great Britain by
CPI Antony Rowe, Chippenham, Wiltshire

British Library Cataloguing in Publication Data
A catalogue record for this book is available from the British Library

Library of Congress Cataloging in Publication Data
Rethinking assessment in higher education: learning for the longer term/
edited by David Boud and Nancy Falchikov.
        p.cm.
    Includes bibliographic references and index.
    1. College students–Rating of. 2. Educational tests and measurements.
    I. Boud, David. II. Falchikov, Nancy, 1939–
    LB2368.R47 2007
    378.1'662–dc22   2006026519

ISBN10: 0–415–39778–2 (hbk)
ISBN10: 0–415–39779–0 (pbk)
ISBN10: 0–203–96430–6 (ebk)

ISBN13: 978–0–415–39778–0 (hbk)
ISBN13: 978–0–415–39779–7 (pbk)
ISBN13: 978–0–203–96430–9 (ebk)

Contents

Illustrations

Tables

Figures

Box

Contributors

Ronald Barnett, Professor of Higher Education, Institute of Education, University of London, UK

David Boud, Professor of Adult Education, University of Technology, Sydney, Australia

Filip Dochy, Professor, Department of Educational Sciences, University of Leuven, Belgium

Kathryn Ecclestone, Reader in Educational Assessment, Centre for Developing and Evaluating Lifelong Learning, University of Nottingham, UK

Nancy Falchikov, Honorary Research Fellow, Higher and Community Education, University of Edinburgh, Scotland, and Honorary Associate, Faculty of Education, University of Technology, Sydney, Australia

David Gijbels, Institute for the Science of Education and Information, University of Antwerp, Belgium

Dai Hounsell, Professor of Higher Education, University of Edinburgh, Scotland

Peter Kandlbinder, Institute of Multimedia and Learning, University of Technology, Sydney, Australia

Margaret Kirkwood, Department of Educational Studies, University of Strathclyde, Scotland

Peter Knight, Professor and Director, Institute of Educational Technology, the Open University, UK

Steinar Kvale, Professor, Department of Psychology, Århus University, Denmark

Mien Segers, Professor of Educational Sciences, University of Leiden, the Netherlands

Katrien Struyven, Centre for Research on Teaching and Training, University of Leuven, Belgium

Kelvin Tan, Department of Leadership and Policy Studies, National Institute of Education, Singapore

Part 1

Setting the scene

Chapter 1

Introduction

Assessment for the longer term

David Boud and Nancy Falchikov

Assessment affects people's lives. The future directions and careers of students depend on it. There are risks involved in changing assessment without considering the consequences. This has meant that there has been very slow movement in the development of new assessment ideas and changes in practice. We face a system of assessment that has been subject to slow incremental change, to compromise and to inertia. We are afraid to change the system because of the risks, but we also avoid looking at it because doing so might entail major effort.

Assessment frames students' views of higher education. It is also a major concern and burden for those teaching them. However, it is such a commonplace matter that we often make assumptions about assessment on the basis of what we have experienced in the past rather than in terms of the new circumstances that confront us. Assessment has also influenced our own paths as learners and has contributed to our gaining the positions we now hold. This means that we have a considerable personal investment in what has appeared to work in the past.

What is at stake here is the nature of higher education itself. Assessment, rather than teaching, has a major influence on students' learning. It directs attention to what is important. It acts as an incentive for study. And it has a powerful effect on what students do and how they do it. Assessment also communicates to them what they can and cannot succeed in doing. For some, it builds their confidence for their future work; for others, it shows how inadequate they are as learners and undermines their confidence about what they can do in the future.

Assessment would be less of a problem if we could be assured that what occurs under the guise of assessment appropriately influenced student learning. However, when we look at the content and approaches used in the dominant assessment practices in higher education, we find that they are often focused on students demonstrating current knowledge, generating material for grading and getting (often inadequate) feedback from teachers. Commonly, assessment focuses little on the processes of learning and on how students will learn after the point of assessment. In other words, assessment is not sufficiently equipping students to learn in situations in which teachers and examinations are not present to focus their attention. As a result, we are failing to prepare them for the rest of their lives.

The beginnings of change

Discussions of assessment are commonly dominated by the needs of certification: what is the best or most efficient method of assessment? How should grades be recorded? How should they be assembled? What constitutes a first-class honours degree? This focus tends to eclipse considerations of the impact of assessment on learning. Time and energy are devoted to assessment activities that are completed too late for them to have an impact on students' learning. In addition, the certi- fication debate has prompted student anxiety and demands that all work be counted for marks and grades. Thus, summative assessment has secured its foothold.

The past ten years has seen a counter-movement to the emphasis on what Peter Knight (2006) has termed 'high-stakes assessment'. Assessment for learning has begun to take a place on the agenda within institutions, although it still takes a secondary place in public policy debates and in the media. One marker of the change of emphasis was the 1998 publication of a substantial literature review by Black and Wiliam. This examined research on formative assessment – that is, how assessment influences learning – and pointed to a number of fruitful directions for development. While this work has had the greatest impact on assessment in schools in the UK, it has also been taken up and used to justify a renewed emphasis on assessment for learning in higher education. Since then there has been a flourishing of papers about assessment for learning in higher education. These have focused on such matters as the role of feedback for learning, the consequential effects of assessment practices on student behaviour, the types of learning that various assessment regimes prompt, the need to align assessment with desired student outcomes and so on. There is now a substantial body of knowledge on which to draw, much of which is addressed in this book.

We are now in a position to step back and challenge the controlling effect of assessment that focuses students on the performance of assessment itself, rather than on what studying in higher education is arguably for: that is, providing a foundation for a lifetime of learning and work in which there is little formal assessment or formal instruction.

The aim of this book

We have been troubled for some time about these problems of assessment. In discussion we came to the conclusion that it was timely to review the state of the assessment debate and consider how assessment can provide an adequate basis for the future. In particular we were concerned that assessment was having a deleterious effect on learning and was not providing a sound basis for learning beyond graduation. What alternatives were there to the common practices we encountered every day? We were aware that there had been many innovations in assessment, some of which have, often partially or indirectly, attempted to address this problem. These have gone under a variety of headings, such as portfolio assessment, self- and peer assessment, authentic assessment and so on.

We identified that, to date, there had been little effort to bring these together around the major purpose of equipping students to learn for the long term. There was, we believed, a need to conceptualise this clearly as an important goal for assessment and to explore the variety of practices that might be utilised to this end. Our view was that students need to develop their own repertoire of assessment-related practices that they will be able to use when confronted with learning challenges throughout their working lives. We realised that, at present, assessment in higher education did not place this as a significant outcome compared to certifying existing knowledge and giving students feedback on current learning.

This led us to begin to formulate a proposal for a book that would look beyond the immediate practices of assessment to consider what assessment would look like if we took seriously the need for it to provide students with a firm foundation for their learning after they had completed their programmes of study. There are now signs that an increasing number of people are willing to confront the challenge of assessment and think differently about it. Momentum has been slowly building towards a more substantial rethinking of assessment than we have seen before. There are many examples of this rethinking in the research literature, but so far they do not seem to have had much impact on overall practice. Indeed, there are few signs that those who most influence assessment policy and practice are even aware that such rethinking is taking place.

We saw a need to bring together some of the most interesting of the reappraisals of assessment and to focus these on the central aim of higher education of preparing students for a lifetime of learning in work and in the community. The key question asked in the book is: how can assessment influence learners in what they do after graduation? It looks to the longer term and explores what can be done in university courses to prepare students for a lifetime of learning and professional work.

Earlier origins

It is easy to portray this book solely as responding to our perceptions of the condition of higher education now. However, all books are located in the experiences and concerns of their authors and are influenced by their biographies. This book emerged from the encounters the editors and contributors have had with assessment during their lives. We have been touched by assessment and it has to a greater or lesser extent affected what we have done and what opportunities we have taken up. While the book aims to be a scholarly contribution to an important current issue, it is also shaped by the experiences of those who write. While the theme of the impact of assessment is taken up later in one of our own chapters, we wish to note here the origins of the book in the experiences of the two editors. This started from our being assessed as students, through our assessing of students as academic staff members and now to investigating assessment as researchers. We digress from the style of the rest of this introduction to portray this experience in the first person.

David Boud writes:

I have strong memories from school and university of feeling frustrated and dismayed by the capricious nature of assessment. In school, I experienced getting the highest marks in some subjects and the lowest in others, of being told that I couldn't write well and failing English, and succeeding almost simultaneously at the highest level in physics in ways that seemed mysterious at the time. I started to realise then that there was a code of assessment to be learned and if I could crack this code, I could do well even when not confident of knowing much about the subject being assessed. At one stage this led me to pass an Open University module (in which, incidentally, the assessment activities were better designed than in many other university courses) with only a perfunctory knowledge of the subject matter. Learning about assessment, I discovered, was as important for success in education as learning what the subject was ostensibly about.

As a research student I was drawn into discussions of assessment and was introduced by John Heron for the first time to the idea of taking responsibility for one's own assessment and working with others on what was termed 'self- and peer assessment'. This was a revelation to me: I realised that I wasn't dependent on teachers and assessors for judgements: it was something I could do for myself. It was only later that I recognised that in spending time working out the assessment codes in formal courses I was involved in a similar process. But that, of course, was about following someone else's agenda, not my own.

So persuaded was I by the value of collaborative courses and self-assessment that I utilised it in the first courses for which I was fully responsible for teaching. Students were surprised and disconcerted to be given significant responsibility for assessment decisions, but I never had any difficulty in persuading them of the value of what they were doing and the importance of it for their professional lives. On moving from what was primarily a teaching position to one that involved research and development in higher education, I started to work with academics across a range of discipline areas to help them introduce forms of self- and peer assessment in their own courses. This resulted in a number of research papers and helped cement self-assessment as a legitimate area of inquiry in assessment.

A fortuitous meeting and discovery of a common interest led me to collaborate with Nancy Falchikov for the first time during her period of sabbatical leave in Sydney. We decided that there had been enough individual studies on self-assessment in higher education by that time (the late 1980s) to undertake a serious review of the literature. This led to one review article (Boud and Falchikov, 1989) and one meta-analysis of the different studies we had been able to identify (Falchikov and Boud, 1989). Unfortunately, the literature then was still dominated by studies comparing teacher with student marks, but it nevertheless provided an impetus for further work that went beyond this. On Nancy's return to Scotland, our interests continued in parallel, as she focused on peer assessment (e.g., Falchikov and Goldfinch, 2000) and I on self-assessment (Boud, 1995).

After my 1995 book that consolidated work on self-assessment up to that point, my interests moved in other directions, and it was only when I was invited to give a series of workshops and presentations in 1999 that I re-engaged with the literature and started to think again about the issues involved in assessment in higher education. Until then I had taken a substantially learner-centred view of assessment and regarded all assessment as ultimately subordinate to learner self-assessment. This was on the grounds that only the learner can learn and therefore any act of assessment that takes place on the student will only influence their learning behaviour if it corresponds to the learner's own self-assessment. There may, of course, also be a short-term compliance effect as well, but I thought that this was unlikely to lead to a permanent change in what learners do.

In order to influence institutional assessment policy I saw that it was necessary to frame assessment not in terms of the individual student's perspective, but in terms of the intentions of the institution. Such a reframing would acknowledge the learner's perspective but direct attention to the concerns of the institution and what it could do. Hopefully, it would address the problem of the fragmented and isolated take up of self-assessment ideas by individual staff members, which had beneficial but limited impact on students, and allow for more systematic development over time. The reframing took the form of developing the idea of sustainable assessment. That is, assessment practices that met the needs of an institution to certify or provide feedback on students' work, but which would also meet the longer-term need of equipping students for a lifetime of learning (Boud, 2000). In this way of viewing assessment, every act of assessment would do double duty in addressing the immediate needs of the institution while also contributing in some way to the development of the skills and capabilities of students to be effective learners.

Nancy Falchikov writes:

In common with many people, I have a strong memory of dissatisfaction regarding the assessment of some coursework while at university. In the first year of my degree, I was one of a large laboratory class that appeared to be run by a small army of Ph.D. students. Being a mature student, I worked diligently and turned in work with which I was satisfied, and which generally received good marks. However, in the lab class, there appeared to be no relationship between the marks I, or any of my fellow-students, received and the quality of the work submitted. The criteria I had identified and applied to other work seemed not to apply in this case, and I couldn't understand why. I guess I had developed a strong capacity for self-assessment and felt resentment at the injustice I perceived to be taking place. I remember discussing the matter with peers, raising this issue and getting nowhere.

Later in my studies at university, another graduate student tutor advised me that I didn't need to work as hard as was my custom, and I was encouraged to take short cuts. I was being nudged towards what I later learned was a strategic approach to studying when I was striving for a deep one. I resisted this pressure, as I was enjoying my way of doing things too much.

Later, while working in what is now a new university, I had the good fortune to hear John Cowan talking about self-assessment, about how his students had been helped to assess their own work. How obvious! How simple! How useful! Of course, students should be encouraged to do this. So, I set about designing a scheme of my own. Looking back, it was very bold, involving both self- and peer assessment by first-year students, and I was lucky that it worked so well. I extended and refined my use of self- and peer assessment across my teaching, disseminated my results within my own institution and published some of my studies.

Some of my published work came to the attention of Dave Boud, with whom I subsequently corresponded on the topic of self-assessment. On one of his frequent visits to the UK, I met him and we planned for me to spend some time working in his unit at the University of New South Wales. Our collaboration led to publication of two papers on the topic of self-assessment – a critical analysis (Boud and Falchikov, 1989) and a meta-analysis (Falchikov and Boud, 1989). During my time in Australia, I also continued to develop my ideas about peer assessment. I had, and have, the belief that, as social beings, we need to relate to other people in all contexts, including assessment. I remembered the solidarity I'd experienced as a first-year undergraduate as we tried to challenge the lab assignment marking. Even though we changed nothing within the formal system, our case was strengthened by our ability to compare our work, to discuss possible reasons for grades awarded. Our resolve was strengthened by our group membership.

After my sojourn in Australia, I returned to teaching in Scotland, where I continued to involve my students in assessment, turning my attention to the role of peers and group dynamics. My background as a psychologist stood me in good stead, providing a theoretical framework within which to locate my work. I felt that a meta-analytic study of peer assessment, a companion to the one I had carried out on self-assessment during my time in Australia with Dave, would be a useful resource for the assessment research community. I thus set about locating and collecting all available relevant peer assessment studies. This venture took some time, but, along with my friend and colleague Judy Goldfinch, a meta-analysis of peer assessment studies was published in 2000. While I appreciated the value of this study, I was also aware that peer assessment involves a great deal more than awarding grades. During my search for studies which had compared teacher and student grades for the meta-analysis, I had found many examples of what I termed 'qualitative' studies which had focused on what people nowadays seem to call 'soft outcomes', the sort of manifestation that helps personal and professional development and is as much focused on the future as on the past or present. I continued to collect these types of study, too.

Concerns within my institution about student attrition and ways of supporting students to reduce this took me into new, though still very student-centred, territory. This ended with my designing and taking part in a study to evaluate the effectiveness of an institution-wide initiative to support students in their first year at university. I also became involved in carrying out and evaluating some peer tutoring initiatives. It is possible to see peer tutoring, involving students in teaching, as a natural development from involving students in assessment, both initiatives being designed to help students develop autonomy within the learning environment.

My work on learning together through peer tutoring culminated in publication of a book on the subject in 2001.

I now turned my attention back to peer assessment, returned to the collection of papers on the topic I had accumulated during the research for the meta-analysis, and added to it very substantially. Peer assessment seemed to have taken off as a subject. In 2005, I published my book on the subject of involving students in assessment.

I met up with Dave on many occasions after our first research and publishing venture. (I've become nearly as regular a visitor to Australia as Dave is to the UK.) Our paths, having diverged for a time, seem to have come together again with our shared interest in peer learning, as well as in involving students in assessment. During a period of his working in the UK, Dave and I began discussions about how we might develop his conception of 'sustainable assessment'. This book, along with a number of other publications (Boud and Falchikov, 2005 and 2006; Falchikov and Boud, forthcoming), is one result of these discussions.

Organisation and themes

In conceptualising assessment for future learning, it is necessary to take account of the context of assessment in higher education. Assessment is a value-laden activity surrounded by debates about academic standards, preparing students for employment, measuring quality and providing incentives. Examination systems are resistant to change as they unreflexively embody many socio-political assumptions about what education is for. Assessment, as we have noted, is also an activity about which strong feelings arise: students are influenced by past experiences of being embarrassed and humiliated or motivated and encouraged by individual examples of supportive assessment, and politicians are exercised by the need to maintain some elusive 'gold standard' of achievement. Discussions of assessment therefore need to consider the social and cultural context of education as much as the direct effects of procedures on learners.

This book takes the perspective that assessment must be judged primarily not on narrow technical grounds, but, as we have suggested, in terms of how it influences the learning for the longer term of those who are assessed. It ranges from philosophical questions about the fundamentally problematic nature of assessment as a human activity through considerations of the socio-political context to issues of educational practice. It not only repositions debates about assessment policy and practice, but illustrates some practical directions for development. It addresses important questions about the relationships between assessment and pedagogy and the appropriate kinds of contribution assessment can make.

A group of international contributors who have made a significant impact on thinking about teaching, learning and assessment in higher education were assembled. All were asked to apply their special expertise to the challenge of rethinking assessment for future learning. It also brings a much wider range of considerations to discussions of assessment than is normally the case and draws on empirical research conducted in a variety of countries in different contexts. It sets the promotion of learning and the impact on students as the benchmark by which assessment practices should be judged. Many of the contributors to the book have been active in changing assessment practices for some years and they have articulated the need for assessment for lifelong learning, the involvement of students in assessment processes and the development of sustainable assessment practices. The book makes these ideas available to a wide audience, explores some of the key issues involved and charts directions for further development in assessment.

Setting the scene

The book is organised into four sections. The first part sets the scene and takes up the central theme of how assessment contributes to learning in the longer term. David Boud in Chapter 2 introduces the idea of the importance of judgement. Starting from an analysis of dominant discourses in institutional assessment policy, he suggests that assessment is best regarded as a process of informing judgement. Not only should assessment inform the judgements of those who make decisions about certification; more importantly, it should also inform the decisions of learners themselves. Boud calls for a new language of assessment in which the idea of informing judgement is central and in which learning rather than certification is foregrounded. His chapter argues that a view of assessment as informing judgement provides an educational foundation for assessment practice and moves it away from an earlier, fruitless focus on measurement alone.

The context of assessment

The second part of the book consists of two chapters. Ronald Barnett in Chapter 3 undertakes a philosophical inquiry into the place of assessment in higher education. He discusses assessment in an age of uncertainty and focuses on the important attribute of commitment. He suggests that, perhaps paradoxically, summative assessment has an important role to play in student learning. The next chapter, by Kathryn Ecclestone (Chapter 4), examines the influence of assessment through seeing students as having assessment careers. What they experience when they are assessed before entering higher education has a profound influence on how they respond to assessment within it. In comparing two quite different pre-university assessment regimes she shows how students are formed in different ways. The chapter prompts us to look carefully at what students bring with them into higher education. Assessment in schools and colleges is changing substantially and assessment in higher education needs to take this into account.

Themes

The central, and largest, part of the book is organised around a number of key themes. These are: the link between assessment and teaching and learning; the role of assessment for certification; the contradictions that occur in assessment today; the operation of feedback in assessment processes; the place of self- and peer assessment; and, finally, the link between assessment and emotions.

In the first of these chapters, Steinar Kvale (Chapter 5) suggests that there are many contradictions in assessment in higher education today. Not only have higher education institutions lost touch with effective assessment practices drawn from much earlier traditions, but they ignore a considerable body of work from the psychology of learning over the past fifty years. He argues that higher education institutions need to look to their social purposes to give sufficient value to assessment for life-wide and lifelong learning in a knowledge society.

The next chapter, by Peter Knight (Chapter 6), focuses directly on assessment used for grading and classification purposes, or what he terms 'warranting' achievements. He suggests that warranting is a professional necessity, but that the attempt to measure all achievements is doomed to failure and focuses attention too much on lower-level attainments rather than the more complex achievements needed for professional practice. He suggests that a greater focus be placed on establishing high-quality teaching and learning environments and less on specific measurements of student performance.

What are the effects of assessment? A team from Belgium and the Netherlands led by Filip Dochy draws on recent research reports on the effects of assessment in Chapter 7. They focus on three occasions: before assessment, after assessment and during assessment. They show the close links between teaching and learning activities and assessment processes, and provide guidelines for how assessment can be engineered into the learning process.

Providing feedback to students is much discussed. Dai Hounsell (Chapter 8) notes that it is often under threat as it is time consuming and is sometimes eclipsed by the requirements of assessment for certification. He discusses the importance of feedback and how it might be conducted in ways that can be sustained in the demanding environment of university courses under resource constraints. He examines ways in which high-quality feedback can be given prominence and structured into courses as a central feature.

One of the major moves to promote assessment for the longer term was through the introduction of self-assessment practices into university courses. Kelvin Tan (Chapter 9) draws on research he undertook on university teachers' conceptions of self-assessment to show that many interpretations and uses of self-assessment are not suitable for promoting learning in general or lifelong learning in particular. He identifies some conceptions of self-assessment that do, however, promote these goals.

The use of peers in assessment has been extensively explored in recent years. Nancy Falchikov (Chapter 10) analyses a range of practices for involving students in assessment and shows that some forms of peer assessment may be detrimental to future learning. Her analysis points to approaches that involve peers in assessment that are more compatible with desired ends. Taking these two chapters together, we can observe that it is not the names given to assessment practices that make them suitable or otherwise for fostering learning, but the particularities of the activities that are undertaken. A focus on assessment *practices* is needed, not simply on labelled *methods* considered independently of their consequences.

The final theme in this section, taken up by Nancy Falchikov and David Boud (Chapter 11), is that of emotion and assessment. They observe how frequently strong emotion is associated with assessment events and that these reactions influence learners for many years after the events that provoked them. They focus on the personal impact of being assessed and the experiences learners report. They suggest that insufficient attention is given to the emotional effects of assessment and that it is necessary to consider the longer-term effects of apparently 'objective' activities on the learning careers of students.

The practice of assessment

The final part of the book looks to practice. It asks the question: what kinds of assessment activities might a focus on longer-term learning lead to? The first two chapters give practical and grounded examples of the use of assessment in particular settings. The chapter by Peter Kandlbinder (Chapter 12) examines assessment issues in a context prompted by the absence of practice in actual work settings in vocationally oriented courses. The challenge of how to assess when the obvious point of contact with future professional practice is removed highlights important considerations about creating any assessment activities. The following chapter by Margaret Kirkwood (Chapter 13) looks at sustainable assessment in the context of continuing professional education. A future orientation is needed not only in undergraduate education, but throughout engagement in professional practice. Through an illuminating case study, Kirkwood shows how some of the principles discussed earlier in the book can be contextualised in a programme for chartered teachers.

The final chapter in the book (Chapter 14) is by the two editors. Rather than attempting to summarise the wide range of earlier contributions and their implications for practice, it takes up the challenge of how to design an assessment scheme that explicitly promotes the formation of judgement across subjects and levels. It proposes a framework of tasks that can be utilised across the curriculum and integrates a number of innovations in assessment practice to this end.

References

Black, P. and Wiliam, D. (1998) Assessment and classroom learning, *Assessment in Education*, 5, 1: 7–74.
Boud, D. (1995) *Enhancing Learning through Self Assessment*, London: Kogan Page.

—— (2000) Sustainable assessment: rethinking assessment for the learning society, *Studies in Continuing Education*, 22, 2: 151–167.

Boud, D. and Falchikov, N. (1989) Quantitative studies of student self-assessment in higher education: a critical analysis of findings, *Higher Education*, 18, 5: 529–549.

—— (2005) Redesigning assessment for learning beyond higher education, *Research and Development in Higher Education*, 28 [special issue ed. A. Brew and C. Asmar]: 34–41.

—— (2006) Aligning assessment with long-term learning, *Assessment and Evaluation in Higher Education*, 31, 4: 399–413.

Falchikov, N. (2001) *Learning Together: Peer Tutoring in Higher Education*, London: RoutledgeFalmer.

—— (2005) *Improving Assessment through Student Involvement*, London:RoutledgeFalmer.

Falchikov, N. and Boud, D. (1989) Student self-assessment in higher education: a meta-analysis, *Review of Educational Research*, 59, 4: 395–430.

—— (forthcoming) The role of assessment in preparing for lifelong learning: problems and challenges, in A. Havnes and L. McDowell (eds), *Balancing Dilemmas in Assessment and Learning in Contemporary Education*, New York: Routledge.

Falchikov, N. and Goldfinch, J. (2000) Student peer assessment in higher education: a meta-analysis of quantitative studies which compare peer and teacher marks, *Review of Educational Research*, 70, 3: 287–322.

Knight, P. (2006) The local practices of assessment, *Assessment and Evaluation in Higher Education*, 31, 4: 435–452.

Chapter 2

Reframing assessment as if learning were important

David Boud

As we have seen, an overall theme of this book is that it is time to rethink what is being done in assessment in higher education in order to foster learning for the longer term. In this chapter I suggest that we not only need to engage in specific assessment reforms, but there should be a major reframing of what assessment exists to do, how it is discussed and the language used to describe it. This requires a central *educational* idea to which participants in higher education can subscribe: that is, a view of the direction in which the enterprise of assessment should be moving. It is only through establishing a counter-discourse to the one that currently dominates higher education that some of the fundamental problems created by current assessment assumptions and practice can be addressed.

In working towards such an idea, I start by examining how assessment is currently referred to within higher education institutions. This represents what can be called the dominant discourse of assessment. This discourse constructs educational practice within and beyond courses. It gives prominence to some purposes and features and obscures others that do not fall within it. One of the characteristics of this discourse is that it creates an entirely self-consistent world of assessment that makes it difficult to see what is excluded and what is given a low priority.

Although the seeds of some alternatives can readily be found, especially in the ways in which the work of Black and Wiliam (1998) on formative assessment has been taken up in higher education, these ideas about assessment and learning have not been sufficiently well located within the dominant discourse and have been marginalised. Indeed, have they become so marginalised that Gibbs and Simpson (2004) write about the decline of formative assessment in higher education and argue cogently for its reinstatement.

I suggest that taking up formative assessment may not go far enough. Often when it is discussed it has not been sufficiently oriented towards developing in students the capacity for future learning beyond the present course of study. I consider which educational features must be central to a sustainable view of assessment that does not, in practice if not in intention, de-emphasise learning for the longer term. These are the key elements of a new discourse of assessment, and I tentatively suggest the beginnings of a framework for thinking about the development of judgement and the idea of assessment being the process of informing judgement. This has the potential to gain the support of those involved in higher education and its assessment as it positions assessment as a key educational imperative.

The dominant discourse of assessment

What is the dominant discourse of assessment in higher education and how does it affect educational practice? One way of determining this is to look at documents that discuss assessment and see where emphasis is placed: the language used to describe assessment betrays what it is used to mean. An easy source of such writing is in university policy documents, which are readily available on websites.

To illustrate current assessment discourse, the following have been extracted from assessment policies available in January 2006. They were found in the top ten rankings for 'assessment policy' in the UK and Australian versions of Google.

City University, London

Assessment is the process by which the University is able to confirm that a student has achieved the learning outcomes and academic standards for the module . . . and/or award for the programme for which he or she is registered.
(http://www.city.ac.uk/acdev/qualifications_
standards_framework/assessment_policy_document.html)

The view of assessment represented here is one of quality assurance, of confirming learning outcomes.

University of New England, New South Wales

An assessment task shall be defined as any compulsory or optional activity or exercise where one explicit intent is to assess student progress or learning achievement in a unit of study. It is considered that many assessment tasks will be designed to accomplish multiple goals with respect to teaching and learning including fostering student learning, assessing student learning, obtaining feedback to provide guidance for further teaching and providing direct and useful feedback to the student to guide their future learning.
(http://www.une.edu.au/offsect/assessment_policy.htm)

Here assessment is seen as an activity of determining achievement. However, a secondary purpose is acknowledged in terms of contributing to learning through the use of assessment in the provision of feedback to teachers and students.

University of the West of England

It is of paramount importance that students, staff, external agencies and employers have confidence in the University's standards and assessment procedures. The University is committed to ensuring that student assessment and its consequences are managed effectively and consistently. The recruitment of an increasingly diverse student population for whom value for money is a growing concern requires vigilance at programme level to prevent assessment overload, particularly where programmes draw on modules from different fields and faculties. Lack of coherence in the selection, implementation and management of assessment can lead to unnecessary student dissatisfaction. The adoption of a University-wide assessment policy and strategies for implementation such as double and anonymous marking is designed to ensure equity and fairness.

(http://www.uwe.ac.uk/aboutUWE/assessment.shtml)

The view here is again one of quality assurance, in terms of ensuring confidence in standards and procedures. A secondary concern here is with regard to inclusiveness in which a context of diversity as well as equity and fairness are stressed.

The final illustration is from the Quality Assurance Agency Code of Practice (2000) that has been created to inform the assessment practices of all UK higher education institutions:

Assessment is a generic term for a set of processes that measure the outcomes of students' learning, in terms of knowledge acquired, understanding developed, and skills gained. It serves many purposes. Assessment provides the means by which students are graded, passed or fail. It provides the basis for decisions on whether a student is ready to proceed, to qualify for an award or to demonstrate competence to practise. It enables students to obtain feedback on their learning and helps them improve their performance. It enables staff to evaluate the effectiveness of their teaching.

(http://www.qaa.ac.uk/academicinfrastructure/
codeOfPractice/section6/default.asp)

The focus here is on measurement of outcomes. The Code first emphasises the sorting and classification of students; then the improvement of performance through feedback; and finally, the improvement of teaching.

It is interesting that in some countries, many universities have a policy that relates to just one form of assessment – the examination. This does not imply that other forms are not used, though it does suggest that the examination is the only one regarded as worthy of scrutiny at an institutional level, and therefore is of special importance. Such policies tend to emphasise the procedural fairness and integrity of the examination process.

In official documentary accounts of assessment, there appears to be a primary focus and a secondary one. The primary focus is characterised by terms such as 'outcomes', 'measurement' and 'integrity'. The secondary focus involves terms such as 'feedback', 'improvement' and 'learning as a process'. There are also some signs of a tertiary focus on future learning, though there is only one example of this in the examples found. There is a ready connection between these distinctions and the common purposes of assessment: assessment for certification (summative), assessment for immediate learning (formative) and assessment for longer-term learning (sustainable). The relative emphasis on these different features is illustrated by drilling down into the details of university assessment policies. Many more words are devoted to the procedures associated with the primary focus than to other foci, with detailed discussions of rules and regulations for examinations, ensuring the identity of students, mechanisms for marking and moderating of scores, avoiding plagiarism and cheating and so on. There is typically little or no discussion of how assessment can contribute to learning, how it can inhibit learning, guidelines for good feedback and similar matters. Notwithstanding the limitations of focusing on publicly available documents, this suggests that the dominant discourse of assessment within institutions remains related to measurement and certification despite a perceived need to acknowledge other purposes. Learning takes the subordinate position in official writings about assessment.

There seem to be no studies that map the expenditure of time and effort on different assessment purposes, though it is reasonable to suggest that most time is spent by university staff on marking assignments and examinations that contribute to final grades. There is also recurring talk of the problem of over-assessment by both students and staff. This is seldom represented in terms of too much time being spent on helping students with their learning – the second and third foci discussed above – but whether too much time is being spent effectively in measurement for certification.

Problems with the dominant discourse

The fundamental problem of the dominant view for assessment is that it constructs learners as passive subjects. That is, students are seen to have no role other than to subject themselves to the assessment acts of others, to be measured and classified. They conform to the rules and procedures of others to satisfy the needs of an assessment bureaucracy: they present themselves at set times for examinations over which they have little or no influence and they complete assignments which are, by and large, determined with little or no input from those being assessed. This may be necessary to fuel the needs of an apparently objective and fair process of classification, but even the objectivity of assessment in apparently 'objective' disciplines is being questioned (Shay, 2005). It is not that in dominant views of assessment students are not expected to be busy in preparing to be assessed, or that they are sometimes allowed choice of assessment task; far from it. It is the nature of that activity and the expectation that it follows the unilateral agenda of authority that is the problem; that is incompatible with the construction of the student as active learner that is needed for a primarily educational view of assessment.

When people face learning demands outside the context of formal study – that is, in the contexts for which higher education is intended to prepare them – they necessarily have to construct themselves as active subjects. They have to determine what is to be learned, how it is to be learned and how to judge whether they have learned it or not. They would not expect to do this independently of others or of expert sources of advice, but it is required that they mobilise themselves and their own resources, taking a much more dynamic position in the tasks of learning and assessment. The passive construction of learners in the dominant assessment focus of higher education does not do this.

The problem is greater than this, however. The secondary focus of assessment, to aid learning, also can tend to construct learners as recipients of information. In assessment policy statements many of the representations of assessment related to learning focus on the role and importance of feedback to students. It is as if feedback were the only process that influences learning. This is a very limited view and one that has inhibited the development of a more sophisticated assessment discourse. When assessment for learning is represented in terms of receiving feedback, this can place students in positions of being passive respondents to the initiatives of others: the teacher identifies what is needed and provides this information to the student. A more thoroughgoing reconceptualisation is needed than one that takes a simplistic view of what assessment for learning is about.

Not only is feedback often construed as a passive act in which teachers supply information to students, but it typically fails to meet the requirements of the practice from which the metaphor of feedback has originally been taken: that is, in control engineering. The original use of feedback was in the context of systems in which the output signal was fed back into the process in order to influence the nature of the output. As Sadler (1998) has pointed out, feedback in education is only worthy of the description if the feedback loop is completed: that is, if teachers can detect in the work of students that the information they have provided has made a difference to what students do. Most comments on student work, even if students read them, occur at times that are the least propitious in terms of influencing subsequent student learning – such as at the end of a unit of study when they are moving on to do something different.

Feedback is important, though, and is discussed further in Chapter 8, but it is not the sole or perhaps the prime consideration. There are other elements that are necessary for sensible discussions of the relationship between assessment and learning because any reconceptualisation of assessment must focus on the importance of learning.

If the dominant focus of assessment in grading and classification has the inadvertent effect of prompting students to adopt an approach to learning with adverse effects, then this is a serious problem that needs to be addressed. While there are many examples of this occurring – for instance, when expectations that a multiple-choice test is to be used encourages students to memorise rather than work to understand concepts, or when students are discouraged because they get lower marks than expected – the dominant focus of assessment does not necessarily promote such approaches (see Falchikov, 2005; Knight, 2002; and Chapter 11). In principle, there is no reason why students could not be prompted by assessment practices to study in positive ways. Unfortunately, this cannot be achieved in practice because teachers and those who design assessment processes have insufficient information about the effects of their assessment practices. The difficulty is compounded by the fact that it is impossible to imagine a normal teaching and learning situation in which one could know enough about student responses to assessment to ensure that formal assessment necessarily had a positive impact on learning.

Consequential validity – that is, a measure of the consequences of assessment on desired learning – has been discussed in the literature (see Boud, 1995; Messick, 1989), but it has seldom been taken up in practice. The adverse impacts of assessment are often noted anecdotally, but little has been done to address them systematically. The challenge, then, is to find ways of thinking about assessment that have a positive consequential influence on learning and then develop the assessment practices that could accompany such a conception.

Towards informed judgement

A productive way to reframe assessment discourse is around the theme of informing judgement (see Hager and Butler, 1996): that is, informing the capacity to evaluate evidence, appraise situations and circumstances astutely, to draw sound conclusions and act in accordance with this analysis. This is an idea that focuses on learning centrally – learning to form judgements – as well as on the act of forming judgements about learning, which may be used for validating purposes. This notion has the potential to incorporate a forward-looking dimension – informing judgement for future decision-making about learning. At one level this is what university courses have always been about and therefore it is not a substantial change. However, with regard to the discourse of assessment, it marks a significant shift of focus away from the process of measuring effects and artefacts and towards what education is intended to be for: that is, the formation of a capable person who can engage in professional work and contribute to society as an informed citizen.

Informing judgement as the central idea of assessment has a multiple emphasis. It relates both to the judgement of others in processes of certification and aiding learning and to informing the judgement of the learner in processes of presenting themselves for certification processes and for learning in the short and long terms. It encompasses the dual focus of summative and formative assessment. However, formatively, it is directed towards informing *learners'* judgement as a key function of assessment as distinct from the present, almost exclusive, focus on informing others. It has the potential to orient assessment towards consequences in that it makes a desired consequence explicit: informing the judgement of learners. It acknowledges the importance of reflexivity and self-regulation through acknowledgement of the centrality of judgement as a process. And it has the potential to contextualise assessment in practice, as judgement always has to be for a particular purpose.

Concerns about measurement, objectivity, standards and integrity are integral to a notion of informing judgement, but in themselves they are secondary to the act of becoming informed. It is this shift from foregrounding measurement to contextualising it as integral to processes of informing judgement that is important. It is not a matter of rejecting the concerns that are presently dominant, but viewing them within an appropriate educational frame that more adequately allows concerns about learning to come to the fore. A view of assessment that places informing judgement centrally is able to include key graduate learning attributes as an intrinsic part of what assessment is for. It gives prominence to students making judgements about their own learning as a normal part of assessment activities, not as the special add-on that, unfortunately, student self-assessment has sometimes come to be.

New ways of inscribing assessment cannot in themselves change assessment and assessment practice, however. A shift will occur only if there is sufficient desire to want to move from one form of discourse to another and if a possible alternative is sufficiently generative to enable other desires to be focused through it. There are signs that an informing judgement discourse has some potential. The above investigation of assessment policy websites revealed that several institutions were seriously rethinking assessment.

While it picks up only one aspect of informing judgement as it has been described here, Griffith University in Queensland does talk about judgement. In its view:

> Assessment is the process of forming a judgment about the quality and extent of student achievement or performance, and therefore by inference a judgment about the learning itself. Assessment inevitably shapes the learning that takes place, that is, what students learn and how they learn it, and should reflect closely the purposes and aims of the course of study.
>
> (http://www62.gu.edu.au/policylibrary.nsf/0/
> 65e95921348eb64c4a256bdd0062f3b0?opendocument)

In the different environment of workplace learning, Beckett and Hager (2000) have argued that the key idea for learning at work is that of making judgements. They argue that we all make judgements of various kinds in work and that we should orient practices in workplace learning around this central feature: 'making better judgments represents a paradigmatic aim of workplace learning, and . . . therefore growth in such learning is represented by a growing capacity to make appropriate judgments in the changing, and often unique, circumstances that occur in many workplaces' (Beckett and Hager, 2000: 302).

Implications of a focus on informing judgement

What then needs to be taken into account in such a view of assessment?

Strong connections between assessment activities and what students learn have been accepted for some time. Assessment activities signal what is to be learned, they influence the approaches to learning that students take and they can indicate the levels of achievement that are required for any given unit of study. In short, assessment frames what students do. It provides an indication of what the institution gives priority to in making judgements, it provides an agenda more persuasive than a syllabus or course outline and it therefore has a powerful backwash effect on all teaching and learning activities. In some settings it has a stronger instrumental effect than others, but it has an effect on learning in all of them. We simply have to imagine how different the experience of a course would be if all the formal assessment activities were removed or changed to become discretionary to begin to see the influence.

While these effects of assessment influence learning, they do not constitute *educational* features. Assessment can have a crucial role to play in an educational framing of learning of all kinds and in all settings and an excessive officially sanctioned focus on grading and classification has distracted attention from what this role can be. The features that the notion of informing judgement should address are threefold.

The first feature connects assessment and learning directly. It takes up the earlier discussion of consequential validity and places the consequences of acts of assessment centrally. Do assessment acts actively promote development of students' capacity to make judgements about their own work throughout the course? Are there inadvertent effects of certification and grading on students' learning that must be countered?

Considerations of the consequential effects of assessment, the influences of assessment beyond the point of graduation, must also be taken into account. Are students better equipped to engage in learning in professional practice? Are they able to deploy assessment strategies positively to influence their own continuing learning? Are they able to utilise the resources of others in this process? Unless it is possible to claim that assessment within higher education contributes in a significant way to these goals, in principle and in practice, then it has an insufficient learning focus.

The second feature of the desirable view of assessment is a focus on fostering reflexivity and self-regulation. These represent two similar ideas, but come from different traditions – reflexivity from social theory (e.g., Bourdieu and Wacquant, 1992; Giddens, 1991) and self-regulation from psychology (Karoly, 1993). What they share is a view that a key to learning in complex settings is to be able to 'look again', to monitor one's own performance, to see one's own learning in the context in which it is deployed and to respond with awareness to the exigencies of the tasks in which one is engaged. Reflexivity and self-regulation are not just about skills, although there is obviously a skill element to them. They involve dispositions and an orientation to both work and learning. They also have an affective dimension. They involve confidence and an image of oneself as an active learner, not one solely directed by others. A focus on reflexivity and self-regulation is a key element in constructing active learners, as these features need to be constructed by both teachers and examiners and themselves.

There have been some assessment initiatives that operate in this general territory. The use of self- and peer assessment practices as a formal part of a course of study is an example (e.g., Boud, 1995). However, not all self- and peer assessment activities have a substantial impact on reflexivity and self-regulation, particularly those of a procedural kind, and reflexivity and self-regulation encompass more than is normally subsumed in self-assessment practices, at least as documented in much of the literature. Peer assessment is sometimes used as a proxy for assessment by staff in the generation of grades and some conceptions of self-assessment are not even associated with the promotion of self-regulation (see Chapter 9). The seeking and utilising of feedback from multiple sources can be part of reflexivity and self-regulation, but if information from feedback is not used explicitly for learning to complete the feedback loop and to contribute to building an understanding of how to utilise information from others effectively, then it is very limited. Some aspects of self- and peer assessment clearly have roles to play in a new conception of assessment for learning, but this is only part of the picture. Unless the fostering of reflexivity and self-regulation is a feature of the normal curriculum and a fundamental part of course design, the impact of assessment on them is likely to be limited. The building of skills for reflexivity and self-regulation through assessment acts is not currently a strong feature of courses.

The third feature of a new focus of assessment is recognition of the variety of contexts in which learning occurs and is utilised. Dominant views of assessment have arisen from traditions in which what is taught is also assessed. In this, assessment is an act of measuring what has been learned from a *course*. The context of assessment, then, is the course itself, typically within an academic programme in an educational institution. Contexts of application in work or professional practice may be used for illustrative purposes, but their influence on assessment is secondary; they are effectively used for background colour. Application of what is learned typically takes place post-graduation, or at least after the unit of study. It occurs after assessment and cannot therefore be fully part of it. This creates an issue, which is often referred to as the problem of transferability of learning: that is, application to any given context is postponed and treated as a separate stage of learning that is not the concern of the educational institution (Boud, 2001; Bowden and Marton, 1998). The context of assessment in higher education is often taken to be the world of the course, not the world of practice, despite lip service being paid to the latter.

The world of the course privileges individual judgements. Acts of assessment judge individuals. Subject content is reified. The role of peers in learning and the nature of practice are downplayed. And knowledge is separated from the world in which it is used (Hager, 2004). Of course, in professional programmes this is often less marked than in programmes in which there is no obvious site of application. Indeed, one of the most significant innovations in professional education, problem-based learning, makes a particular feature of assessing learning in the context of application to problems as authentically constructed as can be achieved within an educational institution (Nendaz and Tekian, 1999).

Again, there are many examples of a partial engagement with the contexts in which knowledge is used, most notably in the increasing use of what is termed 'authentic assessment' (Wiggins, 1989). This refers to assessment practices that are closely aligned with activities that take place in real work settings, as distinct from the often artificial constructs of university courses. This move has progressed a very long way in some vocational education and training systems in which the only legitimate forms of assessment are those that are based upon performance in a real work setting outside the educational institution and judged by an expert practitioner (see Chapter 5). While there are limitations to an authentic assessment approach taken to extremes, the notion that assessment tasks should acknowledge and engage with the ways in which knowledge and skills are used in authentic settings is useful.

Conclusion

What are some of the issues that arise from this articulation and how might they be addressed? Using a new term does not in itself make a difference to practice. However, if the notion of informing judgement is accepted as the guiding principle in all aspects of assessment, it leads to a new set of questions that enable us to determine whether any given set of assessment practices is addressing the central question of improving judgements of both assessors and learners. Practices that may otherwise demonstrate qualities of reliability and validity may not meet the requirement of informing judgement of learners.

If the notion of informing judgement is taken up, the question arises of how assessment that exhibits this feature might differ from assessment that does not. As is implicit in the above discussion, a discourse of informing judgement will always have the dual qualities of a focus on the learning needs of students as well as the legitimate needs of others to have an account of students' learning outcomes. This points to an important shift of emphasis. If judgement is to be informed, which language should be used to do the informing? The current dominant discourse uses the language of marks and grades, as if there were a common understanding of how they might be interpreted. This language destroys detail and obscures meaning. What information is conveyed in knowing that a person gained a 'B' or a credit in a given unit of study? It has meaning only in the context of comparison with other students within the same context because it has its origins in a norm-referenced system of assessment that is becoming outmoded. Grades can be used in a standards-based system but only when grade descriptors are present. If informing judgement is widely adopted, it will be necessary to move to a language of judgement that is both more transparent and more varied than the language of current assessment discourses. While there are still problems in the use of portfolios and qualitative descriptors of outcomes, and while further refinement of them is necessary, this may be worth undertaking, as the alternative has even less to offer.

References

Beckett, D. and Hager, P. (2000) Making judgments as the basis for workplace learning: towards an epistemology of practice, *International Journal of Lifelong Education*, 19, 4: 300–312.
Black, P. and Wiliam, D. (1998) Assessment and classroom learning, *Assessment in Education*, 5, 1: 7–74.
—— (1995) *Enhancing Learning through Self Assessment*, London: Kogan Page.
—— (2001) Knowledge at work: issues of learning, in D. Boud and N. Solomon (eds) *Work-Based Learning: A New Higher Education?*, Buckingham: Society for Research into Higher Education and Open University Press.
Bourdieu, P. and Wacquant, L. (1992) *An Invitation to Reflexive Sociology*, Chicago: University of Chicago Press.
Bowden, J. and Marton, F. (1998) *The University of Learning: Beyond Quality and Competence in Higher Education*, London: Kogan Page.
Falchikov, N. (2005) *Improving Assessment through Student Involvement*, London and New York: RoutledgeFalmer.
Gibbs, G. and Simpson, C. (2004) Conditions under which assessment supports students' learning, *Learning and Teaching in Higher Education*, 1: 3–31.
Giddens, A. (1991) *Modernity and Self-Identity: Self and Society in the Late Modern Age*, Cambridge: Polity Press.
Hager, P. (2004) The conceptualisation and measurement of learning at work, in H. Rainbird, A. Fuller and A. Munro (eds) *Workplace Learning in Context*, London: Routledge.
Hager, P. and Butler, J. (1996) Two models of educational assessment, *Assessment and Evaluation in Higher Education*, 21, 4: 367–378.
Karoly, P. (1993) Mechanisms of self-regulation: a systems view, *Annual Review of Psychology*, 44: 23–52.
Knight, P. (2002) Summative assessment in higher education: practices in disarray, *Studies in Higher Education*, 27, 3: 275–278.
Messick, S. (1989) Validity, in R.L. Linn (ed.) *Educational Measurement*, 3rd edn, New York: Macmillan.
Nendaz, M.R. and Tekian, A. (1999) Assessment in problem-based learning medical schools: a literature review, *Teaching and Learning in Medicine*, 11: 232–243.
Quality Assurance Agency for Higher Education (QAA) (2000) *Code of Practice for the Assurance of Academic Quality and Standards in Higher Education*, Gloucester: Quality Assurance Agency (available at: http://www.qaa.ac.uk/academicinfrastructure/codeOfPractice/section6/default.asp [accessed 18 March 2006]).
Sadler, D.R. (1998) Formative assessment: revisiting the territory, *Assessment in Education*, 5, 1: 77–84.

Shay, S. (2005) The assessment of complex tasks: a double reading, *Studies in Higher Education*, 30, 6: 663–680.

Wiggins, G. (1989) A true test: toward more authentic and equitable assessment, *Phi Delta Kappan*, 71, 9: 703–713.

Part 2

The context of
assessment

Chapter 3

Assessment in higher education

An impossible mission?

Ronald Barnett

In this chapter, I want to make a conceptual argument. I shall do this by drawing on such concepts as authenticity and being. In a nutshell, I shall argue that by taking authenticity and being seriously as educational ends, summative assessment may have a definite role to play in assisting the student's development.

Straightaway, one can sense possible difficulties in such an approach. First, 'authenticity' and 'being' are not exactly part of the stock-in-trade of concepts in the debate on assessment. Second, a conceptual argument in debate over assessment is itself something of a rarity (although not unique: see Davis's (1998) examination of 'The Limits of Educational Assessment' in the context of schools and pupil assessment). Nevertheless, despite its unusual approach, especially in the context of higher education, I hope that what I have to say here and my way of proceeding may have some value.

Assessment in an age of uncertainty

In the contemporary world, as well as it being a means of acquiring high-level knowledge, understanding and skills, higher education should foster the development of human qualities and dispositions, of certain modes of being, appropriate to the twenty-first century. This century, I take it, is one of multiplying frameworks of understanding, of proliferating representations of the world. And those frameworks and representations are both multiplying and contending against each other. It is a world of uncertainty; indeed, of 'supercomplexity' (Barnett, 2000). In such a milieu, the question arises: are the qualities and dispositions characteristically called forth by assessment appropriate to such an uncertain world? It just may be that, characteristically, assessment practices in higher education are not always yielding the educational potential that they might.

To put the matter in this way is to open up not an empirical but a conceptual line of inquiry. The suggestion is that assessment – under any circumstances – is hard put to help advance the qualities and dispositions that might be adequate to an age of supercomplexity. Two specific considerations suggest themselves. First, it may be that assessment in practice does not beckon forth the qualities and dispositions appropriate to a complex world. Here, we would be observing mere limitations in assessment: it is not all that it could be. Second (and a more serious situation), it may be that assessment in higher education invites qualities and dispositions *other* than those appropriate to a complex world. A regime of assessment is not neutral but conjures forms of human development that are inappropriate to the modern age. Here, we would be observing pernicious features of assessment. Either way – whether merely limitations or inherently negative features – we would be voicing concerns about assessment to the effect that assessment was at least not aiding the proper formation of human beings (and may even be injurious to that prospect).

This, then, is the location of this chapter: an interrogative space in which I raise questions about assessment in higher education – simply put, is it fit for purpose? Does the *educational being* that assessment elicits possess a satisfactory form? Could it ever be so?

On educational being

Quickly, we have run into matters deserving of preliminary comment, especially in relation to both words contained in the phrase 'educational being'. 'Being' draws us into the space opened up by Heidegger and subsequently developed by Sartre. It reminds us that human beings are, in the first place, 'beings'; before they are knowing or interactive subjects, they have their being in the world. Of course, as Heidegger drew out, both knowing and interaction with the world are implicated in being: being is in the world and – Heidegger insisted – it develops in and through time. As well as 'being', key concepts for Heidegger were those of authenticity, care and solicitude. In the following passage, all four concepts come into view:

> there is also the possibility of a kind of solicitude which does not so much leap in for the Other as leap ahead of him in his existential potentiality-for-Being, not in order to take away his 'care' but rather to give it back to him authentically as such for the first time. This kind of solicitude pertains essentially to authentic care . . . it helps the Other to become transparent to himself in his care and to become free for it.
>
> (Heidegger, 1998: 159)

As it happens, this set of reflections could be felt to constitute a pedagogical statement, about the solicitude that might characterise a pedagogical relationship; even though Heidegger said little about education as such, much of what he had to say had profound educational implications (Cooper, 2002). However, the value of the passage for us here is that it gives us a sense of being as always having potential, and that that potential can be helped to be realised through solicitude. Through that solicitude, being may come to be authentic and come to exercise proper 'care' towards itself.

Characteristic of this solicitude is its future horizon: it has a concern for the potential of being in the future; it 'leap[s] ahead'. Is this not a nice encapsulation of the committed teacher? She 'leaps ahead', surely, of her students in her solicitude for them. She envisions that each student has in front of him or her latent potential: in such a pedagogical relationship, each student is held in the context of the future, and its possibilities, unknown as they are. The solicitous teacher 'leaps ahead' to stand in each student's future, however hazy that may be.

Sartre (2003) took the story of being further, in showing that being could stand in different stances to the world. In particular, being could take itself unto itself: it could move from being just 'in-itself' to being 'for-itself'. In becoming 'for-itself', being could move from a mode of existence and attain its own authentic essence.

How might these recollections of the work of Heidegger and Sartre help us here? I would suggest that they offer us, in the first place, some pertinent considerations in the framing of 'educational being'. A genuine higher education holds the promise of the attainment of authentic being, albeit a particular kind of authentic being. The authentic being offered by higher education is that state of being in which a student becomes her own person. She is able to take up stances in the world, either in her propositional claims or in her practices, and is able to do so with a measure of authority even though she recognises that any position she holds has to be provisional. To draw on Sinclair Goodlad's (1976) phrase, she moves to a position of 'authoritative uncertainty'.

Crucial here is a sense of the significance of being as such. Yes, in higher education, we look for a student's advancement in her knowledge and understanding and her skills, but neither knowledge nor skills can be developed without a development in the student's being. In making truth claims or in injecting actions in the world, students are giving of themselves as people. That much may be readily accepted so far as actions are concerned, but in the realm of truth claims? Isn't higher education, it may be alleged, precisely a zone in which the personal dimension is to be displaced, so that any partiality or distortion is minimised? The objection has right on its side, but it is itself misplaced. In putting forward truth claims, even in mathematics, the hard sciences or life-concerning professional domains (such as medicine), we want students to align themselves with their claims. We want their claims really to be *theirs*. There should be an identity between the claim being made and the student making it.

To proffer these contentions is to say nothing about originality; about the student being original in her propositional claims or her actions. Originality is a separate matter from that concerning us. The matter before us is rather about first-handedness. In putting forward a claim of any kind, the student puts herself forward; she comes out from herself. The claim stands *there*, independently of the student but with her backing. She commits herself to the claim. At least, that is what the Western idea of higher education calls for: the capacity on the part of the student to inject claims about the world that have her commitment.

Commitment, we may note, is slightly separate from sincerity, although both are important. Commitment is, as we have just seen, the phenomenon in which the individual weds herself to her offering; she imparts herself; she aligns herself to it. Sincerity, on the other hand, betokens a genuineness on the part of the speaker.

We may be clearer about these two terms if we look at their opposites. A lack of commitment is evident when the student does something in a desultory or half-hearted way, whereas a lack of sincerity is evident in the offering not being what it seems. Hiding behind the views of others, even though doing it transparently and in a scholarly way, would count as a weak level of commitment, whereas plagiarism would be an example of insincerity.

As I say, both commitment and sincerity are important, but I want to pick out commitment for now as the more important concept in our present inquiry. The value of the idea of commitment is that it points up the way in which a person's hold on the world, her being, is implicated in her truth claims. I would want to go further and suggest that the student's hold on the world is prior to her claims about the world. To put it formally, ontology precedes epistemology. It is the kind of human being that a student has become that determines the character of her truth claims about the world.

To put the matter another way, behind the utterances that a student makes stand a person and the person's human qualities will modulate the authority of her truth claims. It is already apparent that the making of truth claims calls for certain qualities. We may identify the qualities in question as the following:

- courage (to put one's claims forward as one's own and to be committed to those claims; to hit one note instead of several in the hope that one of them may be right);
- bravery (to be prepared to open oneself to the new);
- determination (to put things as clearly as possible; to follow things through, wherever they may lead);
- persistence (to stick with things; things may be clear only after some years of hard effort);
- integrity (to be true to one's feelings and sentiments);
- sincerity (so that one means what one says, and that what one says is an expression of one's own ideas).

These six qualities help to mark out the student's educational being, albeit an educational being in the making. But without commitment on the part of the student, these qualities are inert: the student's commitment is required in order for our six qualities to come into play. Commitment, therefore, is a kind of super-quality; a meta-quality. A key question before us, therefore, is: not merely does but *can* assessment help to promote such qualities?

The need for assessment

Rather than offer an answer to that question now – although we should not lose sight of it – I want to try another tack: noting that assessment is a necessary feature of higher education. In higher education, we want students to develop themselves in worthwhile ways. The worthwhileness springs from a complex set of considerations. On the one hand, there are considerations that are internal to the intellectual or professional field to hand; and from these considerations emanate internal standards. In turn, we may note that such considerations are doubly contested. First, the internal considerations are themselves debatable; and are debated. The philosophers in the University of Sydney could not agree about the nature of philosophy to such an extent that, for some years, the university had two departments of philosophy. Second, even where there is large agreement on the internal standards, there is often disagreement over their relative weighting. It is in virtue of these two sets of differences of view that tutors can legitimately disagree over the marks to be awarded to students in their assignments.

On the other hand, we are looking to students to develop in ways that are wider than the challenges of any particular field. We may call these wider forms of desirable development personal qualities; and earlier we listed six such qualities. One might be tempted to call those qualities 'academic virtues'; but that phrase is tendentious (see Macfarlane, 2006). It both locates the qualities too tightly in the academic arena, as if they did not have to carry over into life generally, and implies that academic life is especially virtuous.

At the same time, simply to term these qualities 'personal' underplays their significance, implying that the qualities are a matter of individual idiosyncrasy. Courage, bravery, persistence, determination, integrity and sincerity – not to mention commitment – are surely qualities that are characteristic of the forms of the development that we look for in higher education but yet have value in the wider world. These qualities neither have point solely in higher education (their value goes beyond higher education) nor are they developed only in higher education; but they are attributes of the personality structure that we look to higher education to engender. Higher education, therefore, is a set of educational processes in which students are expected to develop in a wide range of ways; and these days, many programmes of study have curricula with highly complex sets of elements of engagement and understanding. Even the term 'interdisciplinary' cannot do justice to some of the complexes of action, capability, understanding, reasoning, interaction and engagement that are required of students. Consider, by way of example, the complexity and range of the forms of human development that might be on the menu within a course entitled 'Music Design Technology'.

The forms of human development embraced by a single course have their own relevant standards – even if, as remarked, those standards are subject to some dispute. Students are therefore obliged to subject themselves to assessment in order to determine whether they have reached the required standards. Standards are inherent in the fields and practices in which the students are engaged. There can be no escape from those standards; there can be no escape from being judged according to those standards.

There is, though, a further sense in which judgement is characteristic of the journeys on which students are engaged. It is not just that standards are internal to the processes and the fields and that students are required to submit themselves to judgement by those standards. It is also that judgement is characteristic of the form of life in which students have their being. Higher education is not academic life but it is linked to academic life. Perhaps the dominant strand to the form of life that is academic life is not – as some might say – that it is dialogical or even that it is critical but rather that it is interrogative. That is to say, any utterance proffered in academic life is susceptible to questioning from other parties. Any utterance has its place in an interrogative space.

The character of the questioning deserves a little filling out. In being potentially subject to questions, utterances are opening themselves to questioning-by-standards. The questions are themselves housed in a space framed by standards. We may term these standards 'critical': they impart a framework for critical questioning. 'Questioning' here may be evident as questions, as rebuttals, as alternative theories, as rival sets of data or as alternative ways of proceeding (in a clinical situation, for instance). Another term here, therefore, is that of 'judgement': utterances and actions propel themselves into a judgemental space.

In this judgemental space lies the price, or indeed the value, of participating in the academic life. Through this judgemental engagement, the soundness of what one has to say may be developed and even improved. But that is again beside the point here. All I want to note here is the interrogative or judgemental character of the academic life.

In turn, then, it follows that one of the tacit aims of higher education is to enable students to subscribe to the judgemental life, albeit a life of judgement that has for its context sets of worthwhile standards. It is a capacity to live well with questioning coming at one – whether affirming or rebuking – that marks out the criticality that, for many, lies at the heart of higher education.

In summary of these last few reflections, we may say that it has emerged that assessment of students is doubly necessary: on the one hand, assessment is necessary in order to judge that students have met sets of standards embedded in the intellectual and professional fields in which their programmes of study are situated; on the other, assessment is necessary at a meta-level, for judgement is characteristic of the academic life as such. As Alvin Gouldner (1979) memorably put it, the academy may primarily be understood through its 'culture of critical discourse'.

Two journeys or one?

It may seem that our story so far has had the effect of characterising the student as moving in opposed directions. On the one hand, we have depicted a journey of increasing authenticity; and hand-in-hand with that authenticity is to be found the formation of human qualities such as courage, bravery, integrity, persistence and determination. On the other hand, we have depicted a journey of increasing adherence to standards and, indeed, a willingness to subscribe to a life of critical judgement. How can it be that the student moves in these two directions at once: on the one hand, increasing singularity; on the other, increasing allegiance to a collectivity? The former journey might imply that assessment of students is otiose: assessment could be counter-productive in the formation of the qualities required of educated being. The latter journey might imply that, after all, assessment is necessary: no assessment, no higher education. Can this conundrum be resolved; possibly even dissolved?

A temptation must be resisted. This is the temptation to distinguish between summative assessment and formative assessment and to place all weight on the latter. In that way, through the more open-ended and forward-looking character of formative assessment – so it might be suggested – daring, individuality and authenticity may all be maintained and even encouraged. Both sides of the conundrum can be held together; the conundrum dissolves.

The problem with that option is that it ducks the issue of the potential value of summative assessment. A second move might then be to suggest that a single assignment may be marked in such a way as to yield both summative and formative outcomes. Let us assume that that is possible; but the potential positive value of summative assessment would still be unaddressed. Is it necessarily the case that summative assessment is injurious to the aim of enhancing authenticity and its associated qualities of human being? Can the educator for whom authenticity is a worthwhile aim at the same time find good grounds for defending summative assessment?

Remember the problem before us: can an individual be helped towards the state of authentic being through judgement, and a form of judgement linked to collective standards at that? Can a student be enabled – through such judgement – to come into herself such that her being becomes 'for-itself'? So that her being is released to take off itself and for itself? Is summative assessment not likely to have the reverse effect? We do not have to posit the case of the student judged to have performed poorly or even to have failed. Even the successful student is being judged against collective standards and is – if only over time – liable to be corralled into a framework, a presupposed mode of thinking and being. Summative judgement is pernicious in that it confines being; it contains being; it brings being into a known form. It renders that which should be strange into the familiar.

Perhaps with precisely some such set of considerations in mind Nietzsche (1968: 14) posed the questions: 'Granted we want truth: why not untruth? And uncertainty? Even ignorance?' Surely, he was urging here the value of breaking free from the bounds of conventions, of sticking within frames liable to produce truth; for such truths – in a sense – however creative they may be, will be limited. Let us encourage daring, boldness and audacity. Hence, too, 'learning is not enough!' (Nietzsche, 1968: 226). We need to have the courage to break out from conventional frameworks and to see and engage with the world in new ways.

This, then, is the perniciousness of summative assessment: that it cabins, cribs and confines, no matter how its supporters may protest to the contrary. The contrary voices may already be heard. It will be said that summative assessment need have no such confining function. If, after all, in a spirit of 'constructive alignment' (Biggs, 2003), open-ended curriculum aims are set and followed through, both in the curriculum and thence in the pattern of assessments, then there is no reason why summative assessment cannot promote Nietzschean-like authenticity.

There are two (albeit linked) problems with that response. First, assessment is a form of classification: it sorts subjectivities into sets, and hierarchical sets at that. It is, to use the term in a sense implied by Foucault (1991), a form of discipline: judgement disciplines its targets. Student subjectivities are controlled and moulded: there is nothing strange about this phenomenon; this, after all, is one of the intentions underlying assessment. Second, as it is developing at least in many of those countries that have spawned national quality agencies, assessment is being asked to comply with national assessment frameworks (perhaps setting out specific expectations in terms of students' knowledge and skills and/or setting out templates as to the form that assessments should take or as where assessments are intended to plot stated 'outcomes').

Our conundrum, then, is intensifying rather than dissolving. On the one hand, the defence of assessment as a virtuous mark of reaching worthwhile standards; on the other hand, the critique of assessment as a form of control, thereby reducing if not altogether expunging the prospect of higher education as an educational process of growing authenticity.

Could there possibly be a way of bridging these two perspectives on assessment in higher education? Is the virtuous reading of assessment – that it just might offer a means of enhancing the student's authenticity – a realistic prospect?

A postmodern reading, at least of a benign kind, might opt for the optical illusion perspective. The optical illusion pertinent here is of a drawing that can be seen in two quite different ways, with neither related to the other: the two apperceptions might even be radically opposed to each other. But that option does not let us off the hook either, for the task before us is still to explain how assessment might have authenticity-enhancing properties. Further, the optical illusion invites us to look in two directions alternately whereas the challenge is to combine the two perspectives – standards *and* authenticity – before us.

The power of authenticity

There just may be a way forward in not just seeing authenticity as one option among many (the postmodern approach) but grasping the potential educational power that authenticity enables us to glimpse.

Through the idea of authenticity, the prospect opens of a student authentically embracing the potential virtues of assessment. Two challenges open up at once. What might it mean authentically to embrace assessment? And how might the potential virtues of assessment be made apparent to students? The first question is one of disposition; the second is one of understanding.

Reasons for embracing assessment in a mode of authentic being are not hard to fathom. Authentic being will embrace assessment for it wishes to test itself, to push itself to its extremes, to live on the edge. Assessment offers three modes of such self-testing. First, and immediately, assessment brings with it possible success or failure. Its embrace, in a spirit of authenticity, is the Everest syndrome in action. Scaling its heights may be exhilarating in part because of the risk of failure. Second, assessment, when rigorous, calls one out of oneself and into a new place. One is stretched into a different place. One is required to travel; and the travel – as we have seen – is as much ontological as it is epistemological. Third, the element of risk – which has to be present if formative assessment is to do its work – characteristically engenders an emotional response. Many students falter at this hurdle, unable to live with the emotional turmoil that summative assessment induces. (This is not a critical comment on such students; merely an underlining of the emotional presences that assessment evokes.)

These three modes of testing – of living with risk, of ontological voyaging, and of emotionality – are possible attractions for authentic being. Through these three modes of testing, authentic being becomes more authentic: it becomes itself, in a Nietzschean spirit.

But this authentic becoming is only possible where the student in her being throws herself forward into her assessments to win the three prizes of becoming (of overcoming risk, of ontological journeying and of emotionality) that await her. There can be no element of the assessing imposing itself, in a regulatory manner, for this educational authenticity to be a real prospect.

Through authenticity, the tables may be turned. The pernicious effect of summative assessment to impose itself, to control and to discipline may be overturned. A liberating potential of summative assessment can be realised if the student, in her authentic being, reaches for it.

Many make much of the distinction between summative and formative assessment. In fact, as I have noted, summative assessment is itself 'formative'. It cannot help but be formative. That is not at issue. At issue is whether that formative potential of summative assessment is lethal or emancipatory. Does summative assessment exert its power to discipline and control, a power so possibly lethal that the student may be wounded for life? Literally so; the student may be disarmed from confronting life; may be robbed of life, her will dissipated. Or, to the contrary, does summative assessment allow itself to be conquered by the student, who takes up a positive, even belligerent, stance towards it, determined to extract every human possibility that it affords?

Possibilities

It is just possible, then, that the circle can be squared: that a student can be propelled – or, more accurately, can propel herself – into a state of authenticity and that summative assessment can play a part in this. Prima facie, this is paradoxical for summative assessment threatens to expunge authentic being. In its propensities to classify, to judge and to place offerings as this or that looms the potential for limiting being, rather than allowing it to become itself.

Characteristically, students will not take up active and engaged stances towards their summative assessments unless they are encouraged to do so. Their authenticity in this educational setting will not simply express itself; it has to be nurtured. Encouragement and nurturing can take and have to take different forms. That encouragement would have to be present at the levels both of the curriculum and of pedagogy as well as of assessment. A curriculum for authentic becoming will contain spaces in which the student will be given a freedom to roam; a pedagogy for authentic becoming will again open spaces for the voyaging of being as well as its affirmation. In other words, long before summative assessment is encountered, the student will have embarked on a voyage of self-becoming and will have reached a point – even if a point still on the way – in which the potential of assessment is understood and relished for the powers of self-understanding that it may impart.

This is no idle wish. Just as we see students who are understandably fearful of formal assessment procedures – and many have been damaged by their experience – so we also see students who advance towards their assignments and the subsequent assessment of those assignments with some *élan*. They propel themselves forward, even while not knowing the outcome. Through their curricula and pedagogical experiences, they have advanced to a position in which they can give an account of themselves without fear (even if the outcome of the judgement that lies in wait is unpredictable). Assessment – *summative* assessment – may have educational properties after all.

But how likely is it that students may approach their assessments in this way? The structure of those possibilities has already been hinted at. It is a structure of possibilities in which all parties are implicated. In the first place, the responsibility lies with the students' educators. As stated, the curriculum will be designed to provide spaces for students for their own becoming and their own self-exciting, and for the formation of their own pedagogical will, their will to learn. This will be achieved in many ways, through problem-based learning, through projects, through group tasks, through optional modules, through activities demanding personal responsibility (in the community, in field trips, in the clinical situation, in the laboratory).

But the pedagogy also has to work to that end: it surely has to be a pedagogy that builds students' confidence in themselves, and their courage and resilience; in short, all the qualities that were identified earlier. Students can be and should be helped to face up to the challenges of assessment and brought to a state of mind in which they are willing to put themselves forward. They come to believe in their abilities and want to test those beliefs. They would feel short-changed if that possibility were suddenly withdrawn. A pedagogy for becoming works in subtle ways, through the smile, through the real engagement where the teacher really listens to the students and takes their words so seriously that they invite even more from the student, and even through firm but explicit guidance and encouragement. Such a pedagogy works in the formation not just of a pedagogical relationship but also through the formation of a *human* relationship.

Both the curriculum and the pedagogical relationship, therefore, are key components of a readiness, even a will, on the part of the student in favour of assessment. But the student also has her part to play: that much is similarly clear from our analysis. In the end, the student has to will herself forward, to come to a perception that assessment is in her educational interests (and not merely her economic interests for the financial capital that her degree will represent). The student may be encouraged to believe in her own abilities and find her programme of studies of personal interest and even delight; but the student has in the end to take her own part in the formation of her positive spirit towards her assessments.

There are, though, clearly elements of power and control here. The student's educators have power over her and control of her curriculum and assessment regime; and have the greater influence over the pedagogy (although, there, the student bears her part, too). The first and major responsibility, therefore, in the eliciting of this positive spirit towards assessment – summative assessment – lies with the student's educators. And that responsibility is unflagging: the encouragement of the student, and the formation of the courage and resilience and other qualities that were identified earlier, is a never-ending challenge. It is *there*, on a daily basis in the working out of the pedagogical relationship.

That responsibility on the part of the educators is also *there*, one might add, in the form of the summative assessments themselves. If summative assessment is really to encourage authentic human being forward, to become more itself, then it is going to have to give space, surely, to individuality. The being of the student is particular to the student, after all. So, summative assessment will itself have to be characterised by experiment and innovation. Doubtless, such assessments for authentic being will face challenges as to reliability and validity but ways through these difficulties are already being developed (see Knight and Yorke, 2003: ch. 7; Murdoch-Eaton, 2005). Students are even going to have to be permitted themselves to experiment with their own modes of writing and textual presentation (see Nolan, 2005).

Conclusion

It is hardly surprising that the matter of summative assessment in higher education has not received the attention it deserves from educators. After all, summative assessment has the power to control, to classify students arbitrarily, to limit their educational development and to impair their own sense of themselves. And we see all of those things happening on a regular basis.

It just may be, however, that an entirely different kind of possibility within summative assessment lies before us. If we can reconceive of summative assessment as an educational site in which students can more fully become themselves – at least their educational selves – then summative assessment may be redeemed as having formative educational potential. Summative assessment may not present itself as an impossible mission after all.

For such an aspiration to be realised, the whole educational process should be understood as a space in which students' educational being can flourish. And that spirit, of educational being and becoming, has to be embodied in educational practices, both within curricula and pedagogy. If such a spirit, of the forming of the students' educational being, can inspire our practices in higher education almost every moment of every day, then the students may catch something of that spirit, too. They may just bring themselves to approach their summative assessments with *élan*, with courage and with daring. For they would feel then that those formative assessments would be a space in which the students' own being can be tested; and they would want, desire, to have it tested. They would be fired up, tackling their assessments with relish, hurling themselves forward into the fray. And in that process, their own authenticity would be enhanced.

In such a set of ways, with both educators and students intent on a joint project of educational becoming, the tables may be turned. The power of summative assessments to humiliate and subject students might be vanquished. Instead, the students would have become themselves and, at the same time, the victors over assessment.

References

Barnett, R. (2000) *Realizing the University in an Age of Supercomplexity*, Buckingham: Open University Press.

Biggs, J. (2003) *Teaching for Quality Learning at University*, 2nd edn, Maidenhead: McGraw-Hill/Open University Press.

Cooper, D. (2002) *The Meaning of Things: Humanities, Humility and Mystery*, Oxford: Clarendon.

Davis, A. (1998) The limits of educational assessment, special issue of *Journal of Philosophy of Education*, 32, 1.

Foucault, M. (1991) *Discipline and Punish: The Birth of the Prison*, London: Penguin.

Goodlad, S. (1976) *Conflict and Consensus in Higher Education*, London: Hodder & Stoughton.

Gouldner, A. (1979) *The Future of Intellectuals and the Rise of the New Class*, London: Macmillan.

Heidegger, M. (1998) *Being and Time*, Oxford: Blackwell.

Knight, P.T. and Yorke, M. (2003) *Assessment, Learning and Employability*, Maidenhead: McGraw-Hill/Open University Press.

Macfarlane, B. (2006) *The Academic Citizen*, London: Routledge.

Murdoch-Eaton, D. (2005) Formal appraisal of undergraduates – worth the effort?, in *01 Issues and News on Learning and Teaching in Medicine, Dentistry and Veterinary Medicine (8)*, Newcastle: Higher Education Academy Subject Centre, University of Newcastle.

Nietzsche, F. (1968) *The Will to Power*, New York: Vintage.

Nolan, K. (2005) Publish or cherish? Performing a dissertation in/between research spaces, in R. Barnett (ed.) *Reshaping the University: New Relationships between Research, Scholarship and Teaching*, Maidenhead: McGraw-Hill/Open University Press.

Sartre, J.-P. (2003 [1943]) *Being and Nothingness*, London: Routledge.

Chapter 4

Learning assessment

Students' experiences in post-school qualifications

Kathryn Ecclestone

There is growing interest among British researchers and policy-makers at levels of the education system in assessment that encourages engagement with learning, develops autonomy and motivation and raises levels of formal achievement. These goals have been influenced by developments in outcome-based and portfolio-based qualifications in post-school education (see, for example, Jessup, 1991; Otter, 1989; UDACE, 1994). There is parallel interest in developing 'learning to learn' skills and encouraging a positive attitude to learning after formal education through assessment that serves what Boud calls 'double duty': namely, meeting immediate goals for achievement while establishing a basis for learners to undertake their own assessment activities in future (Boud, 2000; see also Chapter 6, this volume). More specifically, research offers insights about how to promote a sophisticated understanding of formative assessment that changes how students and teachers regard the purposes of assessment and their respective roles in it in order to enhance learning (see Black and Wiliam, 1998; ARG, 2002; Gardener, 2006).

Yet, despite such compelling goals and the apparently unproblematic nature of principles and methods to encourage them, theoretical and empirical research about the assessment experiences of post-compulsory students in the UK shows that promoting sustainable learning through assessment is not straightforward (see Ecclestone, 2002; Torrance *et al.*, 2005). This work suggests that staff in universities need to understand more about the ways in which students' previous experiences of assessment shape their expectations, attitudes and effectiveness in engaging with different methods and approaches. In turn, this might illuminate some challenges in fostering sustainable learning.

As a contribution to this understanding, this chapter draws on a recent study that explored links between assessment and students' achievement in five post-school qualifications (Torrance *et al.*, 2005). Discussion here focuses on students' experiences in, and attitudes to, two assessment systems: general academic qualifications and general vocational qualifications. First, the chapter summarises the main assessment features of these qualifications. Second, it summarises key concepts from research that explores the evolution of students' 'assessment identities' and 'assessment careers'. Third, it applies these concepts to data from in-depth interviews and observations of assessment activities with four business studies teachers and ten students in two general academic courses, and three tutors and fifteen students in two general vocational courses in two further education colleges. This section discusses students' and teachers' images of achievement and failure, differences between vocational and academic identities and attitudes to formative assessment. Finally, it evaluates implications of discussion for assessment in universities that might seek to foster sustainable learning.

Different assessment systems

Most young people in the UK progress to university from general academic qualifications or general vocational qualifications. Some go to higher education from a work-based qualification. Mature students can take an 'Access to Higher Education' course, while other adult students come from competence-based, workplace vocational qualifications. After compulsory schooling, students can take these qualifications in schools, further education colleges or the workplace. British universities also deal with growing numbers of overseas students who come from a diverse array of assessment experiences.

The past thirty years has seen a huge shift in British post-school qualifications from methods and processes based on competitive, norm-referenced examinations for selection towards assessment that encourages more achievement. There is now a strong emphasis on raising standards of achievement for everyone through better feedback, sharing the outcomes and criteria with students and recording achievement and progress in portfolios. One effect of this shift is a harmonisation of assessment methods and processes between long-running, high-status academic qualifications in subjects such as history, sociology and psychology and newer, lower-status general vocational qualifications such as leisure and tourism, health and social care. General academic and general vocational qualifications now combine external examinations set by an awarding body, assignments or coursework assessed by an awarding body and coursework or assignments assessed by teachers. Some general academic qualifications are still assessed entirely by external examinations.

However, apparent similarities conceal the ways in which day-to-day assessment practices of general and vocational qualifications vary in relation to official specifications and teachers' and students' expectations about whether students can draft formative assignments, receive feedback and negotiate aspects of content and process. For example, general vocational students produce modular assignments prescribed by an awarding body and marked by teachers, supplemented by externally set tests of knowledge and a portfolio of achievement. Students work closely to the official assessment specifications, submitting formative drafts, and are coached closely by teachers to achieve the grade criteria. They can resit unit (module) tests where performance is poor. In general academic qualifications, assessment is still heavily predicated on externally set and marked examinations with some coursework assessment marked by teachers. Formative assessment emphasises the practising of typical examination questions with classroom discussion and feedback. Students can resit some examinations if they have per-formed badly. The ways in which these expectations affect formative assessment practices are explored in more detail below.

Assessment identities and learning careers

In addition to knowing something about differences and similarities in the assessment methods that students have experienced before university, it is also important for staff in higher education to recognise that assessment is still strongly differentiated in post-school qualifications, affecting students' choice of university and universities' choice of students. As Ball *et al.* (2005) show, student decision-making and institutional marketing are both predicated on images of what counts as an appropriate learning identity and culture: these images are strongly class, gender and culturally based.

Other research argues that the notion of 'learning culture' is important in understanding how students and teachers develop implicit and explicit expectations about teaching and learning (see Hodkinson *et al.*, 2004). Taking the notion of culture as a 'socially constructed and historically derived common base of knowl-edge, values and norms for action that people grow into and come to take as a natural way of life', some researchers have examined how assessment methods within different qualifications and the learning cultures of particular contexts combine to construct assessment cultures and assessment careers (Hodkinson *et al.* quoted in Ecclestone and Pryor, 2003: 479).

This work suggests that, while assessment cultures may be particular to a local context, children and young people are socialised in the requirements of formal assessment systems and take certain attitudes and dispositions about assessment and their role in it through compulsory schooling into post-school contexts. A number of studies show that 'learning careers' develop through interactions between personal dispositions and the teaching, learning and assessment strategies that children and young people experience in particular contexts. Dispositions and attitudes cannot be isolated from structural conditions such as employment prospects or the effects of educational selection and differentiation in a local area, the social class and cultural background of students and the educational institutions they choose or are sent to.

Longitudinal, ethnographic studies on primary and secondary school students' learning careers show how attitudes and activities emerge over time, in a complex interplay between the factors summarised above. This work depicts 'pupil career . . . as a particular social product deriving from children's strategic action in school contexts [and] strongly influenced by cultural expectation' (Pollard and Filer, 1999: 22). The experience of successive formal tests as 'key classification events' has a profound effect on children's identity as successful or failing learners (see also Reay and Wiliam, 1998; Torrance and Pryor, 1998). Students' attitudes and strate-gies in relation to their assessment experiences are affected by the ethos of an educational institution, resources, parents' attitudes and the norms of different peer groups. Studies of learning and assessment cultures in further education colleges show that these interactions and their effects on attitudes to learning shift erratically over time, shaped by crises, transformations and changing images of identity in family life, work and relationships (see Bloomer and Hodkinson, 2000; Ecclestone, 2002; Colley *et al.*, 2003). Taken together, these studies suggest that socio-cultural analysis enables researchers to understand the ways in which social context, the forms of knowledge and learning offered in different qualifications, the policy imperatives regulating those systems and day-to-day assessment practices all interact to shape students' identity and assessment practices into 'assessment careers' (Ecclestone and Pryor, 2003; Ecclestone, 2004).

Images of achievement and failure

Notions of assessment careers, identities and cultures were evident among the general academic and general vocational students in the study discussed in this chapter. Images of achievement and failure, and the identity and learning career associated with those images, affected students' and teachers' perceptions about the suitability of a vocational or academic qualification. Ideas about 'achievement' and 'learning' were influenced strongly by official targets to raise attainment of grades, overall pass rates, retention on courses and progression to formal education at the next level. 'Learning' therefore slid easily into targets based on outcomes specified by the awarding body and 'assessment' became the 'delivery of achievement'. These images are reinforced by awarding body procedures for quality control in qualifications and national inspection for further education colleges. As a result, instrumental, target-driven images of learning and achievement were very evident among teachers and students in all qualifications analysed in the study.

Nevertheless, although official indicators of achievement were prominent, academic and vocational teachers and students prioritised different educational goals. Vocational tutors emphasised the importance of an ipsative (self-referenced) achievement based on an ability to develop self-confidence and overcome previous fears and failures from school experience. In some ways, these attributes were more important than the acquisition of skills or subject knowledge:

> [students] develop such a lot in the two years that we have them . . . the course gives them an overall understanding of business studies really, it develops their understanding and develops them as people, and hopefully sets them up for employment. It doesn't train them for a job; it's much more to develop the student than the content . . . that's my personal view, anyway.
>
> (Vocational course leader)

The privileging of personal development in general vocational qualifications reinforces findings from other studies (see Ecclestone, 2002). In contrast, staff and students in general academic courses saw achievement as predominantly about progression in subject-related knowledge and understanding, and gaining suitable grades for university. Academic staff talked much more about their subject than vocational staff did.

Vocational students had a strong sense of identity as 'second chance' learners, an image with which their tutors empathised from their own educational experience. Four students were high achievers, associating their status with other students with consistently good work, conscientious studying and high grades. They referred to themselves in the same language as teachers, as 'strong A-grade students', approaching all their assignments with confidence and certainty and unable to imagine getting low grades. Crucial to their positive identity as successful second-chance students was that other, less successful, students saw them as a source of help when they got stuck. Again, the four high achievers mirrored the characteristics and attitudes of the 'embedded' successful students in earlier studies.

The majority of vocational students worked strategically in a comfort zone, adopting a different grade identity from the high achievers. One said:

> I don't really think about grades and pride is not a motive . . . if I do well, I do . . . Achievement would mean getting a C or above; I'd be happy to get a C but I know I could do better. It works on points so it's easier to set that target and I'll be happy with that because I like to set a lower target and if I get a higher one I'm, like, 'wow'.

Similarly, the general academic students set targets based on a sense of an appropriate grade for them. For example, one pointed out that: 'I'll get an E in this – that's my average. This year I moved it up to a D – I was ecstatic and it's to do with my own barriers. I'm the first child in my family to go to college and I'm not the brightest so I'm doing really well.'

Vocational students displayed high levels of comfort, familiarity and acceptance in relation to the demands of assessment. They were not worried about failure, since none believed that it was possible to fail. As one said: 'you can fail if you just don't do the work on time, or you don't take any notice of the teachers' advice . . . you can drop a couple of the option units if your marks aren't any good and you can still pass the course.'

Similarly, academic students were not worried about failure but they made strategic judgements about what grade to aim for and, in two cases, worked consciously in a comfort zone that was below their potential achievement. Students from academic and vocational qualifications were reassured by the way that poor grades could be retrieved or offset by higher grades in other areas. In academic qualifications students can resit some exams, and in vocational qualifications students can drop their two poorest unit grades because the overall grade is calculated from the average of their best grades. Vocational students believed that they could keep retaking exams until they passed: one was redoing all her first-year exams to get higher grades. However, academic students wanting to go to university saw failure as getting a lower grade than they needed.

Vocational and academic identities

Teachers' and students' attitudes to achievement and failure and their beliefs about students' preferences, capabilities and attitudes correlated to the culture of each qualification track. Vocational and academic students saw clear differences between the two qualifications: academic ones were 'higher status, more well known'. Despite knowing that the vocational course had a lower status, students valued its relevance. As one explained, 'I don't know what AVCE [the acronym for the vocational qualification] means outside here; I just want to learn stuff about business and get some extra knowledge'. None of the vocational students or their teachers saw the general academic qualification as appropriate. Students liked the familiarity of continuing with teaching and assessment methods they had experienced in an intermediate vocational qualification in the final year of school.

Yet, while they saw themselves as 'vocational' students, and despite a progression route from their course to university, none of this group had strong goals for this, and few seemed to know what a business studies qualification could lead to; instead, they liked the image of an 'intelligent-sounding subject', as one student put it. Some had hazy notions that it might be useful if they ever wanted to set up their own business. In the short term, vocational aspirations were erratic: one student wanted to travel, take up hairdressing or apply to the British Broadcasting Corporation; another wanted to train in a craft like plumbing or electrical work. In contrast, academic students said that they and their parents saw the qualification as being 'better' than its vocational equivalent and none had countenanced doing a vocational course.

Attitudes about the purpose and ethos of a qualification and its assessment methods were reinforced by teachers' images of what students liked and wanted. One vocational course leader regarded 'good assessment' as practical activities, work experience and field trips: 'all the things these kids love . . . to move away from all this written assessment'. For her, good assessment should reflect 'the way that [vocational] students prefer to learn . . . they are often less secure and enjoy being part of one group with a small team of staff . . . [assessment is] more supported, it's to do with comfort zones – being in a more protected environment'.

In their beliefs about 'comfort zones' and 'protecting' students, vocational teachers saw assessment as integral to a strong ethos of personal development that minimised stress or pressure: assessment to develop subject knowledge or 'learning to learn' skills was a much lower priority. Teachers and students liked to work in a lively and relaxed atmosphere that combined group work, teacher input and time to work on assignments individually or in small friendship-based groups.

In contrast, teaching and assessment in academic groups in the study were more teacher-centred and didactic and more individualised, partly because students moved between four separate subjects with different cohorts in each. Vocational students compared the familiar, tight-knit atmosphere and a cohesive team of tutors in their course with the experience of two peers taking the first year of an academic qualification. One said:

[the vocational course] is not hard, as long as you do the work; it's a laugh with the class you see all the time. In [the general course], you see other students only once a week and they're boring. Here, you build a culture in the class . . . [In the vocational course], I don't look at the spec from the exam body because we have a good relationship with the teachers and so we trust them. In [the academic course], there's no relationship, it's a big group, no one talks and it's silent. Here we all get on, it's like a family. [Group banter at this point about how sometimes families hate each other.]

Attitudes to formative assessment

Students therefore have different expectations about the 'type' of learner they are, the purposes of assessment as either subject-knowledge or personal development, and the forms of assessment that are suitable for them. In relation to assessment that might encourage sustainable learning, students progressing to university have also had very different experiences of formative assessment. These lead to different expectations about what they can or should expect in terms of feedback and help in improving their work. General vocational qualifications are designed around detailed specifications and assessment criteria, with grade descriptors for each level, and explicit expectations of feedback and targets to improve achievement. Although general academic qualifications have recently adopted a similar format, they have traditionally been seen as norm-referenced, competitive and selective. This ethos has discouraged teachers from giving students the assessment criteria. Different traditions therefore affect teachers' and students' ideas about fair assessment and the place of feedback, help and support.

The study revealed strong differences between these aspects of an assessment culture. Vocational teachers saw their main assessment role as a translator of official criteria. They broke up the strongly framed assignment briefs into sequential tasks to meet each criterion. Students prepared their assignments, working to copies of the official criteria specified for grades in each unit. One college reproduced these in posters on the students' base-room wall. Students could submit a completed draft for feedback, although this had to reflect a best attempt: they could not submit a half-hearted version in the hope of feedback to make it pass. In the study as a whole, there was wide variation in arrangements for this: in some courses, drafting was done numerous times while in others only one opportunity was offered. Lesson time was used to introduce students to each assignment but also to talk through the outcomes of draft assignments, outlined here by one of the college tutors:

I talk through the assessment criteria grid with them and the assignment brief, pinpointing the relationships between P, M and D [pass, merit and distinction] and that it does evolve through to D. The students like to go for the best grade possible and discuss how they could go about getting an M. There again, some students just aim for basic pass and those are the ones who leave everything to the last minute. Then I see a draft work, read through it, make notes, talk to each one, show the good areas in relation to the criteria and explain why and how if they have met them, saying things like 'you've missed out M2' . . . some will action it, some won't. It's generally giving them ideas and giving them a platform to achieve the outstanding M or D criteria.

Vocational tutors marked the draft, starting with grade criteria from the Es through the Cs to the As. Where students had not done enough to get an E, written feedback offered direct advice about how to 'plug' and 'cover' gaps, cross-referenced to the assessment specifications. Less overt advice was given for the Cs and As: as the tutor pointed out, 'students must work these out for themselves – the good grades have to come from them'.

Assignments in the vocational qualification were meticulously organised and staff and students had internalised the language of 'evidencing the criteria' and 'cross-referencing'. They were also very similar in presentation and content, reflecting the prescriptive assignment briefs and demands from the awarding body that they should contain evidence that is easily amenable to formal moderation: teachers and students referred to this as 'moderate-able evidence'.

Yet the formal processes, together with commitment to maximising students' chances of passing and expectations of their capabilities, created a heavy workload for vocational tutors:

> I think we do too much but I say to them 'here are the criteria, there's nothing hidden so why don't you look at them and see if you've done it', but the very nature of some of our students, they can't do that in the first year – well, some do – but the reason they are at the level they are is that they don't have that motivation, but also they're not from backgrounds where they're encouraged in their learning at home . . . They're on their own . . . Some are only used to negative feedback at home.

Vocational students had strong expectations of guidance:

> You do a draft, you get it back and you have a week to change things and hand it back again. If you are lucky and you have just missed a bit, you can improve it – that's good when we don't know what we are doing! You read their comments and try to do what they say like, 'You've missed E1.'

Group affinity, peer support and strong relationships with tutors were integral to how students regarded and dealt with tutors' feedback on their work. Two students who were combining academic and vocational options compared their experience:

> there's no social interaction in economics; the teacher never does group work but in [the vocational course] they do, so you might get some feedback, some criticism about a question, e.g., 'You got this the wrong way round,' and it's

fair enough but because you don't understand it anyway, it doesn't make sense and so we all go 'We'll be lucky if we get an E in this.' It's not just the support you get from teachers but the group – you can ask them but not in [the academic one].

The contrast between one-to-one feedback in a class in the academic qualification and feedback to the whole group in the vocational course affected vocational students' confidence in accepting criticism:

Well, [academic] film studies does lend itself to group interaction and he [the tutor] does try to include the whole group like analysing a film, you can't do that on your own . . . but they don't test you until about a month before the exam and you practise an answer and go through it in class and that's it . . . and he gives your feedback in class, one to one. In [the vocational course], she does it with the group so you don't feel like you're the only one. In [the academic course], you can feel alienated, like it's only you doing it wrong. In [the vocational course], she goes 'some of you didn't do this', it's a few of you and so you can compare . . . You're all in it together.

Expectations and educational goals also affected what tutors regarded as 'fair' assessment. In complete contrast to the close-knit culture of vocational assessment, one academic tutor chose an examination-based course because it made students 'take a chance' in competition with others. It also encouraged students to maintain a reasonable level of performance over two years of the full qualification. For him, too much formative feedback undermined fair assessment:

students [have to] perform and produce material they understand, that's clear and not polluted by me. I don't mark the scripts and that's how it should be: there's no preferential treatment, nowhere for the students to run and hide. In other courses, the coursework can be done by other people, it happens . . . a student can get As on coursework and Ds on examined units . . . I'm confident that if I manage the coursework with students in a particular fashion so that unwittingly I'm scrutinising their ideas, feeding them ideas, letting them bring in different drafts so they could hit the criteria, I could get every one of them an A.

Another strong contrast to the ethos of the vocational course came from his belief that 'if a student who's basically a D got a C [in the exam], and could get an A because of the coursework, that's not right . . . it helps the lazy student'.

Students in academic qualifications practised examination answers that would help them achieve good grades. Written feedback was more general and open-ended than in the vocational course and tutors did not offer direct advice about higher grades. One tutor offered written comments, or comments in class that evaluated the strengths and weaknesses of answers: these comments were strongly critical and occasionally positive. He wrote short comments, questions and queries on individual answers and went through them in class, using question and answer to offer feedback on the quality of responses. On one occasion, he quoted back one student's response as an 'example of "critical analysis" in John's answer just then compared to the "rather descriptive" answer that Liam gave', asking students if they could tell the difference and advising them to look at each other's written answers. In contrast to assessment observed in the vocational courses, this combination of question, answer and feedback was much more robustly focused on eliciting the cognitive skills demanded in the exam.

Unlike the positive consensus among vocational students about assessment, more varied views were evident among academic students. In one college, students saw their tutor's approach to feedback on their practice questions as a tactic to motivate them to do better. Robert pointed out that: 'You never get over 60 per cent from him.' [Interviewer: 'Is that just him, his limitation on marks?'] Robert: 'He doesn't want us to get carried away. He's a hard marker compared to other teachers . . . he sets a culture.' Another said: 'He's the sort of bloke that doesn't use much praise.' Students did not find this feedback motivating or demotivating; instead, it was 'just the way he is' and they accepted it because they felt the classroom atmosphere was good and that he had their educational interests at heart. As with the vocational students, the relationship with the teacher was important in how students responded to assessment. In relation to the robust approach of the academic teacher, one student said: 'It depends if you know the teacher and the mark significantly, it's quite motivating . . . you take the comments on board . . . it's not motivating if you keep getting the same thing [comment].'

Some of the lower-achieving academic students found it hard to relate individual practice answers to oral feedback to the whole group:

> He talks about it in class and we mark it ourselves. But it's really hard because in some subjects, like this one, we barely cover the syllabus let alone know how we're doing . . . some students find it easy to mark their work and anyway, they're really bright already and so they have loads of stuff to tick. If you don't have the ideas, like I don't, because I'm not bright like them, you can't see the weaknesses and so you can't make sense of what he's saying.

Another student added: 'There are loads of questions that could come up in the exam and he [the tutor] adds new ideas, a new angle and it's very verbal and so I don't write it down and so when it comes to remembering later, you forget what you could write.'

Further differences between the assessment cultures of general and vocational qualifications arose over the principle in formative assessment that students should 'internalise' the standards or criteria through processes such as self- and peer assessment. Vocational students could recite the wording of the criteria and locate specific examples of 'evaluate', 'analysis' and 'justify' in their own work. When asked what an A grade meant, one pointed out:

It's analyse, evaluate, and stuff like that. You have to explain things but more in-depth. Instead of just summarising, you have to extend it and make it relevant and link it to what you've already put, it's clear and it flows and it's fully described. Not just going off on a complete tangent. You have to include what they ask, not let it get too theory-based. Mind you, actually doing it's another thing.

Vocational students became proficient at cross-referencing assignment tasks, tutors' comments and the assessment criteria, mirroring the activities of their teachers. Academic students were more vague about the criteria but could, nevertheless, offer a credible account of an A grade: 'It's your style of writing, with evaluation and analysis and synthesis and stuff like that, and you have to show it in your work . . . I can do it to some degree but not totally.' Academic students were well versed in how pieces of work related to different types of tutor comment, or what a strategically placed tick or question mark signified. For example, one pointed to a carefully placed 'Q' over a word on his answers to typical exam questions and said: 'He's asking, "Is that the right word or should I have used another?"' While vocational students used the official assessment criteria during their assignments and carried them with them to accompany their assignments, academic students seemed to work out the demands of different grades in a more haphazard way from the tutor's comments and classroom feedback.

The implications of students' assessment careers for sustainable assessment

The chapter has aimed to show that attempts to make assessment in universities more able to instil sustainable habits of self-assessment while also encouraging achievement have to take into account the practices, identities, expectations and cultures that students bring with them from post-school assessment systems. The subtle shaping of an assessment career combines all four of these dimensions and the dimensions take different forms in the two qualifications discussed here.

Qualifications leading to higher education have some similar assessment processes, but very different assessment cultures. Technical similarities include opportunities to maximise grade achievement, feedback about how to improve, and involving students in understanding the criteria. On the surface, these characteristics might contribute to sustainable assessment. Yet differences in the forms of support offered to vocational and general students affect how these features influence attitudes to learning and assessment.

Further differences arise in teachers' and students' beliefs about the 'type' of learners suited to each assessment culture. In vocational assessment, teachers' interest in students' personal development and confidence over subject knowledge and higher-level cognitive skills manifest themselves in strongly directive formative feedback. This helped students in the study to achieve higher grades and overcome negative images of learning they may have developed at school.

Although a minority flourished through these processes, they also encouraged comforting processes, working below potential capacity and instrumental compliance. General education students had a sense of themselves as 'higher status' than vocational students and they gained higher-level cognitive skills but experienced much less overt formative assessment. The ability of either group to sustain learning on their own through the formative assessment they received during their courses is therefore questionable.

Studies cited in the chapter also show that students accept the assessment systems they experience largely without complaint or dissent and learn to navigate the various demands and processes. Yet they are far from passive recipients of assessment. Instead, attitudes to learning, ideas about their abilities and 'acceptable' teaching and assessment methods and their strategic approach shape assessment practices just as much as the official specifications and teachers' ideas about what is possible. Assessment cultures and the attitudes and activities that emerge from them cannot therefore be separated from these factors.

It is also important to recognise that assessment practices and outcomes reinforce inequality of choice and opportunity. The two groups in the study discussed here were following pre-determined tracks that conformed to and confirmed an existing identity as a 'type' of learner. One danger is that universities replicate segregated tracks based on associated stereotypes about what 'vocational' and 'academic' students expect, want and can deal with. This raises questions about whether higher education encourages broad or narrow assessment and reinforces old learning identities or encourages new ones: for example, pressure to make university familiar and not too uncomfortable in order to widen participation for 'non-traditional' students might also confirm comforting, low-risk images of learning and assessment.

More specifically, analysis in this chapter suggests that students develop particular expectations of appropriate feedback, help and support and of how easy or difficult it is to act on feedback in order to get a 'good grade'. A cultural understanding of formative assessment is useful because techniques such as feedback, explaining the criteria, encouraging student self-assessment and using detailed grade descriptors are seen widely as 'good practice'. Yet, in some assessment cultures, they can encourage superficial compliance with tasks derived from the assessment criteria, bureaucratic forms of self-assessment against the criteria and high expectations of coaching and support.

The chapter has shown that both groups in the study contained some students working compliantly, strategically and superficially to meet assessment criteria, others working happily in a comfort zone lower than their potential achievement and still others working at deep levels of motivation and engagement. In this way, the study lends weight to well-known notions in higher education of deep, surface and strategic approaches to learning. Such strategies are typical of any cohort but they also illuminate how a simple, technical focus on assessment techniques can lead haphazardly to all three approaches. Again, a cultural understanding of students in different assessment systems is important for a more strategic approach to encouraging engaging and sustainable assessment rather than merely instrumental responses.

A particularly salient feature in the study discussed in this chapter is the extent to which post-school assessment systems in the UK now present failure as an undesirable political and educational outcome. Although drop-out and non-completion are official indicators of failure, mechanisms to predict final grades, formative feedback and the chance to repeat poor summative assessments have done much to remove fear of both failure and grading. This is an important cultural shift in the UK, and while assessment still carries high emotional, social and cognitive stakes, students in the study showed a marked lack of anxiety about either assessment or about the possibility of failure.

Arguments in the chapter warn against merely focusing on formative assessment techniques. Instead, a better understanding of assessment cultures and assessment identities would enable universities to address students' expectations about both formative and summative assessment more explicitly. In some cases, this means challenging those expectations. For example, pressure at all levels of the education system to equate achievement and learning with better grades and a climate of university students as 'consumers' in the UK mean that growing numbers of students expect good grades and a good 'assessment experience'.

Finally, the study discussed in this chapter was not merely *for* learning or *of* learning: instead, it *was* learning, especially in the vocational courses. The clearer the task of how to achieve a grade or award becomes, and the more detailed the assistance given by tutors, supervisors and assessors, the more likely the candidates are to succeed; but succeed at what? Transparency of objectives, coupled with extensive use of coaching and practice to help learners meet them, is in danger of removing the challenge of learning and reducing the quality and validity of outcomes achieved. Assessment procedures and practices come completely to dominate the learning experience, and 'criteria compliance' comes to replace 'learning' (Torrance *et al.*, 2005: 46).

In addition to questions about how assessment can encourage sustainable learning, the chapter suggests that we also need to ask to which images and forms of learning and achievement it leads.

References

Assessment Reform Group (ARG) (2002) *10 Principles of Assessment for Learning*, Cambridge: University of Cambridge.

Ball, S.J., David, M. and Reay, D. (2005) *Degrees of Difference*, London: RoutledgeFalmer.

Black, P. and Wiliam, D. (1998) Assessment and classroom learning, principles, policy and practice, *Assessment in Education*, 5, 1: 1–78.

Bloomer, M. and Hodkinson, P. (2000) Learning careers: continuity and change in young people's dispositions to learning, *British Educational Research Journal*, 26, 5: 583–598.

Boud, D. (2000) Sustainable assessment: rethinking assessment for the learning society, *Studies in Continuing Education*, 22, 2: 151–167.

Colley, H., James, D., Tedder, M. and Diment, K. (2003) Learning as becoming in vocational education and training: class, gender and the role of vocational habitus, *Journal of Vocational Education and Training*, 55, 4: 471–497.

Ecclestone, K. (2002) *Learning Autonomy in Post-Compulsory Education: The Politics and Practice of Formative Assessment*, London: RoutledgeFalmer.

—— (2004) Learning in a comfort zone: cultural and social capital in outcome-based assessment regimes, *Assessment in Education*, 11, 1: 30–47.

Ecclestone, K. and Pryor, J. (2003) 'Learning careers' or 'assessment careers'?: the impact of assessment systems on learning, *British Educational Research Journal*, 29: 471–488.

Gardener, J. (ed.) (2006) *Assessment and Learning*, London: Sage.

Hodkinson, P., Biesta, G. and James, D. (2004) Towards a cultural theory of college-based learning, paper presented at the Annual Conference of the British Educational Research Association, Manchester, September.

Jessup, G. (1991) *Outcomes: NVQs and the Emerging Model of Education and Training*, London: FalmerPress.

Pollard, A. and Filer, A. (1999) *The Social World of Pupil Career: Strategic Biographies through Primary School*, London: Cassell.

Reay, D. and Wiliam, D. (1998) 'I'll be a nothing': structure, agency and the construction of identity through assessment, *British Educational Research Journal*, 25: 343–354.

Torrance, H. and Pryor, J. (1998) *Investigating Formative Assessment: Teaching, Learning and Assessment in the Classroom*, Buckingham: Open University Press.

Torrance, H., Colley, H., Garratt, D., Jarvis, J., Piper, H., Ecclestone, K. and James, D. (2005) *The Impact of Different Modes of Assessment on Achievement and Progress in the Learning and Skills Sector*, Learning and Skills Development Agency (available at: https://www.lsda.org.uk/cims/order.aspx?code=052284&src=XOWEB).

Otter, S. (1989) *Learning Outcomes*, Leicester: Unit for Developing Adult and Continuing Education.

UDACE (1994) *Learning Outcomes in Higher Education*, London: FEU/UDACE.

Part 3

Themes

Chapter 5

Contradictions of assessment for learning in institutions of higher learning

Steinar Kvale

> Examinations . . . might be made most important adjuncts in promoting habits
> of . . . self-instruction, voluntary labour, and self-examination.
> *Report to the Oxford Commissioners of Examination Reform*, 1852

Assessment is a field of contradictions. In this chapter I address the question of why the introduction of assessment for learning in institutions of higher learning today is considered an educational innovation. In recent years a variety of assessment forms – such as portfolios, peer assessment, self-assessment and authentic assessment – have been advocated as major innovations to promote student learning. While such learning-enhancing forms of assessment may not have been commonplace in higher education earlier, and may encounter resistance even today, it becomes relevant to discuss the socio-political practice of assessment in a historical and social context.

There exists a contradiction between the designated purpose of institutions of higher education to promote learning and the minor role that assessment for learning has played in these institutions. There is further a contradiction between the negligible application of assessment for learning in the educational system and the extended use of assessment for learning in the apprenticeship training of the crafts. I shall first point out that current innovations in assessment for learning in higher learning – such as extensive feedback, peer and self-assessment and authentic assessment – are well supported by the psychology of learning. Then I shall outline how these principles have been at work in the learning of crafts since the Middle Ages.

In contrast hereto, prevailing forms of assessment in schools and universities have been examinations and grading, which focus on control, discipline and selection. I shall highlight these social functions of assessment with a brief history of examinations and then discuss contradictions between assessment for selection, disciplining and knowledge control and assessment for learning. The historically dominating role of assessment for selecting and disciplining students is at odds with a knowledge-based economy, which requires a learning culture of life-wide and lifelong learning. With the transformation of higher education from an elite to a mass education, and the extension of learning from schools and universities to lifelong learning, assessment for learning comes to the fore. Finally, a contradiction is pointed out between the necessity of educational innovations of assessment for efficient learning in a knowledge economy and a new role of assessment for commensurability and as 'stop watches' to enforce economic accountability.

Principles of efficient learning in the psychology of learning

Assessment of learning can play a key role in promoting learning, according to principles of efficient learning formulated in the psychology of learning. This concerns the role of feedback, goal transparency, intrinsic motivation and key aspects of programmed learning. Educational assessment may thus facilitate learning by providing extensive feedback, clarifying the goals for learning, motivating further learning and encouraging active learning.

- *Feedback.* Within learning psychology it is a well-established phenomenon that feedback furthers learning: 'the simple principle that knowledge of results facilitates learning is one of the few generalisations clearly supported by the research on college teaching' (McKeachie, 1962: 349). The more immediate and precise the feedback is, the stronger the effect on learning. An early example of this is Skinner's (1978) programmed learning in which immediate knowledge of results systematically reinforced learning.
- *Goal transparency.* The more visible a goal of learning is, the better are the opportunities for learning. An educational researcher, Bloom (1981), has even postulated that if the learning goals in school are made sufficiently transparent, and the learners are given sufficient time to work towards the goals, 90 per cent of the pupils will be able to fulfil them.
- *Intrinsic motivation for learning.* Within the psychology of learning an intrinsic learning motivation has long been recognised as superior to extrinsic forms of motivation, such as learning for grades or money: 'Whenever possible, it is advantageous to use goals that are intrinsically related to the learning task' (Hilgard *et al.*, 1975: 261).

These learning principles testify to the learning potentials of innovative forms of assessment in education – such as feedback, peer and self-assessment and authentic assessment – by providing ample, precise and immediate reinforcement of learning performances, illuminating the goals of learning and promoting interest in further active learning. In the following section I show how the current innovations in educational assessment, well in line with principles of efficient learning, have been at work in the practices of craft learning since the Middle Ages.

Assessment for learning in apprenticeship training

In workplace apprenticeships assessment for learning is part of everyday practice, well in line with the principles of efficient learning of modern learning psychology. Here what is today called new modes of assessment has long served to enhance learning (Becker, 1972; Nielsen and Kvale, 2006). In craft apprenticeship selection into the trade is done by the master at the entrance to training, commonly with a reciprocal trial period, and by the ceremonial journeyman's probation test at the end of the training period. Discipline is secured by the strong hierarchy of the workplace and by a rather harsh and rough workplace style. Assessment throughout the four years of an apprenticeship, has, then, largely been free to promote learning of the craft.

Table 5.1 Feedback by assessment in apprenticeship training

Forms of workplace assessment	Concepts from assessment literature
Assessment in relation to goals	Goal transparency and self-assessment
Assessment in relation to models	Goal transparency and self-assessment
Assessment through use	Performance assessment and authentic assessment
Assessment by users	Authentic assessment
Assessment by colleagues	Peer assessment
Assessment responsibility	Self-assessment
Assessment as a task ladder	Reinforcement by access to more complex tasks

In Table 5.1 some key forms of feedback by formative assessment throughout apprenticeship training are depicted in the left column, while in the right column corresponding concepts from assessment and learning literature are indicated.

- *Assessment in relation to clear goals.* The goals of workplace learning tend to be rather transparent, allowing for a significant amount of self-assessment. With clear learning goals the apprentices may themselves assess how their products relate to the quality standards of their trade. Subsequently, self-assessment becomes dominant in their working life.
- *Assessment in relation to models.* Journeymen and masters embody in their work the standards and values of the craft that apprentices identify with and aspire to join. In daily work in the craft shop, the relation of the quality of the master's work to that of the apprentice may be so obvious that assessment from others is superfluous.
- *Assessment through use.* The quality of the work of the apprentices is assessed by the use of their products. A use assessment involves a judgement of the products in terms of their usefulness – does the apprentice joiner's table stand still or rock? Are the tiles even? Does the apprentice baker's bread rise? These types of assessments are made instantly as an integrated part of the work process. In workplace assessment 'the proof of the pudding is in the eating'.

- *Assessment by users.* The assessment of the apprentice's work may also come as a user assessment from customers – are the apprentice baker's pastries sold during the day? The customers' purchases of the apprentice's products are an indicator of the quality of his or her products.
- *Assessment by colleagues.* The work of a novice apprentice is frequently checked with respect to the quality standards of the trade. Whereas the master may often be absent from the workshop floor, the daily assessments will come from the journeymen and also from the older apprentices. Professional assessments are part of the social structure in a workplace, where the apprentice often spends substantial parts of his/her training with a journeyman, who constantly keeps an eye on the quality of the apprentice's work.
- *Assessment responsibility.* The apprentice is, to a large extent, responsible for the assessment of his or her work. By placing assessment in the midst of the work setting, it becomes possible for the learners to test their performances at any time they feel ready, to repeat the testing until a satisfactory quality has been attained, and to ask more experienced colleagues to test them by giving them more demanding tasks.
- *Assessment as a task ladder of increased responsibility.* A significant type of apprenticeship assessment may take place with hardly any verbal comments on the tasks performed, namely by assigning the apprentice to tasks that demand greater responsibility. Wilbrandt (2003) has depicted workplace assessment as a ladder of tasks with increasing responsibility. Recognition for a job well done is indicated when moving the apprentice to more difficult and significant parts of the work process. In particular a request to perform alone a repair job outside the workshop reinforces the apprentice's identity as a craftsperson.

We may conclude that apprentices learn their trade through continuous on-the-job evaluations in an assessment-dense workplace with multiple overlapping 'back-up' assessments, such as feedback from the products, colleagues and users, and through advancement to more demanding work tasks. The forms of assessment in apprenticeship training are in line with key principles for efficient learning derived from modern psychology of learning. The learners receive more or less immediate feedback on their performances, such as whether the product can be used, or by comments from colleagues on the quality of their performance. The assessments throughout an apprenticeship refer to goals that are intrinsic to mastering the trade. They are authentic assessments in that the performances, which are assessed, are appropriate, meaningful and significant tasks of the able craftsperson. The task ladder of increased responsibility in apprenticeship training is in line with Skinner's principles of programmed instruction.

We should be careful not to romanticise the old apprenticeship training: there is the strict discipline of the masters and journeymen, hazing by the older apprentices, and the communality and conservatism of the corporate guilds did not fit in a liberal economy (Black, 1984). Today, mass production, with specialisation and rationalising and the use of piece pay, leaves little time for instructing and supervising the apprentices' work. We should, though, note that apprenticeship training is still found in the arts and in the careers of Nobel laureates in the natural sciences (Kvale, 1997).

Manifold forms of assessment for learning, in line with principles of efficient learning, have for centuries worked well in apprenticeship training. In order to clarify why assessment for learning has not earlier been of paramount importance in institutions of higher learning, and why they are considered radical innovations, it is necessary to turn to the history of examinations and grading and the social functions of assessment.

Assessment in the history of higher education

Throughout the history of education assessment for selection, discipline and knowledge control has dominated over assessment for learning. The prehistory of examinations goes back to the Han Dynasty in China in 200 BCE (see Miyazaki, 1976). The Emperor T'ai-tsung developed a comprehensive civil examination system in the seventh century AD. The exams were based on essays on literature and the thought of Confucius, they were strictly controlled, and only a few of every hundred candidates passed through the provincial examinations to the even tougher final metropolitan palace exam, which was supervised by the emperor himself. The main function of the bureaucratic examination system was to select disciplined and loyal civil servants for the emperor. The founder of the general examination system, T'ai-tsung, thus remarked when observing a procession of the candidates who had passed the final palace exam: 'The heroes of the empire are all in my pocket!' (Miyazaki, 1976: 113).

The examinations introduced at the European universities at the end of the Middle Ages were likewise severe. The ritual public oral disputes could be rather harsh rites of passage. The founder of the university at Paris, Robert de Sorbon, thus in the thirteenth century compared the university exams with the Christian judgement of the Last Day. The main difference he suggested was that the judges over heaven and hell were much milder than the judges at the university (Dürkheim, 1977). The exams of the period were aggressive: thus, at the University of Cambridge the candidates had to swear before the examination that they would never exact revenge on their examiners. The examination rules at the University of Heidelberg from 1501 contained a passage forbidding the candidates to carry long knives at the examination (Kvale, 1972).

The strict and ritual medieval university examinations developed in the modern era into more bureaucratic modes of assessment, where grades attained a key role. The Jesuits introduced to European schools assessment by grades on a scale from 1 to 6. In their school curriculum from 1599 they emphasised competition for grades, whereby the diligence and discipline of the students 'will be, better than through blows, obtained through the hope of honour and the fear of shame' (*Ratio Studiorum*, 1887: §39). In the following centuries grades spread throughout the educational system, where they attained a key role by selection of students for further educational and professional privileges.

Assessment for selection and for discipline has dominated higher education. There have been occasional attempts to use assessment for facilitation of learning. Thus at Oxford a committee in 1852 advocated using examinations in 'promoting habits of . . . self-instruction, voluntary labour, and self-examination' (Cox, 1967: 294); in contemporary terms, promoting self-directed learning, intrinsic motivation and self-assessment. The potentials of assessment for enhancing learning have, though, until recently, generally gone unnoticed in the institutions of higher learning.

In the last few years we find innovations of school assessment, such as portfolios, peer assessment and authentic assessment, presented as 'New insights into learning and teaching' (Birenbaum, 2003). The application of assessment as a tool for learning is regarded as a fundamental change in views on assessment, where 'Aligning assessment, learning and instruction can be seen as one of the most important issues in educational innovation in recent years. Certainly, this goes down to the initiatives at classroom level, such as planned feedback, implementation of peer assessment and increased responsibility of students' (Chapter 7, this volume). Such forms of assessment will, according to well-established principles of efficient learning, contribute to enhanced and enriched learning. In a historical context this 'educational innovation' is, however, not new, but appears from the perspective of the workplace learning as a reinvention of the wheel.

Educational assessment as selection, discipline and control

I shall now turn to social functions of assessment in an attempt to understand why learning-enhancing forms of assessment have not been commonplace in education, and are today heralded as major new insights and educational innovations. Educational assessment has historically served as selection, discipline, knowledge control and, to some extent, as guidance of learning (Kvale, 1977 and 1996; see also Broadfoot, 1996). Assessment for learning has recently come to general attention (e.g., Shephard, 2000). I shall now discuss whether other key functions of assessment may have worked against an optimal use of assessment for learning.

Assessment for certification and selection

The selection of students by means of grade point averages dominates educational assessment today, with formal legal requirements and psychometric criteria of reliability weighing heavier than promotion of learning. A teacher who would neglect the certifying and grading aspects of assessments would quickly receive an official reprimand, whereas passing over the learning potentials of assessment hardly has any consequences.

While selection by grades is formally neutral to social class discrimination, the educational system is built around middle-class values, whereby working-class youth successively falls out. In France the chances of making it to university for children from the social elite have been forty times higher than for working-class kids. Selection to educational privileges by grades in principle obtainable by everyone leads to 'an illusion of chance equality', giving the children left out through social necessity the impression that they themselves have deserved their exclusion from higher educational privileges (Bourdieu and Passeron, 1997). Becker (1972), referring to previous authors, has endorsed the wry hypothesis that nobody learns anything in school, but middle-class children learn enough elsewhere to make it appear that schooling is effective, whereas lower-class children who don't learn the material elsewhere are left to fail.

We may speculate that in the traditional institutions of higher learning – recruiting and forming candidates for a small elite ruling society – a curriculum in the form of an obstacle course, with minimal guidance for learning, would form and let pass only those strong candidates who would learn independently without teaching, and become capable to serve in responsible elite positions in a hierarchical society. With the advent of mass education in a knowledge society, the elite education of the universities has changed drastically, and is addressed below.

Assessment for discipline and control

Examinations control what and how students learn. The ceremonial, secretive, authoritarian and anxiety-inducing forms of traditional university examinations – in particular, the oral cross-examination – involved a strong disciplining of the students. Today power exertion is rationalised through the micromanagement of multiple-choice tests. To many students, assessment is still experienced as a threat, rather than as an incitement to further learning.

In current forms of self- and peer assessment the disciplining of students is transferred to self- and peer control. The external control and surveillance by the examinations are to some extent left to the students themselves, with a responsibility for their own learning and assessment. We may here talk of a modernisation of control with assessment as self-surveillance (Foucault, 1977).

Assessment as censorship and construction of knowledge

Examinations are checkpoints, where the operational decisions that define what knowledge is accepted or excluded in a curriculum are made. The examinations define for the students what knowledge is worthy of acquisition and mastery, what knowledge is inside and what is outside a discipline. While an explicit censorship of knowledge has not been common in the last century, students may nevertheless fear a censorship of ideas. Sartre's observation also pertains to the more recent experiences of Scandinavian students: 'Marx wrote that the ideas of the dominant class are the dominant ideas. He is *absolutely* right. In 1925, when I was twenty years old, there was no chair of Marxism at the University, and Communist students were very careful not to appeal to Marxism or even to mention it in their examinations; had they done so they would have failed' (Sartre, 1963: 17; see also Kvale, 1972).

Today, in some instances, there is a more free joint construction of knowledge by students and their teachers at assessment. Different assessment techniques – orals, essays, multiple-choice tests and portfolios – involve different forms of knowledge construction (see Kvale, 1996).

Assessment for learning

Children are natural-born learners – in their natural environment they learn to walk and talk without institutional or professional assistance; the latter task of mastering the mother language is probably the most complex cognitive achievement of their lifetime. After they have spent ten to twenty years within the educational system it is today considered necessary to encourage and equip them for a lifetime's learning. Taking account of the wide institutional variations of assessment practices, I shall draw attention to some common aspects of educational assessment, which may discourage an efficient, authentic life-wide and lifelong learning: the grade point average as learning goal, the dominance of multiple-choice testing, test anxiety, the frequent lack of feedback and forms of examining and grading which hamper the development of authentic as well as self- and peer assessment.

The grade point average as learning goal

Field studies and interview investigations point to disciplining and competition as predominant in students' perspectives on assessment. In a study from an American college about the grading game, Becker et al. (1968) report that of their 1,100 field observations, 93 per cent indicated that the grade point average was the students' key learning goal, dominating virtually every aspect of college life, whereas an interest in learning for the sake of knowledge was evident in just 7 per cent of the observations. A Danish interview study of assessment in high school likewise reports a dominating grade perspective, where competition for high grades counteracts an interest in deeper and further learning (Kvale, 1980).

The dominance of multiple-choice tests

Assessment in higher education commonly – with variations from institution to institution and country to country – measures precise knowledge as indicated by the true/false alternatives of multiple-choice questions or short-answer questions. While easily and reliably scored for selective purposes, independent and creative thinking hardly lends itself to assessment on standardised tests. There is thus empirical evidence that multiple-choice tests may lead to a simplification of the knowledge taught and acquired, emphasising factual memory rather than more complex cognitive processes (Fredriksen, 1984). While more sophisticated tests can be developed, the conception of knowledge fostered by common standardised testing – with limited alternatives to isolated bits of knowledge – has relatively low ecological validity with respect to the multifaceted demands in professional life, which beyond factual and logical knowledge also encompass ability to act on incomplete, complex, instable, value-laden and paradoxical knowledge. In Fredriksen's (1984: 199) formulation: 'Most of the problems one faces in real life are ill structured . . . But ill-structured problems are not found in standardised achievement tests.' Wiggins later concludes in an analysis of 'Assessing student performance' (1993) that what is educationally vital is inherently at odds with efficient testing with unambiguous test items.

Test anxiety

Assessment has traditionally been associated with negative emotions, primarily with anxiety (Chapter 11, this volume). Examination anxiety was pronounced with the often harsh and humiliating forms of university examinations in earlier centuries. Although the form of the examinations may be milder today, the high stakes for the students in the competition for the grades, which open up educational and occupational privileges, continue to link examinations with anxiety. Strong test anxiety can impair learning, and may for many students, in particular those continually at the lower end of the normal grade curve, imbue assessment and learning with a negative value, something not to be undertaken voluntarily after passing their compulsory formal education.

Feedback

Becker (1972) noted that, in contrast to the ample feedback in apprenticeship learning, while students want to know whether they have learned something as they proceed along the curriculum, the school often fails to tell them whether their understanding is correct, and their skills adequate. According to the psychology of learning, feedback is an essential principle for efficient learning. Feedback solely in the form of a grade gives an indication of how far off the mark a learning performance is, but contains no direction for where to aim future attempts at learning.

A common absence of feedback beyond a grade indicates a lack of reinforcement, which may foster an attitude of futility of learning, conveying to the students an understanding of learning as something which is merely done for passing exams and obtaining good grades.

It is my experience from Scandinavian universities that students frequently complain that they rarely receive any feedback, beyond a grade, on their learning performance; and if they do, the feedback may come a long time after their performance, and is too vague to be useful. Further, it is difficult to motivate teachers to provide ample feedback on their students' learning. The report 'Assessment crisis: the absence of assessment for learning' (Stiggins, 2002) discusses how assessment *of* learning has prevailed over assessment *for* learning in American education, and outlines modes of enhancing formative assessments for learning. In an overview of over 250 studies worldwide linking assessment and learning, Black and Wiliam (1998) conclude unequivocally that classroom assessment for learning can raise pupil achievement. They also found evidence that the gain may be most substantial for lower-achieving pupils. They point out factors of assessment improving learning, well in line with the principles of learning psychology mentioned earlier, such as effective feedback, involving students in their own learning, the profound influence of assessment on the motivation and self-esteem of the pupils and promoting self-assessment. The authors also mention factors inhibiting assessment for learning, in line with the social functions of assessment discussed above, such as teachers' attention to grading at the expense of providing advice for improvement, the demoralising effects on less successful learners of comparing pupils with each other, and teachers' use of feedback for disciplining purposes.

Authentic assessment

Educational assessment practices have generally little external validity with respect to assessments in the workplace and in everyday life. The very term 'authentic', used in relation to current innovations of assessment, suggests that traditional assessment is 'inauthentic', in the sense that the content and form of educational assessment do not match the content and form of the corresponding tasks to be mastered outside of school. Portfolio assignments have been regarded as authentic assessments in that they have been inspired by assessments in working life. While approximating life settings outside of school, the authentic school assessments may become 'as if' replications in schools of activities which in working life have real consequences.

Self- and peer assessment

Common forms of educational assessment foster an other-directed learning. The external evaluations foster a dependency on others which counteracts the self-assessment, which is essential for lifelong learning (Chapter 9, this volume). The examiners' authoritative rankings on the grade scale and the computers' objectified marking of multiple-choice tests contribute to learning that the other is always right, issuing verdicts of no appeal.

While the grades do not give precise information for how to improve learning, they provide exact information on the standing of the pupils in relation to each other. Peer assessment is difficult to practise when a key selection function of assessment rests on competition between individual pupils. Prevalent assessment practises further competition rather than teamwork with cooperative learning and assessment. Cooperation by assessment may be punished as cheating, and cooperation by learning may be counteracted by students' beliefs that when grading along the curve is practised, helping a class comrade may result in he or she taking one's own high position on the grade scale. With a relative grading along the curve, broadly speaking one-third of the students will automatically become losers, acquiring a negative attitude to learning.

When regarded from the perspective of the psychology of learning, traditional features of assessment practices in higher education are at odds with key principles of promoting learning – such as transparency of goals; fast, frequent, specific feedback on performance; intrinsic learning motivation, and authentic assessment with a correspondence of tests of learning to the goals of learning. We may conclude that, in contrast to the apprenticeship learning of the crafts, the learning potentials of assessment have generally been underutilised in institutions of higher learning. In particular there is a strong contradiction between the massive neglect of using feedback for improving learning in educational institutions and the massive empirical evidence that feedback promotes learning. When assessment for learning, until recently, has not been a key concern in institutions of higher learning, this relates to the historical dominance in these institutions of assessment for selection, discipline and knowledge control.

Assessment for learning and for accountability in a knowledge economy

A neglect of the learning potentials of assessment is today at odds with a knowledge society – or learning society. With an increased economic importance of knowledge, more efficient learning of more students for a longer time becomes a key educational goal. In a knowledge economy we encounter a move to assessment for learning, as well as the use of assessment for commensurability and time control for accountability. I shall first address two educational trends leading to an emphasis on the learning potentials of assessment: the transformation of higher education from an elite to a mass education; and the extension of learning from schools and universities to a lifelong learning. Thereafter I shall address assessment for accountability.

Assessment for learning

The institutions of higher learning were previously restricted to a small number of elite students, mainly from the upper and middle classes, who to a large extent were able to learn without much teaching. With higher education today becoming a mass education there is also a massive need to facilitate learning for the many new students who are not already equipped to learn by themselves. We encounter a new emphasis on counselling of students, pedagogical courses for university teachers, educational qualifications by appointments of professors, student evaluations of teachers, as well as assessment to promote more efficient learning for more students.

Furthermore, there is the need for continual learning throughout a lifetime to match the continuing changing demands for workers' competencies and qualifications. An emphasis on traditional examinations of knowledge acquisition may be problematic in an age where knowledge rapidly becomes out of date. In a memorandum on lifelong learning by the European Community Commission (2000) it was emphasised that lifelong learning is a necessary condition for a successful transition to a knowledge-based economy and society. Lifelong learning is required for successive requalifications of workers, and it becomes necessary to foster habits of learning to learn outside formal educational settings and to motivate continual lifelong learning.

Traditional forms of assessment may, as argued above, be counterproductive to facilitation of learning and to foster a lifelong motivation for learning. Innovations in assessment for learning – such as the emphasis on feedback, authentic and self- and peer assessment – represent efforts to facilitate learning and to motivate for the after-graduation learning required in a knowledge economy. Such forms of assessment for learning are, however, not only in contradiction with the traditional functions of educational assessment; they may also be difficult to reconcile with assessments for the new demands of economic accountability in education.

Assessment for accountability

In a knowledge economy there are also requirements of accountability, where assessment attains a key role in government control of value for the money invested in education. This concerns the demands for commensurability favouring quantified assessment as well as the use of assessment as a stopwatch for monitoring the rate of learning.

Strict accountability demands pushes towards objectified quantitative learning outcomes, favouring grades and multiple-choice tests as the decisive measures for accountability. Also in the high-stakes selection pressures in mass education, access from one level to further levels of higher education may be based on grade point averages. Federal demands of benchmarking and competition between institutions require commensurability of learning outcomes, which again supports assessments by grades and multiple-choice measures. The strong accountability demands of educational output are difficult to reconcile with educational innovations in assessment for learning, such as authentic learning and portfolios, self- and peer assessment, which hardly produce the commensurable measurements required for accountability and benchmarking.

Assessment by educational accountability also entails a timekeeping function. Within a Taylorisation of learning at Scandinavian universities, with strict time controls and fine meshed quantitative output measures throughout the curriculum, assessment has served to increase the rate of learning; frequent assessments become 'stopwatches', requiring that students follow the prescribed time allowed for each study unit. The state financing of students through scholarships and loans, as well as the financing of university departments, hinges upon regular assessments for controlling the rate of individual study progress as well as of the production of candidates. Thus, in an early federal Norwegian university reform the new eco- nomic control of the entire university curriculum was to be enforced with frequent examinations as stopwatches for study progress. In the same reform innovations in assessment were suggested to promote positive study relation, so 'There may for example probably be developed solutions with combinations of self-evaluation, students as evaluators, and formally competent evaluators of the discipline' (*Komiteen . . .*, 1970: 42; see Kvale, 1972).

Educational innovations of assessment may here, notwithstanding ideal intentions of the reformers, come to gloss over the harsh disciplining through assessment serving as time controls for accountability demands. While the proposed economic control of student learning progress through frequent exams was soon put into practice, the innovations of evaluation remained suggestions.

In sum, we encounter today a contradiction between the manifold forms of assessment for learning, in line with the promotion of lifelong learning in a knowledge economy, and the new economic accountability leading to standardised measurements and assessment as time control. Thus, while assessment for learning is required for an efficient lifelong learning in a knowledge economy, the very economical means to enforce more learning may, however, be at odds with the aim of enhancing higher forms of learning.

Concluding perspectives

This chapter started with the question of why assessment for learning today is regarded as an educational innovation. Attempts to answer this question lead to a series of contradictions of assessment in institutions of higher learning. First, there is a contradiction between the institutional purpose of promoting learning and a general neglect of the potentials of assessment for promoting learning. There is a further contradiction between the prevalent use of assessment for learning in the apprenticeship training in the crafts and the arts – such as authentic assessment and portfolios, peer and self-assessment – and the minor role assessment for learning has played in institutions of higher learning. These contradictions were in part explained by the dominant functions of assessment as selection, disciplining and knowledge control in the history of education.

Today the rise of a knowledge economy requires efficient learning for more students for a longer time, and forms of assessment to promote efficient learning are coming to the fore. This time a new contradiction arises, between assessment as promoting an efficient and lifelong learning and assessment as a control instrument for economic accountability. The former may lead to educational innovations of assessment for learning – such as authentic assessment and portfolios, self- and peer assessment; the latter leads assessment in the direction of standardised measurements for commensurability and into becoming a stopwatch control of learning rate.

In conclusion, innovations of assessment for learning are not primarily a question of availability or development of assessment techniques, but an issue of what social function assessment plays in institutions of higher learning, and the role of learning in a broader historical and economical context.

References

Becker, H. (1972) The school is a lousy place to learn anything in, *American Behavioral Scientist*, 16: 85–105.

Becker, H., Geer, B. and Hughes, F. (1968) *Making the Grade*, New York: Wiley.

Birenbaum, M. (2003) New insights into learning and teaching, in M. Segers, F. Dochy and E. Cascallar (eds) *Optimising New Modes of Assessment: In Search of Qualities and Standards*, Dordrecht: Kluwer Academic Publishers.

Black, A. (1984) *Guilds and Civil Society in European Political Thought from the Twelfth Century to the Present*, New York: Cornell University Press.

Black, P.J. and Wiliam, D. (1998) Assessment and classroom learning, *Assessment in Education*, 5, 1: 7–74.

Bloom, B.S. (1981) *All Our Children Learning*, New York: McGraw-Hill.

Bourdieu, P. and Passeron, J.P. (1997) *Reproduction*, London: Sage.

Broadfoot, P.M. (1996) *Education, Assessment and Society*, Buckingham: Open University Press.

Cox, R. (1967) Examinations and higher education: a survey of the literature, *Universities Quarterly*, 21: 292–340.

Dürkheim, E. (1977) *The Evolution of Educational Thought in France*, London: Routledge & Kegan Paul.

European Community Commission (2000) A memorandum on lifelong learning, Brussels: ECC (available at: http://europa.eu.int/comm/education/policies/lll/life/memoen.pdf [accessed 3 June 2004]).

Foucault, M. (1977) *Discipline and Punish: The Birth of the Prison*, New York: Viking.

Fredriksen, N. (1984) The real test bias: influences on teaching and learning, *American Psychologist*, 39: 193–202.

Hilgard, E.R., Atkinson, R.C. and Atkinson, R.L. (1975) *Introduction to Psychology*, New York: Harcourt, Brace, Jovanovich.

Komiteen til å utrede spørgsmål om videreutdanning for artianere og andre med tilsvarende grunnutdanning, V (1970), Oslo: Kirke- og undervisningsdepartementet.

Kvale, S. (1972) *Prüfung und Herrschaft – Hochschulprüfungen zwischen Ritual und Rationalisierung*, Weinheim: Beltz.

—— (1977) Examinations: from ritual through bureaucracy to technology, *Social Praxis*, 3: 187–206.

—— (1980) *Spillet om karakterer i gymnasiet – elevinterviews om bivirkninger af adgangsbegrænsning*, København: Munksgaard.

—— (1996) Evaluation as construction of knowledge, in R. Hayhoe and J. Pan (eds) *East–West Dialogue Knowledge and Higher Education*, New York: Sharpe.

—— (1997) Research apprenticeship, *Nordisk Pedagogik – Nordic Journal of Educational Research*, 17: 186–194.

McKeachie, W.J. (1962) Procedures and techniques of teaching: a survey of experimental studies, in N. Stanford (ed.) *The American College*, New York: Wiley.

Miyazaki, I. (1976) *China's Examination Hell: The Civil Service Examinations of Imperial China*, New York: John Weatherhill.

Nielsen, K. and Kvale, S. (2006) The workplace – a landscape of learning, in E. Antonacopoulou, P. Jarvis, V. Andersen, B. Elkjær and S. Høyrup (eds) *Learning, Working and Living: Mapping the Terrain of Working Life Learning*, London: Palgrave Macmillan.

Ratio Studiorum et Institutiones Scholastica Societas Jesu (1887), Berlin: Hoffman.

Sartre, J.-P. (1963) *The Problem of Method*, London: Methuen.

Shephard, L. (2000) The role of assessment in a learning culture, *Educational Researcher*, 29, 7: 1–14.

Skinner, B.F. (1978) *Reflections on Behaviorism and Society*, Englewood Cliffs, NJ: Prentice Hall.

Stiggins, R.J. (2002) Assessment crisis: the absence of assessment for learning, *Phi Delta Kappan*, 83: 758–765.

Wiggins, G.P. (1993) *Assessing Student Performance*, San Francisco: Jossey-Bass.

Wilbrandt, J. (2003) Lærlinge i bevægelse – mellem skole og virksomhed og fra lærling til svend, in K. Nielsen and S. Kvale (eds) *Praktikkens læringslandskab*, København: Akademisk Forlag.

Chapter 6

Grading, classifying and future learning

Peter Knight

Other contributors to this book commend learning-oriented or formative assessment, which is intended to generate information about the task (feedback) and about ways of improving performance on similar tasks in the future (feedforward). Attention also needs to be paid to the practice of 'warranting' or summative assessment. I use 'warranting' to cover all the high-stakes processes of producing grade point averages, classifications and awards. Awards are often licences to practise, although that is just one manifestation of warrants of achievement. Even less attention has been given to the relationship between warranting and future learning, which is the topic of this chapter.

In the first half of the chapter I argue that warranting, as currently practised, is deeply flawed and not conducive to future learning. In the second half I recognise that it is a set of widely embedded social practices that will, in some form, survive. I suggest an approach to warranting achievement that is educationally fertile and sustainable. I begin with a view of the distinctive business of higher education.

The business of higher education

Table 6.1 summarises the set of educational learning outcomes intended to succeed the fifty-year-old classificatory framework known as Bloom's taxonomy.

While much of higher education's business may be with the mundane outcomes described by the top-left categories, I wish to concentrate on the complex achievements that are associated with the bottom-right region. There is a case for saying that a concern for complex achievements distinguishes *higher* education from lower levels and there is some corroboration for that view in employability research which shows that employers value new graduates with strengths in the 'psychosocial' domain, which includes self-efficacy, autonomy, interpersonal relationships and leadership skills, among others (Knight and Yorke, 2004).

Let us now look beyond graduation and consider what is involved in being a professional. My summary of what Dreyfus and Dreyfus (2005) take this to be points, again, to a set of complex achievements:

Table 6.1 A taxonomy for learning, teaching and assessment (after Krathwohl, 2002: 217)

The knowledge dimension	The cognitive dimension					
	Remember	*Understand*	*Apply*	*Analyse*	*Evaluate*	*Create*
Factual knowledge						
Conceptual knowledge						
Procedural knowledge						
Metacognitive knowledge						

a.   A concern with practice.
b.   Making non-routine decisions, as well as routine ones. This involves being accustomed to taking risk.
c.   To a degree 'an expert uses intuition, not calculation, even in reflection . . . With expertise comes a decreasing concern with accurate assessment of isolated elements' (Dreyfus and Dreyfus, 2005: 790).
d.   As appropriate, using research evidence and theories in a systematic way.
e.   Behaving metacognitively, often by 'reflection'.
f.   Forming an individual professional identity, which includes the development of self-theories.
g.   Taking up a social professional identity as a participant in multiple activity systems.
h.   Working with other people's problems, which involves a degree of emotional labour.
i.   A commitment to new learning, often in the interests of clients.
j.   The need to demonstrate fitness to practise through regular recertification and to meet public standards in order to achieve advancement.

(based upon Dreyfus and Dreyfus, 2005)

In so far as universities are involved in the formation of tomorrow's professionals, their business is with the learning that favours the emergence of such achievements. Swanwick (2005: 862), echoing other writers on professional formation, comments on the 'subtle process of change at work as a trainee develops into a professional, a process which itself is more about *being* than *doing*, and this progression may be enhanced by creating a favourable working environment'.

Indeed, social and non-cognitive achievements will arise from engagements in well-designed environments and will not come from formal instruction, although such instruction does contribute to professional formation. Furthermore, much of that learning will be either implicit and accessible to deliberation and metacognition or tacit and concealed from our knowing.

When higher education contributes to the formation of complex achievements it is contributing to people's futures because these are achievements that are valued in professional life and citizenship. How, though, do the practices of warranting contribute?

Consider undergraduate programmes in engineering. Students must know a lot of determinate information and procedures. Plenty of learning-oriented practice, probably done on-demand and online, can help them towards mastery. Many of these mundane outcomes can be reliably assessed by computer. There may be high set-up costs associated with the development of item banks and programming but, in the long run, mundane achievements can be assessed reliably, rapidly and cheaply, and achievement can then be warranted.

However, the UK Engineering Professors' Council's graduate output standard (EPC, 2002) refers to qualities, values and other achievements that we would not or could not warrant by such processes. (I explain why this is the case below.) We could, though, provide plenty of opportunities for feedback and feedforward – for learning-oriented assessment – and encourage students to build evidence-based claims in respect of such complex achievements. The problem is that it will be a professional necessity to warrant many of these complex achievements. I suggest looking at the engineering programme as a whole and deciding which of these complex outcomes the programme team can afford to warrant. If great riches were available, most achievements could be warranted with tolerable reliability. When resources are more limited, carefully planned learning-oriented assessment practices may be economically used, and help students to develop appropriate claims to achievement. In practice, teams make programme-level decisions about which complex outcomes are warranted and which are not.

Warrants without meaning

Warrants don't usually say very much about student achievement. Numbers and grades are pretty meaningless. Consider the case of a student with an upper second-class degree or one whose award is *magna cum laude*. We know nothing about the process standards at work in the programme that the student followed. Let me illustrate this point. As a history external examiner, I saw student essays that had been written with no help from tutors – indeed, in one university, essay topics were quite different from the topics covered in the lectures. In another college I saw student essays that seemed to be of equal quality. However, I knew that these essays were based on recent lectures, had been supported by seminars and were based on close advice from the lecturers about sources and structure. The two sets of essays looked equally good but I knew that the process standards had differed enormously, and so the two sets of essays represented radically different achievements. Complex learning was necessary for success in the first case but might only have contributed to it in the second case. In other words, not all upper seconds are the same.

Some hope that we would better understand the nature of achievement if warrants were complemented by transcripts. However, Adelman (1990) found US transcripts to be far less informative than is often supposed.

Even where universities address common deficiencies with transcripts and produce accounts that describe what students know and can do, warrants will still be limited. They are the product of sets of local practices and can be properly decoded only by those who understand the local practices. Let us return to the upper second degree. Does it come from City University, Hong Kong, which recommends the percentage of first, upper second, lower second and third-class degrees that examination boards should expect to award? Or from Lancaster University, where degree classes are criteria-referenced, not norm-referenced? Unless we know the rules under which warrants are created we cannot know their meaning.

It is sometimes said that the UK system of degree classification is largely responsible for this opacity and that it would be better to adopt a grade point average system (Burgess, 2005). Even so, we would still need to understand the local rules and practices at work. For example, the Student Assessment and Classification Working Group has repeatedly shown that there are considerable variations in assessment practices (Yorke *et al.*, 2004). Table 6.2 shows some of

Table 6.2 Ranges of variation in warranting practices

From:	To:
Grades based solely on coursework	Grades based solely on examinations
Open book and takeaway examinations	Traditional examinations
Tasks require near transfer (that is, they closely resemble ones covered in lectures, seminars and the textbooks)	Tasks require far transfer (they are novel)
Tasks are 'tame' – simplified and structured to help students to tackle them	Tasks are 'in the wild' or authentic: they are messy, as is so often the case in life
There is no external review of departmental grading practices	External examiners adjust marks in line with sector standards
Students allowed to resit any low-scoring units to improve their grade	No resits and no retakes allowed: low grades cannot be improved
In case of illness marks can be adjusted and credit given	No allowances made for illness
Warrants based on final-year grades only	Warrants based on final two years' grades
Criteria-referenced grading	Norm-referenced grading
High proportion of learning-oriented, ungraded assessment	High proportion of warranting, graded assessment

the continua; remember that in the UK system there are further variations arising from the classification system.

In order to understand the significance of these ranges of experience, it is helpful to recall that planned curricula become transformed when they are enacted. Cameron and Heckman (1993) showed how the same planned curriculum, delivered in different ways, led to different learning achievements. The implication is that, whatever the learning intentions of the planned curriculum, students whose warrants are based on practices in the left-hand column will tend to have different outcomes from those whose warrants stem from right-hand column experiences. Unfortunately, neither North American nor British warrants disclose the practices through which grades and classes are created. It is little surprise, then, that it is difficult to communicate achievements to people outside the assessment system and that they, in turn, can find it hard to trust what they are told (Knight, 2006a). An implication is that in order to understand warrants we need to understand the *local* practices of assessment (Knight, 2006b): understanding depends on a double reading (Shay, 2005) – a reading of the assessment criteria and a reading of the contexts of assessment.

Unintended consequences

A stronger criticism of warranting achievement is that it tends, inadvertently, to be toxic to *higher* education.

Warrants, as public and high-stakes statements of competence and other achievement, need to be reliable. This causes difficulties when it comes to complex achievements. They are fluctuating and contested social constructs, not real and stable objects that we might hope to measure. They are *complex*, by which I mean that:

1. their development is not attributable to any one source. The achievement of passing a driving test may be mainly attributed to the quality of driving tuition but, as Pascarella and Terenzini (2005) show, the achievement of something such as critical autonomy is a holistic response to environments and 'sub-environments';
2. it is not certain that a favourable learning environment *will* lead to the development of these complex achievements. This uncertainty is a second feature of complex achievements – there is no linear relationship between inputs and outputs;
3. they are slow to grow, the products of months and years, not of days and weeks; they are the outcomes of whole undergraduate programmes, not of individual units or modules;
4. they cannot be precisely defined. We may recognise when someone gets to the heart of a problem but it is futile to try to define what it means to get to the heart of problems.

Assessment as judgement

In order to build my case I need to distinguish between three approaches to judging achievement: measurement, judicial and aesthetic approaches.

Regardless of the functions of assessment, it is a process of judgement. Just as epistemology distinguishes different forms of knowing, so we can discern different forms of judgement. It is quite common to hear people use 'assess' and 'measure'to mean the same thing. 'Assessment' is actually a broader term than 'measurement' and covers several processes of judgement. Measurements can of course, when they can be properly taken, aid one form of judgement. However, measurement theory expects real and stable objects, not fluctuating and contested social constructs. A common mistake is to apply a form of judgement – such as measurement – to achievements that are not, epistemologically speaking, measurable. For instance, it is no wonder that there are so many problems with attempts to measure 'key' or 'generic' achievements or 'skills': once we move away from the simplest, we are trying to measure the unmeasurable. Such complex constructs are better handled by judicial or aesthetic judgements.

Judicial judgement weighs evidence, following agreed rules, and considers different interpretations before coming to a rule-led verdict on the basis of probabilities or of near certainty. It is a robust form of judgement that can be used with the full range of human thought and action. There are, though, more subjective areas of human experience that are not very well served by judicial judgements. These are areas in which 'connoisseurship' (Eisner, 1985) is an appropriate form of judgement. Connoisseurs are experts with rich knowledge of a field. They offer opinions and argue their points of view. Expert though they are, they often differ because the material in question evokes such different subjective responses. Of course, people making judicial judgements also deploy expertise. However, where judicial judgements operate within a given framework, connoisseurs can invoke different frameworks or sets of rules of judgement; they use expertise to make judgments *and* to decide which rules of judgement to apply. (I owe this point to Dr Shay of the University of Cape Town.)

It is patently impossible reliably to measure complex achievements, which can be described as non-determinate: measurement and non-determinacy are incompatible concepts. Can we make other sorts of reliable judgement about complex achievements? If we use aesthetic judgement, probably not. We might reasonably expect better of aesthetic or judicial judgements, but at a price. Consider the following. First, we cannot expect the certainty that goes with mundane achievements, so 'reliable' judgements of complex achievements will be more provisional than measurements of simpler outcomes. Second, it is complicated to get reliable judgements of complex achievements and makes considerable demands on the judges, who need to be well trained and diligent. Third, it is expensive – the system for judging portfolios that Baume and Yorke (2002) described was abandoned largely because of the cost in staff time and it is very expensive if judgements are any finer grained than 'pass–fail'. Of course, expensive assessment can still be good value, but only under certain conditions, some of which are described below.

I have been claiming that warranting practices are in disarray, especially when it comes to complex achievements. I have argued that warrants frequently lack public meaning and said that inappropriate forms of judgement, notably those associated with judgement-as-measurement, may be deployed. I now suggest that warranting can harm curricula.

Curriculum skew

It may be complicated and expensive to produce tolerably reliable judgements of some complex achievements but how does this lead to the claim that warranting is inimical to such achievements in general? One mechanism is that warranting tries to increase certainty by simplifying the judgement process. For example, 'critical thinking' can be quite reliably judged by means of content-free tests that resemble classic intelligence tests, but this is not critical thinking in any useful sense. Moore (2004) criticises the view, underlying such tests, that critical thinking is some free-floating entity and discusses an alternative that emphasises critical thinking's contexted nature and dependence on a deep knowledge of the field in which it is practised. The costs of assessing critical thinking as a complex contexted practice are considerably greater than the costs of using a computer-graded de-contexted test. For example, in order to enhance the reliability of judgement where such an achievement is involved, programme teams need to establish clear achievement criteria; make sure that students and staff have shared meanings of them; ensure that staff apply them consistently; and assess the same achievement on as many occasions as possible. Costs and complexity are easy to see.

Criteria-referenced assessment, the default attempt to preserve both complexity and reliability, has its own price. Criteria-referencing involves pre-specifying learning outcomes in the form of objectives. The 'objectives war' of forty years ago produced trenchant commentaries on the idea that all human learning can be described in terms of learning objectives (Eisner, 1985). The problem is that attempts to capture the complex achievements in the language of objectives simplify and distort them. Eisner proposed an alternative in the form of descriptions of learning situations likely to evoke certain complex outcomes. While it side-stepped problems with traditional objectives, even calling them 'expressive objectives' did not make it a sufficiently 'scientific' approach for the measure-and-manage breed of quality assurers who have been so influential in higher education practice.

Since it is easier, cheaper and less controversial to assess mundane achievements, they are the ones most likely to be assessed. Given the view that what is assessed gets taken seriously, and the extension that what is assessed for warranting purposes gets taken even more seriously, then it is easy to see how curriculum gets skewed. The planned or official curriculum may pay attention to complex achievements, but if warranting assessment concentrates on the mundane, then the realised curriculum will be decidedly mundane. Furthermore, if assessors simplify a complex achievement to make it feasible to assess it reliably, they are likely to destroy it: for example, whatever reliable, context-free tests of critical thinking are describing, it is not critical thinking as an authentic, complex and contexted practice.

A final objection to a passion for warranting is that even when it is done properly, with attention to the conditions that favour reliable judgements of complex achievements, it tends to displace learning-oriented assessment. Other contributors have shown that learning-oriented assessment takes curriculum time. There is not enough time for it if the curriculum is geared to creating tolerably reliable judgements of complex achievements.

The argument in this first half of this chapter has been that warranting practices are inherently problematic, especially when they address the complex achievements that are the quintessence of higher education. Three main clusters of difficulty are:

- the complex achievements we value in higher education do not admit to measurement, nor can we achieve more than provisional certainty through consensus of experts following judicial or aesthetic principles. In any case, the certainty of proof is not to be had since normal science is about falsification, not proof;
- it is costly to follow the practices of judicial or aesthetic judgement, especially when high degrees of reliability are wanted along with fine-grained judgements. The political economy of assessment means that warranting complex and recalcitrant achievements is costly. Corners are cut and what gets assessed is a mutant of the original;
- warranting is often done badly and tends to snatch up curriculum time that could be used for learning-oriented activities. I also remark upon the poverty of the warrants that are produced – the equivalent of mining tons of rock to get not a diamond but a piece of grit.

Warranting and future learning

Are current practices inimical to future learning?

It is hard to examine common warranting practices and conclude that they are informative, while it is easy to see that a passion for warranting can corrupt the *higher* in higher education. Each conclusion says there is something wrong with undergraduate learning, but should this cause alarm about future learning?

The project of rethinking warranting for future learning implies that we currently have a problem with future learning – that in some way graduates of, say, ten or twenty years' standing are neither well disposed towards nor engaging in future learning. That seems unlikely. Learning is inevitable as they move from job to job and gain promotions; and, even if they stay put, work is changing so fast around us that it is hard to believe that there are many who are not learning. Livingstone (2001: 13), reviewing Canadian literature, said:

nearly all Canadian adults (over 95%) are involved in some form of informal learning activities that they can identify as significant . . . The estimated average number of hours devoted to informal learning by all Canadian adults during 1998 was around 15 hours per week.

Perhaps, though, the project is to rethink warranting for future *formal* learning; we might suppose that graduates of some years' standing have little taste for formal learning partly because they have been put off by undergraduate assessment regimes that were raddled by warranting. Evidence is lacking. Moreover, the proposition is weakened by the strong growth in international demand for taught master's degrees, professional doctorates and other postgraduate awards. The surprise is that warranting is embedded in formal education settings and that it has turned out as well as it has, despite all its problematic features. However, that is no reason to assume that practice is as favourable to future learning as it might be. What follows assumes that we could do better.

There is, I argue, a need for a fresh view of the embedded social practice of warranting, one that emphasises expertise, a sense of proportion and a concern with the programme of engagement leading to an award. In order to develop it I need to range more widely than hitherto. In this chapter I have taken the normal, lifelong social practice of learning and limited it temporally (to the undergraduate years); situationally (to formal and/or university learning); functionally (to assessment); and topically (to warranting). Now, in order to think well about the fragment (warranting), I need to think about the whole (environments that favour complex *and* mundane learning).

Environments that favour complex learning

I propose five elements that distinguish such environments. Participants have:

- valued and feasible goals;
- role variety and stretch – opportunities to engage with others on routine *and* challenging work;
- social interaction *and* challenge through working with diverse people on a variety of tasks, always with the proviso that collaboration has benefits;
- time for metacognitive activity, including working with others to get feedback, feedforward and legitimation;
- an extensive view of workplace effectiveness, including an appreciation of the emotional and interpersonal faces of professional being and doing.

This is a partial description of an environment for complex learning. What sort of curriculum does it suggest? I do not understand curriculum as content and its organisation because these complex outcomes could arise from all sorts of engagements with all sorts of worthwhile content. Here, as in work on employability (Knight and Yorke, 2004), I am saying that it is curriculum processes, which is to say the learning, teaching and assessment processes, that make for complex achievements. Following Pascarella and Terenzini (2005) on subenvironments associated with undergraduate achievement, I suggest that these processes include peer teaching, individualised learning approaches, collaborative learning, co-operative learning, active learning and service learning. A case can be made for others.

In this view of curriculum, the main educational design tasks are to do with creating environments and experiences that afford rich possibilities for development. What roles might assessment play? I give priority to seven on the basis of the earlier suggestions about elements of environments for complex learning:

1. directing attention to opportunities and goals that are valued by the programme;
2. encouraging social interactions, especially academic ones among students;
3. supporting metacognition;
4. consolidating an extensive view of learning;
5. helping students pace their activities;
6. evoking feedback and feedforward;
7. supporting public representations of achievement.

The first half of this chapter argued that warranting practices do not fit this view of assessment and may be dangerous to it.

Towards a new account of warranting

It is worth saying again that a great deal of warranting, mainly of mundane achievements, will be unproblematic and increasingly done by just-in-time, computer-based testing. That is not my concern here. Instead, I return to the warranting of complex achievements through three snippets about the ways in which standards are currently warranted.

There is no shortage of national standards, certification and recertification arrangements, and manuals of criteria and advice on their operationalisation. However, the following snippets suggest that they are not always applied in the rational, objective and reliable ways their authors intended. In medicine I hear of doctors who will pass a competent junior colleague who has problems with one complex achievement, such as communication, because they see medical competence, feel that failure on this element would be too harsh, and believe that they, as senior doctors, lack the skill to help the junior to improve. In teacher education, a colleague reports that standards are consulted when gut feelings suggest that a student is failing – 'you hang them on the standards'. Here standards do not guide judgement but legitimate expert decisions. Brown and Hesketh (2004), looking at assessment centres used to recruit new graduates to blue-chip firms, discern a 'science of gut feeling' behind the centres' fronts of psychometric rigour.

I could not possibly claim on the basis of three snippets that warranting of professional standards always takes this unofficial form. What interests me about them is that they show an alternative approach to judgement to the measurement approach of the psychometricians. I do not see here a dereliction of professional standards. Instead, I see the application of expert judgement – perhaps of connoisseurship – in the holistic way that Dreyfus and Dreyfus (2005) associate so strongly with professionalism. I see a rejection of a 'rational' approach to warranting that involves decomposing performance into competencies, objectives and criteria, each of which is to be observed, certified and then thrown into a warranting pot. Once the pot is full, competence is presumed. (It is sometimes observed that a 'metacompetence' of co-ordinating all the bits wisely and appropriately is usually missed from the pot.) Rational though it may be, the task is Sisyphean because competencies, objectives and criteria proliferate as distinctions multiply and greater precision is sought. In addition, there are many accounts of variations in the use of criteria that are supposed to make for more reliable judgements and convergent warrants. I want to suggest that problems inherent in warranting, combined with criticisms of the unwieldiness of 'rational' approaches to warranting professional competence, are sufficient reason not to pursue this rational approach to assessing professional performance. Could we, though, warrant professional achievements on the basis of expert judgements, taking either the judicial or the aesthetic approach?

If so, I believe that we would have to make a number of 'background assumptions' as philosophers call them. One is that good learning environments will usually lead to good learning outcomes; in other words, where the practice settings are known to be good, we expect that appropriate learning outcomes will materialise. The reason for making this assumption is my radical uncertainty that we can (afford to) make reliable and valid judgements of complex achievements. By extension, we might make a second assumption: namely, that learners in good environments are likely to be competent. Some could say that this assumption puts clients at risk. However, there is no intention of suggesting that teachers and other judges will fail to notice evidence of non-competence. It does mean that effort typically spent on documenting the obvious (that most students are competent) can be spent more profitably and directed at those who give cause for concern.

A third background assumption is that complex achievements grow slowly and should be judged at the level of the programme of engagements leading to an award, not at the level of modules, units or courses. Rather than spend lots of time accumulating evidence of competence in many courses, modules and units, we could presume overall competence in good learning environments unless there were indications of specific shortfalls.

Underlying this are two areas of research. One insists that such achievements take months, if not years, to form (Claxton, 1998). The other reminds us that achievements become more robust and transferable with practice and with opportunities to bring them to bear in a variety of settings (Tuomi-Gröhn et al., 2003). Consequently, assessors need evidence of achievement that comes from a variety of modules, just as students need that variety in order to construct robust achievements.

In practice, experts who judge must meet certain conditions: they must be trained and retrained in the forms of judgement they will be using; they should have lots of opportunities to judge, probably as a rotation as a part of a career pattern; and, ideally, they should be disposed to judge performance in the round, or holistically. They will be judging student performances – essays, displays, simulations and practicals – but they should also be testing the evidence supporting students' claims to achievements.

So, universities would warrant mundane achievements, much as they do now. They would also invest in bringing lots of expertise to bear so that they could say with a high degree of provisional certainty that they judge students to be competent as far as some complex achievements go. However, they would neither wish nor be able to afford to warrant all areas of student achievement. Employers and others interested in achievement in those areas would need to satisfy themselves of the robustness of student claims, although some universities and departments might helpfully say when they judge the evidence backing some student claims to competence to be well founded. Warranting would be put in its place, with universities:

- attesting achievements that they choose to afford to warrant;
- providing learning environments that can be assumed to favour the formation of valued achievements;
- following learning-oriented assessment approaches to create plenty of feedback for learning; and
- educating students in the business of making, documenting and presenting claims to achievement, especially to achievements that, for a variety of reasons, resist warranting.

This is a differentiated approach to assessment and warranting. It is compatible with curricula as sketched above and with a commitment to learning-oriented assessment. It addresses one of the big problems in warranting complex achievements in some tolerably reliable way: namely, that it is very expensive to deploy the expertise to observe students in authentic, 'real-world' or 'in-the-wild' tasks – even more so when they are encouraged to create diverse products (e-portfolios) and negotiate their own goals and criteria. The new approach to warranting recognises that assessing complex learning outcomes requires a proper investment. It appreciates that resources per student are limited and shrinking in many places, and makes it clear that faculty have to make economic decisions about the warranting they can do, as well as moral decisions about the warranting they shouldn't do.

I have proposed that achievements not reached by warranting can be assumed to form either as a result of student engagements with fertile environments or (and) by students making documented claims to achievement. Assessors, as experts, might be asked to rule on the quality of evidence backing these claims *where the programme team judges that they should try to warrant the claim*. They would neither judge nor warrant the achievements themselves, though. In other words, this approach to warranting has the potential to avoid some of the worst problems facing conventional warranting. It might be objected that focusing on the quality of environments is unrealistic in times of intensification, when there are persistent claims that the quality of learning environments is being degraded (for a New Zealand illustration of what is believed to be a global phenomenon, see Houston *et al.*, 2006). Yet that is precisely why such scrutiny is needed, to warrant that environments are fit for the promotion of the complex learning achievements that a programme professes to promote. It is precisely because the degradation of learning environments can lead to 'batch' teaching and the closure of spaces for interaction, exploration and creativity that it is important to have some professed declared curriculum goals.

It could also be said that this new view of warranting is unscientific. However, there is nothing scientific about the 'rational' approach to assessment, which applied the techniques of analytical chemistry (identify the compounds and their quantities) to complex human achievements. Applied to the assessment of complex achievements, the 'rational' approach is philosophically dubious, educationally suspect and practically impossible.

More serious is the criticism that the new view of warranting gives too much leeway to academic teams, who are prone to make glossy *public* representations of their work, their students and their programmes. However, if we believe that students in favourable learning environments will tend to form complex achieve- ments, then surely it makes sense to use assessors, as experts, to warrant the quality of the programme learning environment. This is a check on academic narcissism. The new view of warranting, with its concern for warranting the quality of envi- ronments, is indifferent to a department's research income, selectivity or plant (unless connections with complex achievements can be established). It does not come with a long and mixed list of questions and standards, which external quality assurance agencies love. It envisages assessors, as experts, asking one question: 'What sort of learning does this workplace or practice setting promote?' Some environments will be warranted as fostering complex achievements, but others would be associated with the dysfunctional learning that comes from stale curriculum and discredited assessment practices, of which traditional approaches to warranting *complex* achievements are a super example.

Taking assessment seriously is not enough

This fourfold assessment story – warrant what you can afford to take seriously; value learning-oriented assessment; encourage claimsmaking; and assess the quality of learning environments – suggests an approach to warranting that favours future learning. Notice that there are profound implications for learning and teach- ing practices. In Georgine Loacker's (2005: 3) words, 'only good teaching and learning can make assessment significant and productive'.

References

Adelman, C. (ed.) (1990) *A College Course Map: Taxonomy and Transcript Data*, Washington: US Government Printing Office.

Baume, D. and Yorke, M. (2002) The reliability of assessment by portfolio on a course to develop and accredit teachers in higher education, *Studies in Higher Education*, 27, 1: 7–25.

Brown, P. and Hesketh, A. (2004) *The Mismanagement of Talent*, Oxford: Oxford University Press.

Burgess, R. (Chair) (2005) *The UK Honours Degree: Provision of Information: A Consultation Paper*, London: Universities UK and the Standing Conference of Principals.

Cameron, S. and Heckman, J. (1993) The non-equivalence of high school equivalents, *Labor Economics*, 11, 1: 1–47.

Claxton, G. (1998) *Hare Brain, Tortoise Mind*, London: Fourth Estate.

Dreyfus, H. and Dreyfus, S. (2005) Expertise in real world contexts, *Organization Studies*, 26, 5: 779–792.

Eisner, E. (1985) *The Educational Imagination*, 2nd edn, New York: Macmillan.

Engineering Professors' Council (EPC) (2002) *Engineering Graduate Output Standard: Assessment of Complex Outcomes*, London: Engineering Professors' Council.

Houston, D., Meyer, L.H. and Paewai, S. (2006) Academic staff workloads and job satisfaction, *Journal of Higher Education Policy and Management*, 28, 1: 17–30.

Knight, P.T. (2006a) Assessing learning: trust and universal higher education, in I. McNay (ed.) *Beyond Mass Higher Education: Building on Experience*, Maidenhead: Society for Research into Higher Education and Open University Press.

—— (2006b) Assessment as local practice, *Assessment and Evaluation in Higher Education*, 31, 3: 435–452.

Knight, P.T. and Yorke, M. (2004) *Learning, Curriculum and Employability in Higher Education*, London: Routledge.

Krathwohl, D.R. (2002) A revision of Bloom's taxonomy: an overview, *Theory into Practice*, 41, 4: 212–218.

Livingstone, D.W. (2001) *Adults' Informal Learning: Definitions, Findings, Gaps and Future Research*, Toronto: Centre for the Study of Education and Work, OISE.

Loacker, G. (2005) Enhancing assessment through teaching and learning, paper presented to the First International Conference on Teaching and Learning through Assessment, Hong Kong, 14 July.

Moore, T. (2004) The critical thinking debate: how general are general thinking skills?, *Higher Education Research and Development*, 23, 1: 3–18.

Pascarella, E.T. and Terenzini, P.T. (2005) *How College Affects Students, Vol 2: A Third Decade of Research*, San Francisco: Jossey-Bass.

Shay, S. (2005) The assessment of complex tasks: a double reading, *Studies in Higher Education*, 30, 6: 663–679.

Swanwick, T. (2005) Informal learning in postgraduate medical education: from cognitivism to 'culturism', *Medical Education*, 39: 859–865.

Tuomi-Gröhn, T., Engeström, Y. and Young, M. (eds) (2003) *Between School and Work: New Perspectives on Transfer and Boundary-Crossing*, Amsterdam: Pergamon.

Yorke, M. with Barnett, G., Evanson, P., Haines, C., Jenkins, D., Knight, P.T., Scurry, D., Stowell, M. and Woolf, H. (2004) Self-help in research and development relating to assessment: a case study, *Assessment & Evaluation in Higher Education*, 29, 4: 389–399.

Chapter 7

Assessment engineering

Breaking down barriers between teaching and learning, and assessment

Filip Dochy, Mien Segers, David Gijbels and Katrien Struyven

The complexity of today's society is characterised by an infinite, dynamic and changing mass of information, the massive use of the internet, multimedia and educational technology and a rapidly changing labour market demanding a more flexible labour force that is directed towards a growing proportion of knowledge-intensive work in teams and lifelong learning (Nonaka and Takeuchi, 1995; Tynjälä, 1999). As a consequence, today's knowledge community expects graduates not only to have a specific knowledge base but to be able to apply this knowledge to solve complex problems in an efficient way (Engel, 1997; Poikela and Poikela, 1997). New learning environments based on constructivist theory claim to develop an educational setting in which to reach this goal, making students' learning the core issue and defining instruction as enhancing learning (Lea *et al.*, 2003).

In the early 1990s, Glaser (1990) and Lohman (1993) were arguing that the changing goals, the new methods of instruction as well as the new findings and insights about new learning environments pointed to the necessity of reconceptualising current tests and assessments and critically examining their underlying theory. One of the main arguments for stressing the importance of assessment is the general belief and the empirical evidence from various studies that assessment has an important impact on instruction and learning (Gibbs, 1999; Scouller, 1998). It is argued that, in order to make new learning environments effective, the 'constructive alignment' (Biggs, 2003) between the learning environments' characteristics and the assessment is a 'magic bullet' in improving learning (Cohen, 1987). The main purpose is to make assessment congruent with the instruction and align assessment to what students should be learning (Biggs, 2003). Additionally, it is argued that this alignment might significantly increase the power of assessment as a stimulus and a tool for learning.

The plea for aligning learning, instruction and assessment, within the context of current learning theories, has led to changing insights in assessment. The traditional view that the assessment of students' achievement is separate from instruction and comes only at the end of the learning process is no longer tenable. As assessment, learning and instruction become increasingly integrated, there is strong support for representing assessment as a tool for learning (Dochy and McDowell, 1997). In this respect, Birenbaum (1996) has made a useful distinction between two cultures in the measurement of achievement. In the traditional, so-called testing culture, instruction and testing are considered to be separate activities. The current assessment culture is a consequence of the need to make learning and instruction more in congruence with assessment and can be characterised as follows (Birenbaum and Dochy, 1996). First, there is a strong emphasis on the integration of learning, instruction and assessment. Most assessment specialists like Birenbaum (1996), Nitko (1989) and Keeves (1994) take the position that appropriately used educational assessments can be seen as tools that enhance the instructional process. Additionally, there is a strong support for representing assessment as a tool *for* learning, instead of a tool *of* learning. The view that the assessment of students' achievements is solely something that happens at the end of the learning process is obsolete (Dochy and McDowell, 1997). Second, the position of the student in the learning process is that of an active participant who shares responsibility in the process, practises self-evaluation, reflection and collaboration, and conducts a continuous dialogue with his or her coach, tutor or teacher. Students play far more active roles in the assessment of their achievement. They participate in the development of the criteria and the standards for evaluating their performance, and they document their reflections in a journal and use portfolios to keep track of their academic or vocational growth. Third, various sorts and numbers of measures are included in the assessment, all of which are generally referred to by psychometricians as 'unstandardized assessments embedded in instruction' (Koretz *et al.*, 1994). This implies that reporting practices shift from a single score to a profile; that is, from quantification to a portrayal (Birenbaum, 1996). Fourth, with some modes of assessment there is no time pressure, and a variety of tools that are used in real life for performing similar tasks are permitted. The tasks are often interesting, meaningful, authentic, challenging and engaging, involving investigations of various kinds. Fifth, instead of focusing on tests measuring mainly low levels of comprehension (reproduction), within new learning environments, higher-order thinking skills are assessed. Sixth, assessment does not intend solely to reflect students' cognitive performances but also metacognitive, social and affective learning outcomes. These six characteristics of the assessment culture are schematised in Figure 7.1.

Although many educators support the ideas of the assessment culture and implement them in various ways, researchers (e.g., Segers *et al.*, 2003) argue that much more empirical evidence of the hypothesised benefits of new modes of assessment is necessary. Enhancing the power of assessment is only possible when there is sufficient research-based evidence of the conditions for these new modes of assessment to enhance students' learning. This chapter will present a sample of studies investigating the three discerned effects of assessment. Special attention will be paid to the implications for practice derived from their results. We conclude with some guidelines for the 'engineering' of assessment into the learning process to contribute to longer-term learning.

Generally, assessment focuses little on the processes of learning and how students learn after or before the point of assessment. In other words, a key issue

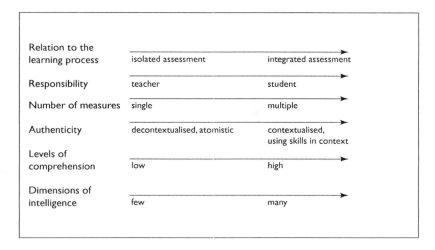

Relation to the learning process	isolated assessment	integrated assessment
Responsibility	teacher	student
Number of measures	single	multiple
Authenticity	decontextualised, atomistic	contextualised, using skills in context
Levels of comprehension	low	high
Dimensions of intelligence	few	many

Figure 7.1 Characteristics of the assessment culture

in this book is that assessment is not sufficiently equipping students to learn in situations in which there are no teachers and examinations to focus their attention. New directions in the area of assessment therefore need to consider the social and cultural context of education as much as the effects on learners.

Effects of assessment: the pre-assessment, post-assessment and pure-assessment effect

In the early 1970s researchers were engaged in studies of student learning at prestigious universities (Snyder, 1971; Miller and Parlett, 1974). They found unexpectedly that what influenced students most was not the teaching but the assessment. Students described all aspects of their study – what they attended to, how much work they did and how they went about their studying – to be completely dominated by the way they perceived the demands of the assessment (Gibbs and Simpson, 2004). Rowntree (1987: 1) stated, 'if we wish to discover the truth about an educational system, we must first look to its assessment procedures'. Both the Snyder and the Miller and Parlett studies additionally highlighted the way students respond to the assessment procedures. Snyder's work gave birth to the notion of the 'hidden curriculum' – the different and unwritten curriculum that students had to discover and pay attention to if they wanted to succeed. As one of Snyder's respondents wrote:

> 'From the beginning I found the whole thing to be a kind of exercise in time budgeting ... You had to filter out what was really important in each course ... you couldn't physically do it all. I found out that if you did a good job of

filtering out what was important you could do well enough to do well in every course.'

(Snyder, 1971: 62–63)

After that, students started to allocate their effort in the utmost economical way: 'I approach the courses so I can get an "A" in the easiest manner, and it's amazing how little work you have to do if you really don't like the course' (Snyder, 1971: 50). These findings show remarkable similarities with the 'strategic or achieving approach' to learning (Entwistle et al., 2001; Entwistle et al., 1991; Entwistle and Ramsden, 1983), which describes well-organised and conscientious study methods linked to achievement motivation or the determination to do well. The student adopting this approach relates studying to the assessment requirements in a manipulative, even cynical, manner. For example:

> 'I play the examination game. The examiners play it too . . . The technique involves knowing what is going to be in the exam and how it's going to be marked. You can acquire these techniques from sitting in the lecturer's class, getting ideas from his point of view, the form of the notes, and the books he has written – and this is separate to picking up the actual work content.'
>
> (Entwistle and Entwistle, 1991: 208)

Depending on the assessment method used, students tend to substitute 'surface' memorising for 'deep' understanding.

Generally, assessment can have an effect on different levels that depends on the function of the assessment (summative versus formative). This aspect is also referred to as consequential validity. It implies the investigation of whether the actual consequences of assessment are the expected consequences. The influence of summative assessment on learning behaviour is mainly proactive. The question 'Do we have to know this for the examination?' will be recognisable for nearly every teacher and illustrates that students tend to adjust their learning behaviour to what they expect to be assessed. These effects can be described as *pre-assessment effects*, since they occur before assessment takes place.

When assessment is formative (integrated within the learning process) and/or summative in nature, it can influence learning because students, after finishing their tasks, reflect on their learning outcomes and learning processes (referred to as *post-assessment effects*). Feedback is the most important cause of these post-assessment effects. Teachers and peers can give students information about the quality of the performance. When students have the necessary metacognitive knowledge and skills, they become capable enough to draw conclusions themselves about the quality of their learning behaviour (self-generating feedback or internal feedback). However, this is not always the case, certainly not in the beginning stage of their study.

An important difference between the pre- and post-assessment effects is that the latter is intentional, whereas the former has often been regarded rather as a kind of side-effect, since the main purpose of summative assessment is not in the first place supporting and sustaining learning but rather selection and certification of students. However, with the increasing implementation of learning environments based on constructivist theories of learning and intending to enhance their scaffolding power, more focus has been placed on the significant role of assessment in steering learning. Therefore, the pre-assessment effect of assessment has received growing attention.

Nevo (1995) and Struyf *et al.* (2001) point to a third kind of learning effect from assessment. Students also learn during assessment itself, because they often need to reorganise their required knowledge, use it to tackle new problems and think about relations between related aspects they didn't discover during studying. When assessment stimulates them to thinking processes of a higher cognitive level, it is possible that assessment itself becomes a rich learning experience for students. This means that, contrary to the old American saying 'weighing the pig doesn't fatten it' in some cases high-quality learning is fostered by simply assessing the learning outcomes. In other words, in some cases, weighing can fatten the pigs. This, of course, applies to formative as well as to summative assessment. We can call this the *pure-assessment effect*. This is somewhat different from the two other effects, in that it can provide for learning, but it does not have a direct effect on learning behaviour prior to the assessment moment, unless under the form of self-feedback as a form of post-assessment effect, as we discussed earlier.

Studies on the pre-assessment effect

Tang (1994) conducted a study in the Physiotherapy Section at the Hong Kong Polytechnic, in the subject of integrated professional studies, with 158 first-year students. The assessment of this subject had traditionally been by written tests consisting of short essay questions (test condition). In order to steer students' learning towards higher-level cognitive preparation strategies, course assignments had been introduced (assignment condition). A qualitative study consisted of interviews with thirty-nine students randomly selected from the sample. The aim was to explore their perceptions of the assessment demands and effects on the adoption of preparation strategies. Path analysis for the test condition demonstrated congruence between the students' study approaches and their assessment preparation strategies. 'Those students who were surface-oriented were more likely to employ low level strategies when studying for the test, while those who were normally deep-oriented had a higher tendency to employ high level preparation strategies' (Tang, 1994: 6). The interviews indicated that deep-oriented students were not disadvantaged in this mode of assessment as they adapted to the perceived low-level demands of the test and 'orchestrated their study approach by adopting the deep-memorising strategy (i.e. surface learning strategies with deep intentions), and hence were able to do the test' (Tang, 1994: 6).

The patterns of relationships for the assignment condition were different from that of the test condition. There was a relative lack of relationship between the students' habitual ways of learning and the subsequent adoption of preparation strategies in writing assignments. Tang suggests that writing assignments is a new experience for most of these first-year students and therefore they cannot readily rely on their habitual strategies to handle the task. 'Under such circumstances, their motives, whether extrinsic, intrinsic or achieving, become a more relevant reference for the decision for the actual strategies to be employed' (Tang, 1994: 8). The results of the interviews demonstrated that high-level strategies, such as understanding, application of information, relating to other subjects and previous knowledge, are requirements perceived to be necessary for both assessment conditions. However, low-level strategies, such as rote learning, memorisation and reproduction, were perceived to be relevant only to the test condition.

Scouller's study (1996) is linked to the Tang study as it focused on students' study approaches related to the mode of assessment implemented. However, she investigated students' perceptions of the assessment demands. Scouller (1996) studied students' learning approaches (classified as either deep or surface) and their perceptions of the intellectual abilities or skills being assessed (classified as lower or higher) within two assessment contexts of the same course: an assignment essay and an end-of-course short-answer examination. The sample consisted of 140 first-year sociology students at the University of Sydney. The main findings revealed that the assessment method strongly influenced the way these students learned and prepared their assessment tasks. The patterns that emerged were more straightforward than those in Tang's study. The sociology students were much more likely to employ surface strategies when preparing for their short-answer examinations than when preparing their assignment essays. In contrast, when writing their assignment essays these students were significantly more likely to employ deep strategies than when preparing for their short-answer examinations. Concerning their learning motives, students were significantly more likely to report surface motives when preparing their short-answer examinations in contrast to their preparation of their assignment essays, when they were more likely to report deep motives. Finally, these students were significantly more likely to perceive the short-answer examination as assessing lower levels of intellectual abilities and skills than the assignment essay. In contrast, students were more likely to perceive the assignment essay as assessing higher levels of intellectual abilities and skills such as analysis and synthesis than their short-answer examination. Probably – in any case more than the Hong Kong students in Tang's study – these students have prior experience with different modes of assessment, including assignments, and therefore can rely on habitual strategies to handle the assignments and thus to be strategic in their approach to learning.

A recent study by Nijhuis *et al.* (forthcoming) further explores the conditions for assessment to steer learning, by investigating the impact of the implementation of a specific new assessment instrument, namely the OverAll Test. This is a case-based assessment instrument and requires students to use knowledge (conceptual models, theories) as a tool to define, analyse, solve and evaluate the problems presented in novel, authentic, ill-structured case studies. On the basis of a set of multiple-choice questions and open-ended questions, students have to analyse various case studies of companies applying the knowledge they had acquired during the course. Specifically, they have to relate information presented and ideas explored in the case studies to the main concepts and theories learned during the course. Furthermore, students are asked to give specific advice to the company described in the case, based on relevant arguments. More than in the aforementioned studies, explicit attention is paid to the alignment of learning, instruction and assessment.

In the course under study, the OverAll Test is implemented as an integral part of a redesigned learning environment. The main differences between the original and the redesigned learning environment are the format of learning tasks (*study* tasks in the original course and *problem* tasks in the redesigned course) and the mode of assessment (a knowledge reproduction test in the original course and a combination of a knowledge reproduction test and an OverAll test in the redesigned course). In order to unravel the mechanism through which assessment steers learning, two variables, indicated as relevant in the aforementioned studies, are taken into account: students' intended learning strategies as an indicator for their general, habitual learning strategies (Tang, 1994) and their perceptions of the assessment demands (Tang, 1994; Scouller, 1996). Two questions are central. When comparing the original and the redesigned learning environment, is there a change in the students' intended learning strategies, their perceptions of the assessment demands and their actual learning strategies? And what is the association between these three variables in both conditions, the original and the redesigned learning environments?

The results indicated that, contrary to expectations, the students in the original course adopted more deep learning strategies and fewer surface learning strategies than the students in the redesigned course. Although the students were informed about the differences in the various course information resources, there were no significant differences between both groups of students in the learning strategies they intended to employ as well as in their perceptions of the assessment demands. In both conditions, the correlation indices indicate that students who intend to employ surface learning strategies perceive the assessment demands as surface and actually use surface approaches to learning. The results show clearly that those students who express their intentions to employ a certain learning strategy perceive the assessment demands as such and actually employ a related learning strategy. This association between the intended learning strategies and students' perceptions of the assessment demands and their actual learning strategies is clear within both conditions.

Similar findings on the effects of redesigned learning environments are expressed in the research of Struyven *et al.* (2006). This study investigated the effects of the learning/teaching environment on students' approaches to learning (i.e., combination of intention and learning strategies), and compared lecture-based and student-activating settings within the first year of elementary teacher education. The lecture-based environment made use of a multiple-choice test, whereas four student-activating groups were assigned to one of four assessment modes: namely, portfolio assessment; case-based assessment; peer/co-assessment; and multiple-choice test. Data collection from a sample of 790 students was carried out using a pre-test/post-test method. Though students' approaches were similar at the start of the course, a clear distinction was found after experiencing the lecture-based and student-activating teaching/learning environments. However, the direction of change was opposite to the premise that student-activating instruction deepens student learning. Instead, the latter pushed students towards a surface approach to learning and students' monitoring of study approaches suffered significant lowering. Neither the student-activating instruction nor the three new modes of assessment (peer assessment, portfolio assessment and case-based evaluation) were able to enhance deep(er) approaches to learning.

These results indicate that the introduction of new modes of assessment, although they are in alignment with the learning environment, does not directly lead to desired changes in student learning. Various factors might mediate the effect of new learning environments on student learning. A related study by Nijhuis *et al.* (2005) refers to the role of students' perceptions of the learning environment. The results indicated that those students who showed a higher level of surface learning perceived the redesigned learning environment as less positive in terms of clarity of its goals, the usefulness of the literature resources and the workload. These findings are confirmed in the study of Struyven *et al.* (2006).

However, though the assessment methods did not deepen the approaches to learning, Struyven *et al.* (2005) found a positive effect of the hands-on experience of the modes of assessment on the assessment preferences of their students. At the start of this research project, students were largely unfamiliar with the four assessment methods and the results from 612 students show negative students' responses to these unknown evaluation methods. Students indicate feelings of uncertainty, not knowing what to expect. This makes them feel uncomfortable with and critical towards the expected assessment method. However, as familiarity with the assessment tool grew and students became better informed of its characteristics and effects, students' preferences concerning this tool changed positively. Moreover, the results indicated that the students' perceptions of the appropriateness of the assessment method are congruent with students' preferences. Interestingly, conclusions apply to both traditional tests, such as multiple-choice testing, and new modes of assessment, such as case-based assessment, peer evaluation and portfolio assessment. Considering the unpopularity and widely perceived critiques that this traditional tool has suffered during recent years, these results are rather surprising. This finding is probably due to the good use of the assessment method and its orientation towards knowledge construction, including the skills to apply content to practice-relevant situations and to solve real-life problems.

Studies on the post-assessment effect

A study by Gijbels et al. (2005) investigated the effect of assessment on students' performance in final exams. They took a small but progressive step towards the integration of assessment, learning and instruction by integrating written assessment tasks in the learning process. In order to get more insight into the effects, they formulated two research questions. First, do students who complete the assessment tasks do better in their final exam compared to students who do not? Second, what are the most important concerns in students' and teachers' perceptions of the assessment tasks? Students' final exam results were used to find out whether students who complete the assessment tasks do better than students who do not. Answers from questionnaires and semi-structured interviews were used to discover the most important concerns in students' and teachers' perceptions of the assessment tasks. A total of 205 students, following a course on public law in the second year of their law degree, participated. Out of these students, 164 completed six assessment tasks. The results showed that, when corrected for differences in prior academic performance, students who submitted all the assessment tasks successfully during the course performed significantly better (achieving higher grades) on their final exam compared to students who did not complete the assessment tasks. This was the case for both those parts of the final exam that were related to the assessment tasks as well as non-related questions, indicating that the assessment tasks seem to have influenced the general learning approach of the students.

From the questionnaires and interviews, it appeared that both the students and the teachers see the benefits of the assessment tasks. Students reported studying more, more critically and more systematically as a result of them. Moreover, better time management was related to higher final exam grades. All the students reported that the feedback they received was very useful. Tutors reported that assessing a piece of work and giving appropriate feedback was only possible by checking it thoroughly. Furthermore, they thought it was important for students to receive sound and detailed feedback. They found it inappropriate not to check students' work thoroughly and to look only for evidence of sufficient effort, as was suggested when starting the project in an attempt to reduce the time needed to correct the assignments. However, for many tutors, this resulted in a larger than planned amount of time in their evaluation of the tasks. The presence of a well-constructed correction model was, according to the tutors, very helpful and reduced time in giving feedback. In conclusion, tutors perceived a time-management problem and were concerned about the feasibility of the whole project. Nevertheless, the authors conclude that small steps in the change of the assessment system can result in relatively big improvements in students' learning and results.

The role of practice and feedback has been evidenced in research on peer assessment. The study by Sluijsmans et al. (2002) focused on the influence of peer assessment training on the peer assessment skills as well as on performance. This study was conducted with 93 second-year students in a teacher training college, with students randomly assigned to control groups and experimental groups. The experimental groups were trained in defining performance criteria, giving feedback and writing assessment reports, using peer assessment tasks. Analysis of the students' peer assessment reports indicates that the experimental groups outperformed the control groups in the quality of their assessment skills. Additionally, they outperformed the control groups in their scores for the final end-of-course products.

Studies on the pure-assessment effect

Portfolio assessment has been advocated as a valuable tool for learning through assessment. Tillema argues that:

> Portfolios as one of the more prominent instruments can be used as learning tools for competence development because they provide opportunities to monitor and appraise changes in performance . . . During the compilation of evidence, the portfolio as a tool offers a framework to monitor and coach performance improvement, often with the aid of mentors or coaches who provide feedback on the portfolio evidence. This kind of deployment of the portfolio instrument makes it especially suitable as a tool for learning.
>
> (Tillema, 2001: 126–127)

Tillema (2001) conducted a study in the context of a training programme for small business and retail managers. The portfolios were used to collect data on progress in entrepreneurial competencies. In three different samples (cohort staff teams), the portfolio assessment tool was designed differently: a dossier portfolio with a portfolio guideline that specified precisely what products of work-related performance were to be included as evidence of accomplishments in the work environment; a course-related learning portfolio defined as a detailed description of targets to be attained as well as the collection of evidence about attained performance in practice settings; a reflective learning portfolio defined as a learner report on professional growth in competence. The 137 participants in the study were asked about the perceived benefits and problems while collecting and learning from the portfolio. Additionally, overall performance ratings of the portfolio collector were obtained from supervisors in the work and training settings.

The results of the study indicate that there is a clear difference in performance change among portfolio types. The reflective portfolio shows the most gains, correlating with the highest functional feedback as perceived by the students. The dossier portfolio and course-related portfolio show lower levels of behavioural improvement. This may be explained by the fact that they are primarily focused on appraisal and testing of performance rather than on improvement. The reflective portfolio, far more than the dossier and course-related portfolio, was evaluated by the students as providing more insights about performance and, additionally, showed lower levels of acceptance and use of feedback recommendations.

Engineering assessment into the learning process: some guidelines

We previously called 'longer-term learning' outcomes 'learning lasting for life' outcomes, which refer to outcomes that are durable, flexible, functional, generalisable and application-oriented (Dochy, 2005). Such learning is characterised by increasing self-directedness and self-assessment and is more discovery-oriented, using authentic problems or cases. As such, it profits from contextualisation and increased motivation (Dochy, 2005), and such learning requires 'engineering' the assessment into the learning process more intensively.

In conclusion, we indicate some guidelines for the engineering of assessment into the learning process. Faced with the powerful (direct and indirect) impact of assessment (which may be either positive or negative), assessment should be used strategically, engineered to have educationally sound and positive influences.

Three issues related to assessment can help teachers in engineering assessment as a true tool for learning (Gibbs and Simpson, 2004). First, assessment can influence the quantity and distribution of student effort. This is the case when the assessed tasks capture sufficient study time and effort and distribute this effort evenly across the topics and weeks. Second, assessment can influence the quality and the level of the students' effort. When the tasks engage students in productive learning activities and communicate clear and high expectations to the students, assessment supports student learning. Third, assessment can be accompanied by timely and sufficient (peer) feedback. Feedback should be provided quickly enough to be useful to students and should be given both often enough and in enough detail. The quality of feedback is important. It should focus on learning, be understandable for students and linked to the purpose of the tasks and the criteria. Students' response to feedback should be taken into consideration. Feedback should be received by and attended to the students and students should act upon the feedback in order to improve their tasks or their learning.

In general, research suggests that traditional modes of assessment, such as multiple-choice examinations, lead to (generally undesirable) surface approaches to learning whereas new modes of assessment (such as working with more authentic tasks) lead to (generally desirable) more deep approaches to learning. Nevertheless, this should not make us jump to the conclusion that the implementation of new modes of assessment always leads to more deep-level learning (e.g., Nijhuis et al., forthcoming; Struyven et al., 2006). It seems that students need to perceive the new mode of assessment at least as clear in its goals, useful and appropriate regarding the workload demands in order to influence students' learning in the desired way. This probably implies the engineering of a blend of different (old and new, formative and summative) modes of assessment. Continuing along this line involves efforts from different players in the field. First, departmental audits or accreditation audits should not be limited to a screening of external standards in summative tests. They should also include an inventory of the amount and nature of formative assessments and new modes of assessment, and consider the realisation of the aim of spreading optimal learning and principles of good teaching practice. Second, teacher pre-service and professional development programmes should include instruction in how students learn and how learning can be assessed as a major component in most programmes. The focus should be on the proper integration of learning and assessment in teachers' educational experience (Black and Wiliam, 1998; Hamilton, 2003; Pellegrino et al., 2001). Finally, it is up to the teachers to struggle with and overcome the difficulties in bridging the gap between the new developments in the assessment culture and the daily educational and assessment practice.

References

Biggs, J. (2003) Teaching for Quality Learning at University, 2nd edn, Buckingham: Open University Press.

Birenbaum, M. (1996) Assessment 2000: toward a pluralistic approach to assessment, in M. Birenbaum and F. Dochy (eds) Alternatives in Assessment of Achievement, Learning Processes and Prior Knowledge, Boston, MA: Kluwer Academic.

Birenbaum, M. and Dochy, F. (eds) (1996) Alternatives in Assessment of Achievement, Learning Processes and Prior Knowledge, Boston, MA: Kluwer Academic.

Black, P. and Wiliam, D. (1998) Assessment and classroom learning, Assessment in Education: Principles, Policy and Practice, 5, 1: 7–74.

Cohen, S.A. (1987) Instructional alignment: searching for a magic bullet, Educational Researcher, 16, 8: 16–20.

Dochy, F. (2005) Learning lasting for life and assessment: how far did we progress?, presidential address at the European Assocation for Research on Learning and Instruction conference, Nicosia, Cyprus (available at: http://www.earli.org/about/articles/EARLI 2005%20presidential%20address%20FINAL.pdf).

Dochy, F. and McDowell, L. (1997) Assessment as a tool for learning, Studies in Educational Evaluation, 23, 4: 279–298.

Engel, C.E. (1997) Not just a method but a way of learning, in D. Boud and G. Feletti (eds) The Challenge of Problem Based Learning, 2nd edn, London: Kogan Page.

Entwistle, N.J. and Entwistle, A. (1991) Contrasting forms of understanding for degree examinations: the student experience and its implications, Higher Education, 22: 205–227.

Entwistle, N.J. and Ramsden, P. (1983) Understanding Student Learning, London: Croom Helm.

Entwistle, N., McCune, V. and Walker, P. (2001) Conceptions, styles, and approaches within higher education: analytical abstractions and everyday experience, in R.J. Sternberg and L.F. Zhang (eds) Perspectives on Cognitive, Learning and Thinking Styles, Mahwah, NJ: Lawrence Erlbaum Associates.

Entwistle, N.J., Meyer, J.H.F. and Tait, H. (1991) Student failure: disintegrated patterns of study strategies and perceptions of the learning environment, Higher Education, 21, 2: 249–261.

Gibbs, G. (1999) Using assessment strategically to change the way students learn, in S. Brown and A. Glasner (eds) Assessment Matters in Higher Education: Choosing and Using Diverse Approaches, Buckingham: Open University Press.

Gibbs, G. and Simpson, C. (2004) Does your assessment support your students' learning?, Journal of Learning and Teaching in Higher Education, 1: 3–31.

Gijbels, D., van de Watering, G. and Dochy, F. (2005) Integrating assessment tasks in a problem-based learning environment, *Assessment and Evaluation in Higher Education*, 30, 1: 73–86.

Glaser, R. (1990) Toward new models for assessment, *International Journal of Educational Research*, 14: 375–483.

Hamilton, H. (2003) Assessment as a policy tool, in R.E. Floden (ed.) *Review of Research in Education*, 27: 25–68, Washington, DC: American Educational Research Association.

Keeves, J.P. (1994) Methods of assessment in schools, in T. Husèn and T.N. Postlethwaite (eds) *International Encyclopedia of Education*, Oxford and New York: Pergamon Press.

Koretz, D., Stecher, B., Klein, S. and McCaffrey, D. (1994) The Vermont portfolio assessment program: findings and implications, *Educational Measurement: Issues and Practice*, 13, 3: 5–16.

Lea, S.J., Stephenson, D. and Troy, J. (2003) Higher education students' attitudes toward student-centred learning: beyond 'educational bulimia'?, *Studies in Higher Education*, 28, 3: 321–334.

Lohman, D.F. (1993) Teaching and testing to develop fluid abilities, *Educational Researcher*, 22: 12–23.

Miller, C.M.I. and Parlett, M. (1974) *Up to the Mark: A Study of the Examination Game*, Guildford: Society for Research into Higher Education.

Nevo, D. (1995) *School-Based Evaluation: A Dialogue for School Improvement*, London: Pergamon.

Nijhuis, J., Segers, M. and Gijselaers, W. (2005) Influence of redesigning a learning environment on student perceptions and learning strategies, *Learning Environments Research*, 8: 67–93.

—— (forthcoming) Redesigning a learning and assessment environment: the influence on students' perceptions of assessment demands and their learning strategies, *Studies in Educational Evaluation*.

Nitko, A.J. (1989) Designing tests that are integrated with instruction, in R.L. Linn (ed.) *Educational Measurement*, New York: American Council on Education, Macmillan Publishing Company.

Nonaka, I. and Takeuchi, H. (1995) *The Knowledge-Creating Company*, New York: Oxford University Press.

Pellegrino, J.W., Chudowsky, N. and Glaser, R. (2001) *Knowing What Students Know: The Science and Design of Educational Assessment*, Washington, DC: National Academy Press.

Poikela, E. and Poikela, S. (1997) Conceptions of learning and knowledge – impacts on the implementation of problem-based learning, *Zeitschrift für Hochschuldidactic*, 21, 1: 8–21.

Rowntree, D. (1987) *Assessing Students: How Shall We Know Them?* London: Kogan Page.

Scouller, K. (1996) Influence of assessment method on students' learning approaches, perceptions and preferences: the assignment essay versus the short answer examination, in *Different Approaches: Theory and Practice in Higher Education*, proceedings of HERDSA conference, Perth, Western Australia, 8–12 July (available at: http://www.herdsa.org.au/confs/1996/scouller.html).

—— (1998) The influence of assessment method on students' learning approaches: multiple choice question examination versus assignment essay, *Higher Education*, 35: 453–472.

Segers, M., Dochy, F. and Cascallar, E. (2003) *Optimizing New Modes of Assessment: In Search for Qualities and Standards*, Boston, MA: Kluwer Academic.

Sluijsmans, D.M.A., Brand-Gruwel, S. and Van Merriënboer, J. (2002) Peer assessment training in teacher education, *Assessment and Evaluation in Higher Education*, 27, 5: 443–454.

Snyder, B.R. (1971) *The Hidden Curriculum*, Cambridge, MA: MIT Press.

Struyf, E., Vandenberghe, R. and Lens, W. (2001) The evaluation practice of teachers as a learning opportunity for students, *Studies in Educational Evaluation*, 27, 3: 215–238.

Struyven, K., Dochy, F. and Janssens, S. (2005) The effects of hands-on experience on student teachers' preferences of assessment methods, paper presented to the International Study Association on Teachers and Teaching conference, Sydney, Australia, 3–6 July.

Struyven, K., Dochy, F., Janssens, S., Schelfhout, W. and Gielen, S. (2006) On the dynamics of students' approaches to learning: the effects of the learning/teaching environment, *Learning and Instruction*, 16, 4: 279–294.

Tang, C. (1994) Effects of modes of assessment on students' preparation strategies, in G. Gibbs (ed.) *Improving Student Learning: Theory and Practice*, Oxford: Oxford Centre for Staff Development.

Tillema, H. (2001) Portfolios as developmental assessment tools, *International Journal of Training and Development*, 5, 2: 126–135.

Tynjälä, P. (1999) Towards expert knowledge? A comparison between a constructivist and a traditional learning environment in the university, *International Journal of Educational Research*, 33: 355–442.

Chapter 8

Towards more sustainable feedback to students

Dai Hounsell

Anyone engaged in a demanding activity, however experienced they are, can from time to time benefit from constructive and well-targeted feedback – the counsellor advising needy clients, the coordinator of a large and interprofessional team of colleagues, the help desk manager who constantly has to prioritise enquiries and requests for assistance. In such situations, periodic feedback can help individuals take stock of how well they are doing, and consider ways in which, for example, their effectiveness might be increased, their workload made more manageable, or their job satisfaction heightened. But when the activity concerned is not a wholly familiar one but involves significant new learning, as in educational settings, the role of feedback is particularly powerful. Indeed, in higher education, which is our focus here, well-crafted feedback can enhance learning in three significant ways:

- by *accelerating learning*, i.e., speeding up what can be learned by the students concerned within a given period of time, and so enabling learning to take place more rapidly, or in greater depth or scope, than would otherwise be the case;
- by *optimising the quality of what is learned*, i.e., helping to ensure that the learning outcomes achieved and evinced by the students meet the standards hoped for or required (e.g., in terms of precision, appreciation of complexity, applicability to real-world problems and so on);
- by *raising individual and collective attainment*, through enabling the students to attain standards or levels of achievement higher than those which they might otherwise have reached, i.e., without recourse to the scaffolding afforded by feedback.

Yet in contemporary undergraduate education, the sustainability of feedback is under threat, as evidence continues to emerge of pervasive student concerns about the provision of feedback in an era of mass higher education. In Australia, for example, three successive quinquennial surveys (Krause *et al.*, 2005) have consistently shown dissatisfaction with the adequacy of feedback on the part of two out of five first-year undergraduates, while surveys in Hong Kong by Carless (2006) have disclosed not only significant disparities in student and staff perceptions of feedback but student discontent with the level of detail in the feedback provided and with its contribution to helping them improve their performance. British findings are if anything even more compelling. One major source is a recent national survey of graduates' perceptions of their experiences at university, in which feedback emerged as a major focus of student concern (National Student Survey, 2005). Another source is an analysis of the reports of nearly 3,000 quality assurance visits over an eight-year period. In the great majority of the sixty-two subject areas reviewed, reviewers had commented on 'the failure of a significant number of institutions to provide adequate feedback on students' work' (QAA, 2003: 28). Similar indications of discontent were evident in three out of the four subject areas surveyed in a large-scale investigation of undergraduate courses as teaching–learning environments (Hounsell *et al.*, 2005). Students' concerns about guidance and feedback ranged widely, encompassing not only the consistency and helpfulness of tutors' comments but the timing and frequency of feedback and the adequacy of guidance about assessment expectations and criteria.

To a significant extent, this groundswell of student discontent with feedback can be seen as a product of the onset of mass higher education, which has brought in its wake soaring student enrolments and intakes much more diverse than hitherto (see, for example, SFC, 2003; McInnis *et al.*, 2000). In Scotland, for instance, the proportion of young people going into higher education rose from one-fifth to almost one-half between 1980 and 2000, and there were similar rates of growth elsewhere in the UK and in Australia (Scottish Executive, 2003; NCIHE, 1997; DETYA, 2005). Not surprisingly, expansion on this scale was only practicable by driving down unit costs, with the consequence that student–staff ratios almost doubled between 1983 and 2000 (DfES, 2003) and funding per student fell by 40 per cent over a similar period (NCIHE, 1997: 45). That, in turn, has meant that staff marking and commenting loads have increased sharply, while students have been set fewer coursework assignments, and opportunities for interaction in tutorials and practicals have shrunk (DfES, 2003) – and this in a period when, it might reasonably be assumed, addressing a much wider spectrum of student capabilities and aspirations would call for greater rather than fewer opportunities to gain practice on assessed tasks and more rather than less guidance and support.

A further potentially dysfunctional development has been the shift towards modularised and semesterised curriculum structures. Since this can result in course units which are compressed into a few weeks rather than extending over a full academic year, assignments and assessments tend to bunch together towards the end of a unit. And when assessment is 'end-loaded' in this way, a module or unit may be close to finishing – or may have finished – before the students receive any significant feedback on their work, with the consequence that there is little or no opportunity to capitalise on what could be learned from that feedback in subsequent assessments (Yorke, 2001; Higgins *et al.*, 2002; Gibbs, 1999).

In such circumstances, a downward spiral is all too easily generated. Student disenchantment mounts when the feedback they get on their undergraduate work is too uninformative, or unconstructive, or comes too late to be of much practical use. Their faith in its value to them as learners therefore begins to wane. At the same time, staff who are already hard pressed to mark and comment systematically on assignments and assessments find growing indications of students not taking feedback seriously, alongside diminishing evidence that their feedback has 'made a difference' to the quality of work students produce (Hounsell, 2003). Some students, it appears, do not even bother to collect work that has been marked and commented upon, while others do collect it but seem interested only in what mark they received. Staff commitment to providing helpful feedback can therefore become increasingly undermined.

The aim of this chapter is to explore how this downward spiral might be reversed, and the long-term sustainability of feedback in higher education safeguarded. In its most immediate sense, this would mean restoring the position of feedback as a pedagogical resource that was prized by staff and students alike for its role in supporting the achievement of curriculum aims and learning outcomes. But in a more fundamental sense, the sustainability of feedback would, like sustainable assessment (Boud, 2000), be a function of its contribution to equip students to learn prospectively, in their lives and careers beyond graduation.

In the sections which follow, three pathways towards more sustainable feedback of these twin kinds are explored:

- greater focus on the provision of high-value feedback;
- transforming the role of students in feedback;
- enhancing the congruence of guidance and feedback.

Greater focus on providing high-value feedback

The distinction recently drawn by Knight (2002) between 'high-stakes' and 'low-stakes' assessments has quickly proved to be conceptually and practically worthwhile: it is framed from the students' eye-view, and it cuts across the more familiar but rather shop-worn formative/summative divide in a way that opens up fresh perspectives and insights. It may be equally fruitful to suggest distinguishing between 'high-value' and 'low-value' feedback, where what is in focus is the relative potential impact of the feedback being offered in relation to the learning of the students concerned: that is, to what extent it seems likely to have a significant effect on the quality of their learning, at that point in time, in their ongoing academic studies, and in their longer-term development. From this standpoint, then, the more telling or lasting the feedback, the more 'sustainable' it is considered to be.

One way of deploying this distinction is in appraising the nature and quality of the written comments made by tutors on returned work. While there have been relatively few analyses of such feedback comments, those which can be identified suggest wide variations between tutors not simply in the quantity of comments made, but in their scope, focus, tone and clarity (see, for example, Ivanic *et al.*, 2000; Chanock, 2000). Thus, low-value comments may be concerned with relatively minor matters of language (spelling, punctuation, syntax), factual precision, or bibliographic finesse. Low-value feedback may also be relatively cryptic: the ubiquitous tick in the margin, orthographic shorthand such as '?', '!' or '(. . .)' , or the use of bald imperatives and assertions – 'Explain', 'A bit confused', 'Linkage?' (Lea and Street, 2000). Most fundamentally, feedback comments may lack transparency (Lillis and Turner, 2001), invoking a set of academic conventions and ground-rules for communicating within the subject which are largely tacit rather than explicit and of which students may have only an incomplete and uncertain grasp (Hounsell, 1987). As Lee and Street (2000: 40) observe:

> Faced with writing which does not appear to make sense within their own academic framework, they [tutors] are most likely to have recourse to what feel like familiar descriptive categories such as 'structure and argument', 'clarity' and 'analysis', in order to give students feedback on their writing. In reality, their own understanding of these categories may be bound by their own individual disciplinary perspective, but they may be less meaningful outside this framework and therefore not readily understood by students unversed in that particular orientation of the discipline.

Research into students' perceptions and experiences of feedback comments reveals a similar picture. While confirming the need for transparency, there is also a concern on the part of students that feedback should not only highlight strengths and weaknesses but point to how they might go about improving their work. In a questionnaire survey of history students, for instance, Hyland (2000: 244) concludes that:

> Many students stressed that while they were 'always trying to achieve a higher standard', they rarely knew 'how to set about it'. And this was primarily due to 'not knowing what is meant' when tutors use terms such as 'structure', 'analysis' and 'original thought' in criticism of a history essay; not receiving clear, precise and practical advice about how to make improvements; and not having the benefit of tutorials to talk about learning problems and achievements.

However, the extent to which feedback can support students in raising the quality of their work is not solely a function of the nature of the comments made by tutors on assignments and assessments. It is also bound up with the timing and phasing of feedback – assessments crowding towards the end of a semester in the way already noted – and with the salience of the feedback *beyond the task to which the feedback relates*. For feedback is likely to have much greater longevity if that particular assignment or assessment is imminently to be repeated, forms part of a linked chain of assessments within a module or course unit, or enhances students' evolving grasp of a core component (a key concept, say, or skill in interpreting data) of a wider programme of study. This is not fanciful, for concrete examples can be pinpointed. They are most readily to be found in postgraduate research supervision, where the gestation of a thesis is closely bound up with recursive cycles of dialogue and feedback: a draft of a chapter or part-chapter is submitted for comment, critiqued and suggestions made for improving it, and it is then reworked by the student prior to resubmission – which then may also reveal to supervisors how well their feedback has been grasped and addressed. Transposing this recursive approach directly to undergraduate taught courses is not so straightforward, except in the case of the honours dissertation or final-year project (where, ironically, the potential for recursive feedback is sometimes unrealised because of staff concerns that it might improve the quality of the finished work). However, McCreery (2005), with an example from a history course, has shown how even in a first-year undergraduate module it is possible to incorporate an opportunity to revise ongoing work in response to tutors' comments and group discussion, by reconfiguring tutorial provision to build progressively towards a full-blown essay. Another promising approach lies in refocusing written course-work around the 'patchwork text' (Scoggins and Winter, 1999), where a series of assigned tasks are carefully interwoven and interspersed with opportunities for recursive comment-and-revision. There may also be untapped potential in many courses for *anticipatory* feedback, where the lecturer not only posts past exam questions on a website but alerts students to potential 'traps for the unwary' and offers suggestions about how particular questions might fruitfully be approached (McCune and Hounsell, 2005). In informing their revision strategies for forth-coming exams, such feedback can be put to direct and practical use by students.

In all of these examples, feedback has metamorphosed into *feedforward*, exemplifying Black's argument that feedback can serve learning fully only 'if it involves both the *evoking* of evidence and a response to that evidence by *using* it in some way to improve the learning' (Black *et al*., 2003: 122). But it should also be observed that high-value feedback need not only be a matter of providing comments that are substantive, timely and directly usable. A thoroughgoing approach to guidance and feedback would also incorporate what Sadler has called 'exemplars of performance': in other words, authentic illustrations of completed work by students that represents high-quality achievement in the subject at that level and on that kind of assigned task. Such exemplars may be crucial in helping students to come to hold what Sadler would regard as a prerequisite for high achievement: namely, 'a concept of quality roughly similar to that held by the teacher' (Sadler, 1989: 121). Indeed, as Sadler argued later, this would accord with the ultimate goal of most educational systems, which is:

> to help students not only grow in knowledge and expertise, but also to become progressively independent of the teacher for lifelong learning. Hence if teacher-supplied feedback is to give way to self assessment and self monitoring, some of what the teacher brings to the assessment act must itself become part of the curriculum for the student, not an accidental or incon-sequential adjunct to it.
>
> (Sadler, 1998: 82)

Transforming students' roles in feedback

A second route towards more sustainable feedback lies in a transformed role for students in feedback, and in a variety of forms: in targeting, generating and interpreting feedback, and in communicating and engaging with it. While the rationale for student self- and peer assessment generally has been eloquently articulated by Boud, Falchikov and others in a series of studies (Boud, 1995; Falchikov, 2001; Brew, 1999) there has also been vigorous advocacy in the formative assessment literature of the particular benefits of student involvement in the processes of feedback. Indeed, for most of those working in this field, an active and substantial feedback role for students is seen as indispensable if higher-quality learning outcomes are to be achieved. For Askew (2000), the conceptual frame of reference is constructivist theories of learning, in which the making of meaning rests primarily with the student, and where feedback needs to engage both teacher and students in a reflexive, collaborative dialogue. For Nicol and Macfarlane-Dick (2006), on the other hand, it is self-regulation in learning which provides the conceptual cornerstone to a set of principles of good feedback practice. The capacity of students to self-regulate – to monitor, direct and prioritise their learning activities – can be powerfully facilitated through well-designed feedback and formative assessment, and can empower students to generate their own internal feedback more effectively. But perhaps the most seminal figure in this field has been Sadler (1989 and 1998). In his conceptualisation of formative assessment, two interrelated actions that need to be engaged in by the learner are pivotal: the perception of a gap between what he or she understands or can do and a desired level of understanding or skill; and the taking of action to close that gap (Sadler, 1989). As elaborated by Black and his colleagues, for whom Sadler's ideas have been especially influential:

> The learner first has to understand the evidence about this gap and then take action on the basis of that evidence. Although the teacher can stimulate and guide this process, the learning has to be done by the student. It would be a mistake to regard the student as the passive recipient of any call to action: there are complex links between the way in which a message is understood, the way in which that perception motivates a selection among different courses of action, and the learning activity that might follow. These arguments made it clear theoretically that the development of self-assessment by the student might have to be an important feature of any programme of formative assessment.
>
> (Black *et al.*, 2003: 14)

Extrapolating, then, from any or all of these conceptual standpoints, an authentic and significant student engagement in and with feedback would be a *sine qua non* of sustainability. But the rationale need not be wholly driven by conceptualisations of assessment in formal educational settings, for there are pragmatic grounds, as well as arguments based on employability and lifelong learning, which are also pertinent. The ostensibly pragmatic argument for student engagement in feedback stems from the use of student peers in the marking of laboratory reports or mid-semester class tests – tasks which could create an infeasibly large workload if marked by the teacher, but which are also low-stake assessments and predominantly formative in function. In such instances (where students follow peer-marking schemes and model answers provided by the teacher) spreading the marking load can give students access to feedback which it might otherwise not have been practicable to provide, as well as a toe-dipping acquaintance with peer feedback.

Key to the employability and lifelong learning argument is the notion that expertise in giving as well as receiving feedback is prized in the workplace (Jaques, 2000), and can be put to a variety of valuable uses in everyday life beyond the academy. Cohen and colleagues (2001: 249) have crisply encapsulated what expertise in feedback calls for:

> The giver of feedback has to identify what constitutes good work in a given subject area and express these ideas in a coherent form, while also communicating effectively with the prospective receivers about their feedback needs. The recipient of feedback benefits from identifying and articulating these needs, from receiving detailed comments from a peer who has faced a similar challenge and from responding appropriately to the feedback.

There are various ways towards greater student engagement that can help generate rich feedback. One example rests on the premise that the traditional approach to inculcating a grasp of assessment criteria (through individual and small-group practice, imitation, feedback and discussion) is increasingly impractical in contemporary mass higher education. The alternative approach reported (Rust *et al.*, 2003) seeks to impart tacit as well as explicit knowledge about criteria through a blend of exemplars, practice in peer marking and dialogue between staff and students. Another possibility is via peer involvement in recursive feedback, where in a series of meetings students use previously identified criteria to supply feedback to peers on increasingly polished versions of a piece of written work (Falchikov, 2001). A third, an initiative in honours-level English literature (Mallett, 2004), demonstrates how with more advanced students a challenging blend of various possibilities for drawing students more directly into the feedback process can be crafted. In the first of two essays which these students submit, they complete a self-assessment sheet in which they not only identify the essay's strengths and weaknesses and suggest what mark it merits, but indicate what aspects of their work they would most like to have feedback on from the tutor. For the second essay, students mark each other's essays:

> to criteria and ground rules they choose themselves. (Students can, for example, ask the peer-marker to note only what they admire, or only what they wish to dispute.) They can, if they wish, then revise the essay, and submit both the peer-assessed piece (which now becomes a draft) and the final version;

if the latter shows signs of making good use of the peer's comments, the writer rather than the marker is given credit for that.

(Mallett, 2004: 28–29)

Fourth, Robinson and Udall (2006) discuss an approach to greater student engagement with the curriculum which combines interactive 'learning conversations' between tutor and students about feedback with self-assessment against outcomes and critical reflection. The approach is being used in three universities in a range of subject areas and course units. Through the learning conversations in particular, the co-authors suggest, students are encouraged to develop a greater sense of ownership of, and thus greater autonomy in, their learning.

Enhancing the congruence of guidance and feedback

The last of the three pathways towards more sustainable feedback lies in fashioning teaching–learning environments which seek to maximise the degree of 'congruence' (McCune and Hounsell, 2005; Hounsell *et al.*, 2005) between high-quality learning outcomes and opportunities for formative feedback. The concept of congruence grows out of Biggs's (2003) model of 'constructive alignment', sharing its concern with goodness-of-fit between curriculum goals and teaching–learning and assessment strategies as a prerequisite of pedagogical effectiveness, while acknowledging both a wider array of contextual influences and the need to take due account of localised constraints and opportunities, which influence what may be feasible and practicable in a given institutional setting.

Strictly speaking, the two pathways already mapped out – higher-value comments and a more central student role in the trafficking of feedback – could each help to open up richer opportunities for formative feedback in a course or programme of study. But the wide-angle lens afforded by looking at teaching–learning environments in the round can also draw other salient features into the field of view. Foremost among these is recognition of the complementary benefits of *intrinsic* and well as *extrinsic* feedback (Hounsell, 2003). In this fundamental distinction, first drawn by Laurillard (2002), extrinsic feedback is that which is provided *ex post facto*, on a task – archetypally the coursework assignment – that has been largely or wholly undertaken by the student outside of timetabled face-to-face teaching–learning activities. By contrast, intrinsic feedback occurs incidentally and concurrently (Nicol and Macfarlane-Dick, 2006), and is woven into day-to-day teaching–learning encounters, where students are, for instance, working on a question or problem, and get virtually instant feedback in the form of the teacher's comments and suggestions on their approach to the question or problem or the quality of their answer or solution. It is, of course, the former, extrinsic kind of feedback which has hitherto been the prevailing focus of attention, and by bringing intrinsic feedback out of the shadows, it becomes apparent that the formative potential of this form of feedback could be capitalised upon much more fully. The most striking way in which this has begun to happen is through the use of 'personal response systems' (where students use a hand-held electronic device to signal their responses to fixed-choice questions) for instant monitoring of students' understanding of key points in lectures (see, for example, Draper, 2004; Boyle, 2004). But this should not be seen as a phenomenon which only technology has made possible. The well-established small-group tutorial or seminar can also offer rich possibilities for intrinsic feedback, especially when it is used to assist students to mould their discussion contributions towards progressively more refined exemplifications of academic discourse in the discipline or subject area concerned (Anderson, 1997).

A no less powerful means of creating feedback-enriched teaching–learning environments also entails rethinking conventional conceptions of what feedback is and how it can be nurtured. There is growing evidence of the accelerant effects on learning of activities which might collectively be called 'collaborative and on-display assignments' (Hounsell and McCune, 2003; Hounsell, 2003). These are assignments in which the end-product or completed work is not privately and individually vouchsafed to the lecturer or tutor but openly visible to some or all of the students. One instance of such assignments occurs when students are working co-operatively, in teams or groups, on a shared task, and therefore learn from and with each other in pooling not only perspectives and insights but strategies for tackling such tasks – for example, ways of dissecting a question, marshalling evidence, deciding on an optimal structure for a draft of an exposition or analysis, bringing an argument to a decisive conclusion (Hounsell, 1998). Another instance is to be found in individual as well as group-focused activities, where the task culminates in an oral or poster presentation. Even where students have prepared their work individually, their eventual presentations to an audience of their fellow course participants are on open display, and can enable them to perceive alternative ways of tackling the same task or a similar task, as in the following illustrative comments, drawn from group interviews with physical science students who had made oral presentations to their peers (Hounsell and McCune, 2003):

STUDENT 1:   You've got hands when you're presenting, it's so good.

STUDENT 2:   I was noticing that when I was doing [my presentation].

STUDENT 1:   No, but you used your hands when you were talking about the Northern Hemisphere and the Southern Hemisphere, and it was great because you don't actually have to describe the Northern Hemisphere at the top of the earth, and you don't have to give all the details of describing . . . and like a diagram you can point to bits.

STUDENT 1:   Your slides were like really packed . . . [Student B] had quite a few overheads which had little bits on and [Student C] just had a load of pictures. I had a load of slides and [Student D] had a few slides just with bullet points and he talked around them. So really there were five different types of presentation but I think they all came across really well.

The nub of the argument being made here is that, in breaking the long-established conventions of individually and privately transacted 'set work', collaborative and on-display assignments can function as proxies for feedback, emulating it in their capacity to prompt students to consider alternative strategies for communicating insights and findings, while also acquainting them at first hand with examples of high-quality work by their fellow students.

Lastly, teaching–learning environments could become more fertile sites for feedback if it were made a much more visible and more central component in teaching and assessment policies and strategies. The inconsistencies in provision which, as noted earlier, students often experience, come about in part because feedback has generally been perfunctorily treated, a *sub silencio* practice and one which has been begrudged where it has been viewed as an administrative chore rather than a pedagogical necessity. University teachers and their institutions go to considerable lengths to ensure that their examination practices and procedures are rigorous, consistent and on a par with those in comparable universities. Yet the quality of feedback, a key determinant of high attainment, frequently goes unevaluated in module questionnaires, unmonitored in course and programme reviews, and unscrutinised by external examiners, while taking steps to help newcomers acquire expertise in the giving of feedback – or older colleagues to review and refine their expertise – is too rarely seen by academic departments or faculties as something to be carried out with due diligence. Reversing this Cinderella status, by drawing feedback into the mainstream of institutional structures and processes, would therefore be a strategic necessity. But perhaps the truest mark of feedback's rehabilitation would mean considering it not simply as a worthwhile means to an end (the achievement of course aims and learning outcomes) but as an invaluable end in itself, beyond as well as within the university. In other words, expertise in feedback – accomplishment in learning from and with it, and in being skilled at deploying it constructively – would itself become an outcome of a higher education.

References

Anderson, C. (1997) Enabling and shaping understanding through tutorials, in F. Marton, D. Hounsell and N. Entwistle (eds) *The Experience of Learning*, 2nd edn, Edinburgh: Scottish Academic Press.

Askew, S. (ed.) (2000) *Feedback for Learning*, London: RoutledgeFalmer.

Biggs, J. (2003) *Teaching for Quality Learning at University*, 2nd edn, Buckingham: Society for Research into Higher Education and Open University Press.

Black, P., Harrison, C., Marshall, L. and Wiliam, D. (2003) *Assessment for Learning: Putting It into Practice*, Maidenhead: Open University Press.

Boud, D. (1995) *Enhancing Learning through Self-Assessment*, London: Kogan Page.

—— (2000) Sustainable assessment: rethinking assessment for the learning society, *Studies in Continuing Education*, 22, 2: 151–167.

Boud, D. and Falchikov, N. (2006) Aligning assessment with long-term learning, *Assessment and Evaluation in Higher Education*, 31, 4: 399–413.

Boyle, J. (2004) Using immediate feedback in class: the New Approaches to Teaching and Learning in Engineering (NATALIE) project [Case Study 5], in C. Juwah *et al.* (eds) *Enhancing Student Learning through Effective Formative Feedback* [SENLEF Project], York: Higher Education Academy (available at: http://www.heacademy.ac.uk/senlef. htm).

Brew, A. (1999) Towards autonomous assessment: using self-assessment and peer-assessment, in S. Brown and A. Glasner (eds) *Assessment Matters in Higher Education: Choosing and Using Diverse Approaches*, Buckingham: Society for Research into Higher Education and Open University Press.

Carless, D. (2006) Differing perceptions in the feedback process, *Studies in Higher Education*, 31, 2: 219–233.

Chanock, K. (2000) Comments on essays: do students understand what tutors write?, *Teaching in Higher Education*, 5, 1: 95–105.

Cohen, R., Boud, D. and Sampson, J. (2001) Dealing with problems encountered in assessment of peer learning, in N. Falchikov, *Learning Together: Peer Tutoring in Higher Education*, London: RoutledgeFalmer.

Department for Education and Skills (DfES) (2003) *The Future of Higher Education* (Cmd 5735), London: Stationery Office (see esp. paras. 1.19 and 1.31).

Department for Education, Training and Youth Affairs (DETYA) (2005) *Higher Education Students Time Series Tables*, Canberra: Department of Education, Training and Youth Affairs (available at: http://www.dest.gov.au/highered).

Draper, S. (2004) Feedback in interactive lectures using an electronic voting system [Case Study 3], in C. Juwah *et al.* (eds) *Enhancing Student Learning through Effective Formative Feedback* [SENLEF Project], York: Higher Education Academy (available at: http://www.heacademy.ac.uk/senlef.htm).

Falchikov, N. (2001) *Learning Together: Peer Tutoring in Higher Education*, London: RoutledgeFalmer.

Gibbs, G. (1999) Using assessment strategically to change the way students learn, in S. Brown and A. Glasner (eds) *Assessment Matters in Higher Education*, Buckingham: Society for Research into Higher Education and Open University Press.

Higgins, R., Hartley, P. and Skelton, A. (2002) The conscientious consumer: reconsidering the role of assessment feedback in student learning, *Studies in Higher Education*, 27, 1: 53–64.

Hounsell, D. (1987) Essay-writing and the quality of feedback, in J.T.E. Richardson *et al.* (eds) *Student Learning: Research in Education and Cognitive Psychology*, Milton Keynes: Society for Research into Higher Education and Open University Press.

—— (1998) Learning, assignments and assessment, in C. Rust (ed.) *Improving Students as Learners*, Oxford: Oxford Centre for Staff Learning and Development.

—— (2003) Student feedback, learning and development, in M. Slowey and D. Watson (eds) *Higher Education and the Lifecourse*, Buckingham: SRHE and Open University Press.

Hounsell, D. and McCune, V. (2003) Students' experiences of learning to present, in C. Rust (ed.) *Improving Student Learning Theory and Practice – Ten Years On*, Oxford: Oxford Centre for Staff and Learning Development.

Hounsell, D. *et al.* (2005) *Enhancing Teaching–Learning Environments in Undergraduate Courses: End-of-Award Report to the Economic and Social Research Council on Project L139251099*, Universities of Edinburgh, Durham and Coventry: ETL Project (available at http://www.ed.ac.uk/etl/publications).

Hounsell, D., McCune, V., Litjens, J. and Hounsell, J. (2006) *Biosciences Subject Overview Report*, Universities of Edinburgh, Durham and Coventry: ETL Project (available at: http://www.ed.ac.uk/etl/publications).

Hyland, P. (2000) Learning from feedback on assessment, in A. Booth and P. Hyland (eds) *The Practice of University History Teaching*, Manchester: Manchester University Press.

Ivanic, R., Clark, R. and Rimmershaw, R. (2000) What am I supposed to make of this? The messages conveyed to students by tutors' written comments, in M.R. Lea and B. Stierer (eds) *Student Writing in Higher Education: New Contexts*, Buckingham: Society for Research into Higher Education and Open University Press.

Jaques, D. (2000) *Learning in Groups: A Handbook for Improving Group Work*, 3rd edn, London: Kogan Page.

Knight, P.T. (2002) Summative assessment in higher education: practices in disarray, *Studies in Higher Education*, 27, 3: 275–286.

Krause, K., Hartley, R., James, R. and McInnis, C. (2005) *The First Year Experience in Australian Universities: Findings from a Decade of National Studies: A Project Funded by the Higher Education Innovation Programme, Department of Education, Science and Training: Final Report*, Melbourne: University of Melbourne (available at: http://www.cshe.unimelb.edu.au/).

Laurillard, D. (2002) *Rethinking University Teaching: A Conversational Framework for the Effective Use of Learning Technologies*, 2nd edn, London: RoutledgeFalmer.

Lea, M.R. and Street, B.V. (2000) Student writing and staff feedback in higher education: an academic literacies approach, in M.R. Lea and B. Stierer (eds) *Student Writing in Higher Education: New Contexts*, Buckingham: Society for Research into Higher Education and Open University Press.

Lillis, T. and Turner, J. (2001) Student writing in higher education: contemporary confusion, traditional concerns, *Teaching in Higher Education*, 6, 1: 57–68.

McCreery, C. (2005) Less is more: rethinking assessment in a first-year history unit, *Synergy* [University of Sydney], 22: 23–26 (available at: http://www.itl.usyd.edu.au/synergy/).

McCune, V. and Hounsell, D. (2005) The development of students' ways of thinking and practising in three final-year biology courses, *Higher Education*, 49: 255–289.

McInnis, C., James, R. and Hartley, R. (2000) *Trends in the First Year Experience in Australian Universities*, Canberra: Department for Education, Traning and Youth Affairs, Higher Education Division.

Mallett, P. (2004) Self and peer-assessment of written work in English [Case Study 6], in C. Juwah *et al.* (eds) *Enhancing Student Learning through Effective Formative Feedback* [SENLEF Project], York: Higher Education Academy (available at: http://www.heacademy.ac.uk/senlef.htm).

National Student Survey (2005) (available at: http://www.thestudentsurvey.com/ [accessed 9 November 2005]).

National Committee of Inquiry into Higher Education (NCIHE) (1997) *Higher Education in the Learning Society: Report of the National Committee of Inquiry into Higher Education* [Dearing Report], London: HMSO.

Nicol, D. and Macfarlane-Dick, D. (2006) Formative assessment and self-regulated learning: a model and seven principles of good feedback practice, *Studies in Higher Education*, 31, 2: 199–218.

Quality Assurance Agency for Higher Education (QAA) (2003) *Learning from Subject*

Review, 1993–2001: Sharing Good Practice, Gloucester: Quality Assurance Agency for Higher Education (available at: http://www.qaaa.ac.uk).

Robinson, A. and Udall, M. (2006) Using formative assessment to improve student learning through critical reflection, in C. Bryan and K. Clegg (eds) *Innovative Assessment in Higher Education*, London: Routledge.

Rust, C., Price, M. and O'Donovan, B. (2003) Improving students' learning by developing their understanding of assessment criteria and processes, *Assessment and Evaluation in Higher Education*, 28, 2: 147–164.

Sadler, D.R. (1989) Formative assessment and the design of instructional systems, *Instructional Science*, 18: 119–144.

—— (1998) Formative assessment: revisiting the territory, *Assessment in Education*, 5, 1: 77–84.

Scoggins, J. and Winter, R. (1999) The patchwork text: a coursework format for education as critical understanding, *Teaching in Higher Education*, 4, 4: 485–499.

Scottish Executive (2003) *A Framework for Higher Education in Scotland*, Edinburgh: Scottish Executive Education Department.

Scottish Funding Councils for Further and Higher Education (SFC) (2003) *Higher Education in Scotland: A Baseline Report*, Edinburgh: Scottish Funding Councils for Further and Higher Education.

Yorke, M. (2001) Formative assessment and its relevance to retention, *Higher Education Research and Development*, 20, 2: 115–126.

Chapter 9

Conceptions of self-assessment

What is needed for long-term learning?

Kelvin Tan

Introduction

Many writers have emphasised the general importance of student self-assessment in higher education. It has been argued that self-assessment should be a continuing focus throughout undergraduate education (Burgess *et al.*, 1999) and a main goal of higher education (Dochy *et al.*, 1999). The development of self-assessment ability is also recognised as a distinct outcome of higher education (Dearing, 1997; Stefani, 1998) and a critical educational tool for learning beyond university education (Tamir, 1999; Taras, 2001).

One of the arguments for promoting student self-assessment in higher education is that it equips students to become 'lifelong learners who can evaluate their own performance after they have finished formal study' (Brown and Glasner, 1999: 116). The notion, and the promotion, of lifelong learning is increasingly used as a basis for student self-assessment in higher education (Burgess *et al.*, 1999). It is argued that self-assessment practices encourage students to become 'lifelong learners who reflect continuously' (Sluijsmans *et al.*, 1998: 15). Likewise, Bartels (1998) argues that self-assessment allows students to form the habit of personal reflection in lifelong learning. There are three common ways that self-assessment practices are related to the development of students as lifelong learners.

Critical skills

Learning for present purposes such as fulfilling the requirements of a course of study focuses on students' ability to perform well in assessments conducted by their teachers. In contrast, lifelong learning may be said to require a different emphasis on skills; in particular, skills that equip students to conduct and evaluate their own learning. The ability of students to assess their progress and outcomes of learning are described as a core educational skill for lifelong learning (Boud, 1994). Self-assessment is considered to be far more suited to developing such skills as opposed to traditional forms of assessment which do not allow students to make their own judgements on their learning (Somervell, 1993).

Self-directed learning

One of the terms that is frequently associated with lifelong learning is 'self-directed learning'. The argument is that students must be able to plan and direct their own learning in order to be able to pursue learning situations without the assistance of the teacher. Hence, the ability to self-direct one's own learning is fundamental to lifelong learning (Sutherland, 1998). In this context, self-assessment is considered to be fundamental to preparing students for lifelong learning because its practices encourage students to self-direct their learning. Self-assessment develops students' ability to plan and direct their own learning and develop in their working lives (Hanrahan and Isaacs, 2001) and prepares students for lifelong learning by preparing them to become self-directed learners (Patterson *et al.*, 2002).

Responsibility for learning

Finally, there has been an emerging recognition of the need for students to assume responsibility for their own learning in undergraduate education in order to pursue their lifelong learning beyond higher education (Hinett and Weeden, 2000). Consequently, it is incumbent on tutors to provide students with the opportunity to discuss what constitutes an acceptable quality of work and to make judgements against explicit criteria in their undergraduate courses. In this context, self-assessment practices train students to make their own judgements of their learning in order to utilise the same skills when pursuing learning outside the higher education institution.

At the same time, the introduction of self-assessment activities forces students to re-examine their existing attitudes to their learning roles and responsibilities (Williams, 1992). Sambell and McDowell (1997) observed that self-assessment opportunities allowed their students to gain more confidence to assume greater levels of responsibility in directing and evaluating their future learning.

Is self-assessment sustainable?

One of the ways of examining the efficacy of assessment practices for enhancing lifelong learning is to evaluate its sustainability beyond its immediate practice. In the context of lifelong learning, Boud (2000: 151) defines sustainable assessment as 'assessment that meets the needs of the present without compromising the ability of students to meet their own future learning needs'. One of the key requirements for students in relation to their future learning needs is the ability to self-assess their learning. The literature exhorts self-assessment ability as being central to students' capacity for engaging in lifelong learning. The development of students' self-assessment ability beyond higher education is an emerging need for further development and research. Likewise, there is a need to design self-assessment practices that can develop and sustain students' self-assessment ability beyond its immediate programme of study. While the concept of sustainable assessment may be well articulated, the concept of sustainable self-assessment is not as fully expounded. This limits the general understanding of self-assessment skills to meeting immediate and short-term learning needs. There is no guarantee that these benefits for learning are long lasting as well if they are not designed specifically to sustain students' post-higher education learning.

My view is that the value and practice of self-assessment in higher education should be demonstrated to be sustainable before it can be claimed to be relevant to learning occurring beyond university education. While there is much support for self-assessment being consistent with, and beneficial to, the general idea of lifelong learning, there is less emphasis on how present self-assessment practices may relate to future learning contexts.

This chapter reports the results of an investigation into academics' conceptions of the scope of their student self-assessment practices in terms of students' learning and suggests a set of increasingly sophisticated meanings and practices of student self-assessment. In addition, the study examines whether self-assessment practices in higher education may relate to achieving and sustaining future learning beyond higher education programmes and what this might mean for academics. I conclude with a discussion on four issues which need to be addressed in order to develop students' capacity for long-term learning through self-assessment practices in higher education.

Academics' conceptions of student self-assessment

The purpose of this study was to identify and describe qualitative differences between the ways academics understood and used student self-assessment in relation to enhancing their students' learning. The qualitative differences, or conceptions, of student self-assessment in turn suggest how self-assessment practices may contribute to enhancing and sustaining students' long-term learning beyond higher education. The investigation utilised a phenomenographic approach to identify qualitatively different conceptions of student self-assessment. The conceptions describe the critical aspects of understanding and using student self-assessment in a particular way for enhancing learning.

Sixteen academics from three universities in New South Wales, Australia, representing twelve different disciplines were interviewed on their self-assessment practices. Three different conceptions of student self-assessment were identified in terms of representing a progressively greater scope of self-assessment for learning. These three conceptions offer a lens for viewing how self-assessment practices limit or enhance lifelong learning for students in qualitatively different ways. Table 9.1 illustrates the relations between the three conceptions of student self-assessment as a nested hierarchy.

The conceptions are envisaged as evolving subsets, each subsuming and building on the previous conceptions. The greater number of critical aspects of student self-assessment in a conception implies a more sophisticated way of understanding

Table 9.1 Conceptions of student self-assessment as a nested hierarchy

	1. Teacher-driven SSA	*2. Programme-driven SSA*	*3. Future-driven SSA*
Critical aspects of student self-assessment	Focus on teacher's authority ✓ Compliance/control of student behaviour ✓ Contingent judgement of knowledge	Focus on completing programme of study ✓ Compliance/control of student behaviour ✓ Contingent judgement of knowledge ✓ Feedback on requisite standards of programme of study ✓ Development of requisite proficiency to complete programme of study	Focus on sustaining self-assessment ability ✓ Compliance/control of student behaviour ✓ Contingent judgement of knowledge ✓ Feedback on requisite standards of programme of study ✓ Development of requisite proficiency to complete programme of study ✓ Sustainability of self-assessment beyond programme of study

and using student self-assessment. In this context, the future-driven conception of student self-assessment may be seen as the more complete and sophisticated way of understanding and using student self-assessment for students' long-term learning. The conceptions are described in the next section with illustrative quotations from interviews.

Teacher-driven self-assessment

Teacher-driven self-assessment emphasises students learning how to be compliant with their teacher's expectations through self-assessment practices. Students do not judge their learning in the context of the requisite standards of the programme of study. Instead, the teacher acts as the sole benchmark for the students' judgements of their learning and does not refer to the requisite standards of the programme of study when judging students' self-assessment outcomes. Consequently, students may focus only on their teachers' expectations in self-assessment practices without relating such expectations to the expected standards of the programme of study. The following quotes illustrate the emphasis on the teacher controlling and regulating the students' judgements of their learning in student self-assessment.

'What would indicate to you that student self-assessment has largely been successful?'

'The students attend. You must learn if you are there. It's self-evident. *If they don't turn up, then they learn nothing.*'

'The outcome of the self-assessment is it's either an assessment that is ready to be handed in or not . . . it's a binary response. It's either yes or no. *And essentially it has to get to a yes before they hand it in.*'

Teacher-driven self-assessment is limited to the emphasis on the students' judgements complying with the academic's expectations. The academics essentially understand student self-assessment to be a form of limited involvement for students to make inconclusive judgements of their learning. Student self-assessment is experienced as an opportunity for students to make tentative judgements of their learning which are subject to the academics' authoritative judgements.

In teacher-driven self-assessment, the role of the teacher primarily focuses on assessing whether students' judgements of their learning are compliant with the teacher's expectations. However, the teachers do not necessarily refer to the programme of study as a basis for assessing students' self-assessment outcomes. Student self-assessment is useful for teachers as a way to ensure a minimal level of competence in students' work before such work is accepted and assessed. Student self-assessment functions as a form of a prerequisite for learning and assessment rather than as a basis for teachers to discuss the quality of students' learning and self-assessment outcomes. Nor is the teacher concerned about students understanding the requisite standards of the programme of study as a basis for the students' judgements of their learning. As such, the students' standards and proficiency within the programme of study and the sustainability of their capacity for self-assessment beyond the programme of study are not present in the academics' awareness of self-assessment. Self-assessment is relevant as an instrument of control in discrete activities. It is not discerned as being relevant to the programme of study. Such a conception of student self-assessment has little capacity for lifelong learning. Instead, its practices develop students' dependency on the academics and stymie their judgement abilities. The lack of development of students' self-assessment abilities in turn restricts their ability to self-assess their learning needs in the future.

Programme-driven self-assessment

In programme-driven self-assessment, the programme of study is the benchmark for students' judgements of their learning. The programme encapsulates the collective criteria for evaluating students' judgements of their learning. The conception of programme-driven self-assessment emphasises the gap between students' standards and the requisite standards of the programme of study. The sustainability of self-assessment beyond the programme of study is not within the academics' awareness of the phenomenon. Instead, academics with a programme-driven conception are more concerned that students have incorrect and inadequate standards for judging their learning. The role of the teacher primarily focuses on using students' self-assessments to educate them on the requisite standards of the programme of study. The following quotes illustrate the focus on the programme of study acting as the composite set of standards and proficiency which benchmark and develop the students' judgements of their learning.

> 'So maybe you could set up a self-assessment once they have got really familiar with the standards. *This early stage, they don't have standards.* This is the first opportunity for them to establish a notion of standards.'

> 'On the back, the student receives assessment grades as indicated for grades by university . . . So they can get an idea of where they're strong and where they've got to improve. *And then they look at that with the one they'd done and they identify areas where there is noticeable difference.*'

In the conception of programme-driven self-assessment, learning is defined by and limited to the expectations and assessment requirements of the programme of study. Academics who experience programme-driven self-assessment focus on providing feedback on students' judgements of their standards within the programme of study in order to appreciate what the requisite standards are. The overall aim of this approach is to assist students to progress and complete the programme. In contrast with future-driven self-assessment, programme-driven self-assessment does not explicitly focus on students learning for purposes beyond the programme of study.

The effect of focusing students' judgements of their learning on the programme of study is that students are not encouraged to consider their learning needs beyond the programme. This is inconsistent with the notion of lifelong learning as learning well beyond formal higher education. Programme-driven self-assessment is also characterised by a high degree of regulation over how self-assessment is conducted and judged. Students' scope for learning and self-assessment ability in programme-driven self-assessment is focused on the requirements of the programme of study but may not extend to external standards which are not explicitly emphasised in the same programme. Because it emphasises the programme's assessment requirements over the students' independent judgements of their learning, it is limited in its effectiveness in preparing students to be autonomous professionals capable of appraising the quality of their work beyond the prescribed standards of the programme of study.

Future-driven self-assessment

Future-driven self-assessment may be understood as a form of assessment that has the power to sustain itself beyond completing the programme of study. The future need for students to be able to self-assess their work in professional working contexts is the benchmark for students' judgements of their learning in the programme of study.

In future-driven self-assessment, the emphasis is on understanding and using student self-assessment to develop students' capacity for exercising their own judgements without depending on the academic. The role of the academic with a future-driven conception of student self-assessment is to utilise the programme of study to develop students' self-appraisal skills in terms of constructing and refining assessment criteria. Through a developmental process, students may be able to construct their own assessment criteria, negotiate the criteria against externally laid standards and eventually make judgements based on the developed criteria. This process permits students to focus beyond the expectations of the teacher and the programme of study and judge their self-assessment criteria against professionally prescribed standards and conventions. Such skills in turn form the basis for students to sustain their self-assessment capacity independently of the academic in future contexts. The following quotes illustrate the focus on sustaining students' capacity for self-assessment beyond the programme of study.

> 'Because it is professionally imperative for nurses, for doctors, for teachers, for everybody, that you're able to realistically self-assess . . . That *ability to self-assess is the springboard for your lifelong learning.*'

> 'Because it is *essential for lifelong learning* . . . if they never learn to accurately self-assess, then they will never *know when they have a deficiency that needs to be recovered once they've left the sort of structures of a university.*'

A characteristic of future-driven self-assessment is that students have to confront their pedagogy and judging ability in the present programme of learning in order to learn how to make defensible judgements of their professional work in the future. Academics who value future-centred self-assessment approach student self-assessment with the intention for their students to learn to self-appraise their proficiency levels and identify areas for development beyond the programme of study.

Some writers have highlighted the tension between assessment and reflection in that the former rewards certainty and achievement while the latter encourages doubt and questions (Brew, 1999; Hinett and Weeden, 2000). In this context, teacher-driven and programme-driven self-assessment accentuate such tensions by emphasising the certainty of the teacher's and the programme's expectations respectively. Students are encouraged to judge their learning in order to be certain that their outcomes are acceptable to their teacher or adequate for the programme. This discourages them from exploration or even questioning the assumptions underlying the teacher's or the programme's assessment practices and values system. In contrast, future-driven self-assessment permits greater reflection by forcing students to look beyond the academic and the programme of study when judging what and how well they had learned. This seems to provide students with more scope to reflect critically on their learning as well as their assessment practices.

How can student self-assessment lead to long-term learning?

The three levels of student self-assessment may be differentiated in terms of the scope of self-assessment as an assessment practice. The scope of teacher-driven self-assessment practice is limited to the individual teacher's preferences and expectations. The teacher is the assessor as well as the yardstick of students' self-assessment practice. The scope of programme-driven self-assessment is the seemingly objective assessment requirements of the programme of study. However, since these requirements are mainly interpreted and communicated by the academic, it is the academic who largely decides whether students are self-assessing satisfactorily. What teacher-driven and programme-driven self-assessment have in common is the limitation of self-assessment as an assessment activity that perpetuates the existing mechanisms of assessment. Students' self-assessment is judged against existing assessment practices and assessment reliability is emphasised by maintaining the status quo. In contrast, I see future-driven self-assessment as encompassing the principle of self-assessment as an assessment ability that involves students understanding, questioning and challenging existing assessment practices. By focusing beyond the academic and the programme of study, future-driven self-assessment looks beyond the notion of reliability within formal programmes of study to embrace a more critical and reflexive view of student assessment and self-assessment.

The three conceptions of student self-assessment also represent increasingly broader scopes of what students may learn from self-assessment. When self-assessment is limited to the teacher's expertise in teacher-driven self-assessment, there is a risk that students may learn and self-assess in a way that pleases their teachers without going on to think about the requisite standards of the programme of study. When self-assessment is tailored to meet the needs of the programme in programme-driven self-assessment, there is a risk that students' inclination to learn only for the purpose of completing the programme is accentuated. Students correspondingly learn as much and as well as the programme requires them to.

I would argue that such limitations to students' future learning capacity are largely absent in future-driven conceptions of student self-assessment. In future-driven self-assessment, there is less emphasis on students being able to match the teacher's or the programme's judgements exactly. When student self-assessment is future driven, it focuses on utilising the programme of study to prepare students to develop sustainable self-assessment ability.

My view is that the three conceptions of student self-assessment provide a structured and systematic way of identifying the increasing scope of understanding and using student self-assessment for long-term learning. Future-driven self-assessment possesses the broadest scope of self-assessment and presents the best opportunity for sustainable assessment.

In this next section, I identify and discuss four issues which are necessary for understanding and using self-assessment for sustaining students' long-term learning beyond the programme of study.

Power

It has been popular to advocate student self-assessment practices as a means of 'empowering' students in the assessment process. The conventional argument has been that self-assessment counters the dominant influences of the teacher's power by allowing students to exercise some of that power for themselves. In this regard, reducing the teacher's power over students is a basis for the practice of student self-assessment (Boud, 1995; Butcher and Stefani, 1995; McMahon, 1999; Rainsbury and Hodges, 1998; Somervell, 1993; Stefani, 1998).

In the past few years, some writers have questioned the assumption that self-assessment practices will automatically empower students in the assessment process (Race, 1995; Reynolds and Trehan, 2000; Tan, 2004). These writers argue that the potential of student self-assessment to empower students for learning depends on how it is understood and used by academics and students. The findings of this study offer insights into the qualitatively different ways that academics may understand and use power in relation to enhancing their students' learning.

In teacher-driven self-assessment, the focus is on the teacher's retention and exercise of his or her commodity of sovereign power over students. In programme-driven self-assessment, the focal awareness on the programme of study emphasises the academic as an agent or a proxy of the commodity of epistemological power as well as being a subject of the same epistemological power situated in and within the programme of study. The programme of study represents a point at which epistemological power is applied on the students (through the academic) and on the academic.

In contrast, I would see future-driven self-assessment as extending beyond the meaning and practice of power as a commodity. The greater awareness of more critical aspects of self-assessment is illuminated by dealing more reflexively with issues of power beyond the teacher's sovereign authority and the epistemological boundaries of the programme of study. Academics are also aware of the disciplinary effects of self-assessment practices and attempt to minimise these effects by allowing students some discretion in the types of self-judgements they may elect to show the academic.

Alternatively, some academics allow their students the option of not participating in self-assessment activities at all in order to lessen the disciplinary effects of self-assessment. For example, Leach *et al.* (2001) are of the view that self-assessment should be optional for learners and the freedom to choose whether to assess themselves represents a form of empowerment.

I am generally hesitant about the notion of optional self-assessment being empowering for students. I view the future-driven conception of self-assessment as characterising self-assessment and empowerment as a critical and mandatory practice. What the emphasis on making self-assessment mandatory in future-driven self-assessment seems to suggest is that if self-assessment ability is mandatory in the future, then self-assessment activity should not be optional in the present programme. Students who choose not to self-assess are not necessarily empowered since this decision may be a sign of their docile and disciplined condition in the first place. After all, it is conceivable that students will decide against self-assessing their work because they lack confidence, in themselves or in the teacher, to do so.

Second, reducing self-assessment to an option contradicts the general consensus that self-assessment should be a central focus and attribute of higher education. I argue that self-assessment cannot be a critical element and an optional practice at the same time. If students are expected to be able to judge their own learning, then self-assessment cannot be presented as an option for them to dismiss. Conversely, if self-assessment is a practice that can be ignored by students, then it is difficult for academics to claim it to be central to the idea of higher education and professional practice. I would recommend self-assessment as mandatory practice in order to ensure its use in developing and sustaining students' self-assessment ability for long-term learning contexts.

Formative assessment to enhance learning beyond the programme of study

Student self-assessment is also identified closely with effective formative assessment or assessment practices that emphasise the enhancement of learning. Both Sadler (1998) and Black and Wiliam (1998) emphasise the need for formative assessment to involve students in generating and understanding feedback that explains the gap between the state revealed by feedback and the desired state. Sadler (1998: 79) goes further by arguing that 'any formative assessment that is not self-assessment involves communication . . . [and] that the communication is from the teacher to the learner'. In these contexts, self-assessment plays the critical role of ensuring that feedback given in formative assessment is not unduly dominated by the teachers' views.

While the importance of formative assessment for learning is commonly recognised in higher education, the place and use of formative assessment for long-term learning is not as obvious. Boud (2000: 159) had identified formative assessment practices to be vital to achieving sustainable assessment but observed that discussion of formative assessment in the literature and in practice 'has made relatively little contribution to current assessment thinking' and that 'new thinking is therefore required to build sustainable assessment'.

When used formatively, student self-assessment is assumed to enhance the quality of feedback by involving students in the assessment process that generates and constructs such feedback. However, the potential of student self-assessment to enhance the quality of formative assessment also depends on the specific ways that academics understand and use student self-assessment in each context.

The three conceptions of student self-assessment may offer a new way of understanding how self-assessment affects formative assessment practices to enhance lifelong learning. Compared to future-driven self-assessment, teacher-driven self-assessment is more likely to produce feedback that is similar to unilateral teacher assessment practices. The distinction between programme-driven and future-driven self-assessment suggests that formative assessment may be conceptualised in terms of whether the feedback designed to enhance students' learning is targeted at their learning within and/or beyond the programme of study. In programme-driven self-assessment, academics primarily focus on using self-assessment to assist students to enhance their progress in the programme of study. The efficacy of self-assessment and its formative uses are confined to the objectives of the programme. Likewise, it is suggested that formative assessment and/or self-assessment practice with a primary focus on the programme is limited in assisting students' learning beyond the programme of study and beyond university education.

From reliability to reflexivity

The progressive levels of awareness of student self-assessment also indicate that academics with greater awareness of critical aspects seem to relate in a more reflexive manner to their own power as well as in resisting power that surrounds them. For example, academics in future-driven self-assessment are reflexive, and encourage their students to be reflexive, about existing assessment and self-assessment practices. The scope of self-assessment is enlarged to include students' judgements of assessment practices in addition to and in relation to their judgements of their learning. However, emphasising reflexivity in assessment and self-assessment practices may affect the practice and place of other assessment principles, such as assessment reliability.

A traditional notion of assessment reliability refers to the consistency of marks obtained with the same assessors and the same test conditions. In contrast, future-driven self-assessment would appear to emphasise students being reflexive about the assumptions underlying the assessment process rather than being concerned about the reliability of the assessment itself. While reliability requires the assessment mechanisms to be unchanging and unchallenged in order to be a non-variable, reflexivity encourages students to modify and question existing assessment practices. Academics may have to allow, or perhaps encourage, their students to question and challenge the relative reliabilities of existing assessment and self-assessment practice in order to sustain their future ability to conduct their own self-assessment. The sustainability of self-assessment means that students' self-assessment ability must be developed in the present in order to be present in the future.

From self-assessment activity to self-assessment ability

There are many practices in higher education which advocate students assuming more participation and responsibility for their learning. The trend towards problem-based learning, for example, typically requires students to confront a 'problem' specifically designed to drive their learning. Students are responsible for defining their objectives, planning what and how they need to go about learning, and judging the extent to which they achieve their objectives. Likewise, the use of learning contracts and self-directed learning methods emphasise students assuming significant, if not primary, responsibility for conducting and appraising their learning. These learning strategies or methods place a premium on students being able to plan and conduct their learning independently of the teacher. A large part of such independence involves students being able to judge the extent of their learning without the direct assistance of the teacher. Because such independent learning processes in future-driven self-assessment is identified by teachers and eventually students with enhanced learning, the related aspect of self-assessment activity was also viewed in terms of enhancing the general quality of learning as well. Consequently, self-assessment ability as well as explicit self-assessment activities is emphasised.

As noted earlier, sustainable assessment can be understood as 'assessment that meets the needs of the present without compromising the ability of students to meet their own future learning needs'. Perhaps the most critical need for students to meet their own future learning needs is their capacity to judge what their own learning needs are and how they can go about meeting them. Self-assessment ability is therefore a critical ingredient for students' lifelong learning. The arguments and the research findings of this study suggest likewise: that the development of students' present and future self-assessment ability is the main focus of academics who hold a future-driven conception of self-assessment.

Conclusion

The three progressive conceptions of student self-assessment represent three increasingly broader scopes of what students may learn from self-assessment. When self-assessment is limited to the teacher's expertise in teacher-driven self-assessment, the focus is on students learning to please their teachers. When self-assessment is tailored to meet the needs of the programme in programme-driven self-assessment, there is a risk that students' inclination to learn only for the purpose of completing the programme is accentuated. Students correspondingly learn as much and as well as the programme requires them to.

It would seem that future-driven self-assessment possesses the broadest scope of self-assessment and presents the best opportunity for students to enhance their learning. It forces students to learn beyond pleasing the individual teacher and beyond satisfying the assessment requirements of the present programme of study. Unlike the previous two conceptions, there is no emphasis on students being able to match the teacher's or the programme's requirements exactly. Sustainable self-assessment connotes going beyond the academic's personal expectations and the programme's requisite benchmarks for judging students' judgements of their learning. When student self-assessment is future-driven, it focuses on utilising the programme of study to prepare students to develop sustainable self-assessment ability. A conceptual distinction between programme-driven formative assessment to enhance present learning within the programme and future-driven formative assessment for learning beyond the programme is recommended.

References

Bartels, J.E. (1998) Developing reflective learners – student self-assessment as learning, *Journal of Professional Nursing*, 14, 3: 135.

Black, P. and Wiliam, D. (1998) Assessment and classroom learning, *Assessment in Education: Principles, Policy and Practice*, 5, 1: 7–74.

Boud, D. (1994) The move to self-assessment: liberation or a new mechanism for oppression?, in P. Armstrong, B. Bright and M. Zukas (eds) *Reflecting on Changing Practices, Contexts and Identities*, papers from the 24th Annual Conference of the Standing Conference on University Teaching and Research in the Education of Adults, University of Hull, 12–14 July, Leeds: Department of Adult Continuing Education, University of Leeds.

—— (1995) *Enhancing Learning through Self-Assessment*, London: Kogan Page.

—— (2000) Sustainable assessment: rethinking assessment for the learning society, *Studies in Higher Education*, 22, 2: 151.

Brew, A. (1999) Towards autonomous assessment: using self-assessment and peer assessment, in S. Brown and A. Glasner (eds) *Assessment Matters in Higher Education*, Buckingham: Society for Research into Higher Education and Open University Press.

Brown, S. and Glasner, A. (1999) Towards autonomous assessment, in S. Brown and A. Glasner (eds) *Assessment Matters in Higher Education*, Buckingham: Society for Research into Higher Education and Open University Press.

Burgess, H., Baldwin, M., Dalrymple, J. and Thomas, J. (1999) Developing self-assessment in social work education, *Social Work Education*, 18, 2: 133–146.

Butcher, A.C. and Stefani, L.J. (1995) Analysis of peer, self- and staff-assessment in group project work, *Assessment in Education: Principles, Policy and Practice*, 2, 2: 165–186.

Dearing, R. (1997) *Higher Education in the Learning Society* [summary report], London: HMSO.

Dochy, F., Segers, M. and Sluijsmans, D. (1999) The use of self-, peer and co-assessment in higher education: a review, *Studies in Higher Education*, 24, 3: 331.

Hanrahan, S. and Isaacs, G. (2001) Assessing self- and peer-assessment: the students' views, *Higher Education Research and Development*, 20, 1: 53–70.

Hinett, K. and Weeden, P. (2000) How am I doing?: developing critical self-evaluation in trainee teachers, *Quality in Higher Education*, 6, 3: 245–257.

Leach, L., Neutze, G. and Zepke, N. (2001) Assessment and empowerment: some critical questions, *Assessment and Evaluation in Higher Education*, 26, 4: 293–305.

McMahon, T. (1999) Using negotiation in summative assessment to encourage critical thinking, *Teaching in Higher Education*, 4, 4: 549–554.

Patterson, C., Crooks, D. and Lunyk-Child, O. (2002) A new perspective on competencies for self-directed learning, *Journal of Nursing Education*, 41, 1: 25–31.

Race, P. (1995) What has assessment done for us – and to us?, in P. Knight (ed.) *Assessment for Learning in Higher Education*, London: Kogan Page.

Rainsbury, E. and Hodges, D. (1998) Academic, employer and student collaborative assessment in a work-based cooperative education course, *Assessment and Evaluation in Higher Education*, 23, 3: 313–325.

Reynolds, M. and Trehan, K. (2000) Assessment: a critical perspective, *Studies in Higher Education*, 25, 3: 267–278.

Sadler, D.R. (1998) Formative assessment: revisiting the territory, *Assessment in Education*, 5, 1: 77–84.

Sambell, K. and McDowell, L. (1997) The value of self and peer assessment to the developing lifelong learner, in C. Rust (ed.) *Improving Student Learning: Improving Students as Learners*, Oxford: Oxford Centre for Staff and Learning Development.

Sluijsmans, D., Dochy, F. and Moerkerke, G. (1998) *The Use of Self-, Peer- and Co-Assessment in Higher Education: A Review of the Literature*, Heerlen: Educational Technology Expertise Centre, Open University of the Netherlands.

Somervell, H. (1993) Issues in assessment, enterprise and higher education: the case for self-, peer and collaborative assessment, *Assessment and Evaluation in Higher Education*, 18, 3: 221–233.

Stefani, L. (1998) Assessment in partnership with learners, *Assessment and Evaluation in Higher Education*, 23, 4: 339–350.

Sutherland, L. (1998) Developing students' meta-cognitive awareness through self-evaluation: a South African perspective, in C. Rust (ed.) *Improving Student Learning: Improving Students as Learners*, Oxford: Oxford Centre for Staff and Learning Development.

Tamir, P. (1999) Self-assessment: the use of self-report knowledge and opportunity to learn inventories, *International Journal of Science Education*, 21, 4: 401–411.

Tan, K.H.K. (2004) Does student self-assessment empower or discipline students?, *Assessment and Evaluation in Higher Education*, 29, 6: 651–662.

Taras, M. (2001) The use of tutor feedback and student self-assessment in summative assessment tasks: towards transparency for students and for tutors, *Assessment and Evaluation in Higher Education*, 26, 6: 605–614.

Williams, E. (1992) Student attitudes towards approaches to learning and assessment, *Assessment and Evaluation in Higher Education*, 17, 1: 45–58.

Chapter 10

The place of peers in learning and assessment

Nancy Falchikov

In this book, we are concerned with learning after graduation and how this might be encouraged during higher education. We know that assessment can influence learning in both beneficial and not-so-beneficial ways and that this influence can be very long lasting, as we shall see in Chapter 11. In this chapter, I argue that peer involvement in assessment during higher education has the power to aid learning both when it takes place and in the future. As work plays an important part in most of our lives, I start by examining what we know about learning in the context of apprenticeship learning and about how assessment is carried out there. I then examine some higher educational practices involving students in assessment that may be said to parallel practices found in apprenticeship learning. Next, I examine the relationship between self- and peer assessment and look at how the two can work together to support learning throughout life. Finally, I consider ways in which some forms of peer assessment may be detrimental to future learning and recommend aspects of peer assessment likely to support assessment and learning beyond higher education.

The role of peers in learning: theoretical background

Humans, being social animals, learn with and from others from the moment of birth. Much of this learning is informal, particularly in the years when we are not engaged in formal education. During formal learning, the teacher takes on an important role, particularly where the learning context is traditional. Peer learning, in which we learn with and from one another, may be less easily observed, but it is rarely absent. However, there have always been those who explicitly value and understand the role of peers in learning. John Dewey's declaration concerning education indicates his strong belief in the importance of the social context and of the people within it. He asserted:

> I believe that the only true education comes through the stimulation of the
> [student's] powers by the demands of the social situations in which he finds

himself. Through these demands he is stimulated . . . to conceive of himself
from the standpoint of the welfare of the group to which he belongs . . .
Through the responses which others make to his own activities he comes to
know what these mean in social terms. The value which they have is reflected
back into them.

(Dewey, 1897: 77–80)

Similarly, Piaget and Inhelder (1966: 156) asserted that social interaction in
which 'the individual contributes as much as he receives' is an important factor
in mental development. Other educators have also argued for the importance of
both peers and interactive activity in learning. Bruner's (1960) work, for example,
is influential in the context of adult learning. In fact, current views on the
importance of scaffolding in cognitive apprenticeships may be said to derive from
his belief that teaching and learning of structure are central to learning. As
in workplace apprenticeships, cognitive apprenticeships involve 'modeling,
coaching and providing and fading structure for a cognitive or metacognitive
process' (Starr, 1991: 428). Brown *et al.* (1989) also acknowledged the debt owed
by proponents of situated cognition and cognitive apprenticeships to activity
theorists such as Vygotsky (1978), who maintained that the range of skill that can
be developed with adult guidance or peer collaboration exceeds what can be
attained alone.

Building on such work, Lave has also argued that learning is a function of the
activity, context and culture in which it occurs (Lave, 1999; Lave and Wenger,
1991). Lave, too, believes that learning is a social activity, requiring social interaction and collaboration. Moreover, he argues that knowledge needs both an
authentic context and a structure, as did Dewey, Piaget and Bruner. Learning
involves active participation in a 'community of practice' in which members of
the community determine and structure their own practices, and construct identities
in relation to these communities (Wenger, 1999). In the same way that traditional
apprentices move ever nearer to autonomy, expertise and membership within their
trade or craft, newcomers to a learning community start out as 'apprentices' and
move towards full participation in its socio-cultural practices by means of a process
of 'legitimate peripheral participation'.

Learning at work: apprenticeship learning

Learning at work is typically characterised by activity and social interaction within
a context. The apprenticeship model is often held up as the 'natural way to learn'
(Collins *et al.*, 1991: 1). According to Collins *et al.*, in traditional apprenticeships
the expert shows the apprentice how to do a task; the apprentice observes and then
practises the skills involved. As the apprentice's expertise develops, the master
gradually cedes more and more responsibility to the apprentice, who is eventually
able to carry out the task independently. This transition involves four important

aspects: modelling, scaffolding, fading and coaching, where coaching is 'the thread running through the entire apprenticeship experience' (Collins *et al.*, 1991: 2). The aim of this type of learning is to help apprentices develop self-monitoring skills and advance towards expertise. Of course, in the workplace, learners observe not only the expert at work, but other learners with varying degrees of expertise, divers skills and different levels of pay and status. According to Collins *et al.*, observing peers with differing levels of ability and expertise encourages individuals to see learning as an incrementally staged process. Peer learning is not limited to apprenticeship learning. For example, Boud and Middleton (2003) noted that, within the academic profession, informal interactions with peers are the predominant ways of learning.

Kvale (2006) has observed that workplace learning is assessed in a variety of ways. It may be accomplished by reference to goals or models and through use. However, peers also have an important role in the process. The learner, too, plays an increasing part in workplace assessment, taking on more and more responsibility for self-assessment. Kvale also explored how features of workplace assessment may be fostered during higher education, identifying peer and self-assessment as playing an important part in this.

It is important also to be aware that, although we may learn a great deal about both workplace learning and learning more generally by scrutinising the apprenticeship model, not all workplace learning fits it. Indeed, the term 'apprentice' might be alienating in some contexts. It has also been argued that the conceptual framework of communities of practice, on which apprenticeship learning is predicated, may be insufficient to encompass much workplace learning (e.g., Boud and Middleton, 2003).

Similarly, it can also be argued that apprenticeship learning and assessment can go only so far in meeting the needs of learning and assessment within formal education. Collins *et al.* (1991) argued that application of the apprenticeship model to higher education, known as cognitive apprenticeship learning, is not the only way to learn. Activities such as active listening or reading can help develop skills that apprenticeships cannot. Similarly, working on one's own, planning and conducting research, choosing what to study, identifying one's own problems and so on may also be achieved by means other than modelling and scaffolding, even though these activities may be very beneficial in other respects.

Let us now look at the cognitive apprenticeship model found within formal learning.

The higher education context: the cognitive apprenticeship model

Kvale (2006: 1) asserted that 'important innovations of learning by assessments in school – such as feedback, formative assessment, peer assessment and self assessment – have been key parts of the apprenticeship training in European crafts since the medieval ages'. Similarly, peer tutoring, another modern teaching 'innovation', which involves students teaching and learning with their peers, also has roots that go deeper than the last century, certainly to the late eighteenth and early nineteenth centuries, when Lancaster and Bell introduced the monitorial system into schools.

The cognitive apprenticeship model draws from traditional apprenticeship learning, but incorporates elements of schooling, linking better-prepared (or more advanced) students with the less well prepared (or less advanced) in learning and thinking activities. As with workplace apprenticeships, cognitive apprenticeships provide the novice with an insight into the processes experts use to handle complex tasks. In the context of higher education, these processes include, in addition to the variety of cognitive activities used to solve a complex task, self-monitoring and reflection on the differences between expert and novice. Cognitive apprenticeships are particularly suited to collaborative learning situations (e.g., Starr, 1991).

Learning from and with peers in higher education

Peers are playing an increasingly prominent role in current higher education, where learning with others forms a part in most, if not all, university courses. Moves towards co-operative activities have been driven in large part by criticisms from employers who have noted that many university courses are not preparing students to work with others in teams. Teachers perceive (or pay lip service to) the learning benefits of group work, as well as being aware of its more pragmatic use as a means of reducing coursework marking. A cursory inspection of the literature points to a mushrooming of papers on the subject of group work over the past few years. Co-operative learning, which has some important features not necessarily present in much group work, is also espoused as an ideal in some contemporary higher education research (e.g., Co-operative Learning Center, 2005). Group working and co-operation are also supported by other current higher education initiatives that have given rise to a plethora of publications (e.g., by bodies such as the UK's Higher Education Academy: HEA, 2005).

Some higher education institutions pay lip service to the ideas of team working and co-operation in their policy documents. However, as we noted in Chapter 2, it often seems that more time, energy and document space are concentrated on honing procedures for certifying individual students than on promoting co-operative ventures.

While it might be argued that many activities, such as the many forms of group and teamwork found in higher education today, have the power to encourage co-operation, two stand out as particularly beneficial and influential: peer tutoring and student involvement in assessment. While some students provide their own informal social/emotional and academic support, in the form of activities such as study groups, peer reading of drafts and discussion of topics and problems, others do not do this, and thus miss out on a valuable source of support and many learning opportunities. Formal support, in the form of peer tutoring or peer learning more widely, can provide some of these opportunities (e.g., Boud *et al.*, 2001; Falchikov, 2001). In their seminal review of peer teaching in higher education, Goldschmid and Goldschmid (1976: 29) argued that peer tutoring 'may be particularly relevant when one seeks to maximise the student's responsibility for his own learning and active participation in the learning process, and to enhance the development of skills for cooperation and social interaction'.

As I have argued elsewhere (Falchikov, 2001), peer tutoring schemes may take a variety of forms, have differing aims and objectives and encompass a variety of organisational structures. They do, however, share a basic belief in the efficacy of peer learning and benefits of one-to-one or small-group learning experiences.

Not all examples of peer tutoring are equally beneficial. Sometimes, the roles that students take up can begin to interfere with learning. For example, Gillam *et al.* (1994: 165) noted that, when acting as tutor, 'a student may identify with the system which placed her in the position . . . and invested her with "a certain institutional authority"'. In this way the degree of similarity between partners is decreased. I have found that, in such circumstances, the tutee's liking for both the tutor and the method of learning is also decreased. Thus, it is important that roles within peer tutoring are not fixed. Cohen and Sampson (2001) also emphasised the importance of reciprocity within practices, noting that difficulties may arise if students do not accept each other as peers.

Another means of providing rich learning opportunities and social support is by involving students in assessment. This activity may be said to resemble students teaching each other in that, in both, teacher roles need to change in similar ways. Both can also be empowering for students.

Peer assessment

My review of the assessment literature (Falchikov, 2005) suggests that students are becoming involved in assessment in more and more ways. The most frequently encountered variety, however, is peer assessment. This takes many forms, often takes place in the context of group work and frequently entails the provision of feedback.

Peer assessment requires students to provide either feedback or grades (or both) to their peers on a product, process or performance, based on the criteria of excellence for that product or event which students may have been involved in determining. Within the literature on implementation there is much variation. There appear to be two main classes of feature: benefits to learners and reliability and validity issues. There is a necessary a tension between the two. I shall briefly discuss each in turn.

Characteristics associated with the first, student-centred class are improvements to cognitive and metacognitive competencies, skills development, personal and intellectual development, improved social competencies, beneficial effects on 'affective dispositions' (Birenbaum, 1996: 4), such as confidence, and benefits to the assessment process itself. Some teachers also report personal benefits in that they gain professional satisfaction from the benefits enjoyed by their students. In addition, some have commented that working with students to identify criteria explicitly has also been practically helpful to their own assessment practice. Others have seen that the transparency associated with the best examples of student involvement is beneficial to all.

My survey also found that some assertions made by teacher–researchers concerning the benefits they claimed were not supported by strong evidence. For example, at the end of one such study, the author asserted that students were more confident about self-assessment but provided no evidence to support this impression. However, improved confidence was also reported in well-designed questionnaire studies (see Falchikov, 2005). Some studies provided compelling evidence to support their claims: evidence derived from statistical analysis, analysis of questionnaire and self-report data. Statistical evidence supporting the benefits of peer assessment tended to centre on performance. For example, Bangert's statistical analyses (1995) indicated significantly better performance by peer assessors than by students who had not participated. Similarly, Greer (2001) found better examination performance by peer assessed students than was achieved by previous non-peer assessed cohorts. Student-derived questionnaire data provided other indications of benefits in terms of students taking responsibility for their learning (e.g., Dochy et al., 1999). More recent studies emphasise the importance of feedback and negotiation (e.g., Hunter and Russ, 1996; Sluijsmans et al., 2001). Improvements in skills development featured prominently: presentation skills (e.g., Price and Cutler, 1995); professional skills (e.g., Topping, 1998); trainee teaching performance (e.g., Anderson and Frieberg, 1995); listening skills (e.g., Falchikov 1995a and 1995b); increased involvement in learning and development of critical and independent thinking skills (e.g., Falchikov, 1986). Repeating the experience of peer assessment was seen as beneficial by participants (e.g., Sivan, 2000). Attitudinal data supported the benefits of practice, in that participants with more experience rated peer assessment as more beneficial than participants with a single experience of it.

There was also some indication in the survey that the experience of peer assessment within higher education was thought by students to be likely to have relevance for their future careers (e.g., Trevitt and Pettigrove, 1995). Peer assessment is sometimes thought to promote lifelong learning skills (e.g., Challis, 1999). Other studies associate the practice of peer assessment with enhancement of particular skills which often appear in lists of desirable attributes of graduates, some of which we have encountered already:

- reflection (e.g., Alverno College, 2001);
- autonomy and independence (e.g., Beaman, 1998);
- self-efficacy (e.g., Bangert, 1995);
- responsibility (e.g., Dochy et al., 1999).

There are yet other skills developed by peer assessment that have usefulness beyond higher education: transfer of learning (e.g., Catterall, 1995); enhanced diplomatic skills (e.g., Falchikov, 1994, 1995a and 1995b); problem-solving (e.g.,

Dochy *et al.*, 1999). In addition, several 'affective dispositions' (Birenbaum, 1996: 4) seem to benefit from the experience of peer assessment. For example, stress can be reduced (e.g., Zakrzewski and Bull, 1998) and, as we saw above, maths test anxiety might decrease (e.g., Bangert, 1995). Increased confidence in those taking part in peer assessment has been noted (e.g., Lapham and Webster, 1999). In addition, peer assessment is thought to improve internal (intrinsic) motivation (e.g., McDowell, 1995).

The second category of peer assessment study focuses on reliability and validity issues. Thus, marks and grades play a prominent part in the assessment process. We know that these have a particular salience for students. Not only do marks influence the timing and focus of student work effort, but they can present problems to students involved in peer assessment studies. It is not uncommon for students to question their own competence in relation to awarding marks, or for them to express concerns about marking fairly and responsibly (e.g., Sluijsmans *et al.*, 2001). This anxiety is amplified when marks are required which carry a significant proportion of the overall mark for the course or module.

We would all do well to be wary of marks. We know that teachers have difficulty in achieving reliability in marking (e.g., Newstead and Dennis, 1994). We know that students are overly fixated on this aspect of feedback. The mark is the academic equivalent of Gollum's 'precious'. It has the power to corrupt all who come into contact with it, not least the learner. Assessment should always be more than marking. If certification is essential in a particular context, there seems to be some degree of safety in numbers as regards generating marks. Mathews (1994) and Magin (1993 and 2001), for instance, suggest that marks derived from multiple assessors are more reliable than single marks. Peer assessment readily provides multiple marks.

In some ways, students resemble beginner teachers who also express concern about reliability and standards. The problem of lack of confidence is solvable, however. As I have argued elsewhere (Falchikov, 2005), students need support in order to learn how to become thoughtful and reliable assessors and partners in assessment, whether marks are required or not. Training is essential to help develop necessary skills, as is practice in assessing. It is frequently reported by teachers that initial student reluctance and lack of confidence quickly dissipate. For example, Sluijsmans *et al.* (2001) found that, at the beginning of a peer assessment exercise, only 7 per cent of students felt comfortable assessing their peers, while over 70 per cent said they were in favour of it once they had practised it and knew what was involved. As we have seen, other studies report increases in confidence resulting from peer assessment.

The relationship between self- and peer assessment

Peer and self-assessment are often included as parts of a single assessment innovation in higher education. This suggests one of two things: that practitioners appreciate that self- and peer assessment have different roles or that they use the phrase 'peer and self-assessment' as a catch-all. In what ways are the practices of self- and peer assessment similar and how do they differ? What is the relationship between the two?

Cowan (1988: 192) described self-assessment as a process of passing responsibility for the learning 'which both preceded and followed assessment to the students themselves'. Students apply standards and make judgements about their own learning. Often they have been involved in deciding the criteria by which their learning is to be judged. In peer assessment, students make judgements about the performance of peers. The two activities may be combined. For example, Heron (1988) described a situation in which each person in a group assesses herself or himself before the group, using common criteria, and then receives feedback from members of the group on both whatever is being assessed and on the process of self-assessment.

Peer assessment is sometimes seen as a means of developing self-assessment skills. Indeed, it has been argued that it is a necessary step towards this end. Peer assessment has power to be more than this, however. Peers are necessary partners in learning at any stage. The value of peers in learning and development is stressed by educators and psychologists alike.

Peer assessment to support future learning

In this chapter, I have emphasised the advantages of peer assessment as practised in higher education and noted that peers are a key feature of learning in the workplace and in professional practice. In fact, learning with and from peers is the dominant mode of everyday learning. Peer assessment in higher education can take many forms and fulfil many useful functions. Whatever the form of peer assessment practised, the method should enable learners to make reasonable judgements about the extent to which they have achieved expected outcomes (see Nightingale et al., 1996). In this way, peer assessment can help learners prepare for a lifetime of learning.

Apprenticeships, as we saw above, are characterised by coaching, modelling, scaffolding and fading. Cognitive apprenticeships share these features and Collins et al. (1991) argued that teaching methods to encourage effective learning should give students opportunities to observe, engage in, invent or discover expert strategies within a context. This is equally true for assessment methods. An important feature of traditional apprenticeship learning is its open, transparent nature. Recent increases in the use of group and co-operative learning in higher education, often involving peer and self-assessment, as well as other forms of learning with and from one's peers, may be seen as creating a context in which previously hidden features of learning are made explicit. Apprenticeship learning has the aim of producing a new autonomous expert. Similarly, some examples of formative peer assessment are explicitly designed both to promote independence and autonomy and to aid learning in the future. Apprentices acquire and practise skills. Some implementations of peer assessment are explicitly designed to encourage growth of skills identified as desirable by professional bodies and employers. Hughes and Large (1993: 379), who implemented self- and peer assessment to help prepare their students for both professional life as pharmacologists and for employment more generally by improving their written and oral communication skills saw peer and self-assessment as valuable, 'since our employer contacts advise us that such assessments are expected relatively early in an employee's career'. Working with peers helps develop skills such as teamworking, interpersonal skills, group problem-solving and communication (e.g., Harvey *et al.*, 1997; Brennan *et al.*, 2001; Hawkins and Winter, 1995). Peer assessment can take many forms and carries many benefits, as we have seen above. For a full review of peer assessment methods currently in use, along with a review of their benefits, see Falchikov (2005).

Much practice of self- or peer assessment is characterised by personal invest-ment and mutual dependency within environments that readily foster a sense of ownership. Characteristics of peer assessment practices that are likely to encourage and support future learning may be seen to parallel the four aspects of traditional apprenticeships elaborated by Collins *et al.* (1991). That is to say, 'good' peer assessment should provide opportunities for modelling, scaffolding and fading, and, by means of support from peers working within reciprocal relationships, provide similar benefits to those stemming from the coaching which occurs in both traditional and cognitive apprenticeships (see Kvale, 2006).

Peer assessment and modelling

Many peer assessment studies describe preparatory activities that may be seen as a form of modelling. For example, in Ewers and Searby's (1997) implementation of peer assessment in musical composition, students worked in small groups to identify criteria to encourage ownership of these, with the lecturer present with the power to intervene if 'any serious oversights were being made'. While this is not exactly the parallel of the apprentice observing the master at work, the lecturer expert is at hand with explicit criteria to help the students should it be necessary. In any case, the students may be seen as already having some expertise themselves, as they have been assessed before on many occasions.

Peer assessment and scaffolding

Dochy (2001) identified scaffolding as an essential criterion of what he terms any 'new assessment'. Scaffolding within current practice of peer assessment, as with the modelling example above, is frequently associated with selection and use of criteria to help learners make judgements. The simplest form of scaffolding takes the form of a teacher-prepared marking scheme (e.g., Catterall, 1995) or checklist (e.g., Freeman, 1995) for use by students. Another scaffold might involve some discussion of supplied criteria (e.g., Kelmar, 1992) or expansion of teacher-supplied criteria (e.g., Orsmond *et al.*, 1996). Kelmar (1992) found a good correlation between peer and teacher marks, although teachers used a greater range than students and peer marks exceeded teacher marks in general. Similarly, Orsmond *et al.* (1996) reported that, although a good correlation between teacher and peer assessment was present overall, several discrepancies in marking were found at the level of individual criteria. These 'apprentices' have further learning to do before they may be regarded as experts in assessment.

Peer assessment and fading

The type of fading described by Collins *et al.* (1991) is also discernible within the corpus of peer assessment literature. Frequently, students are provided with support and help at the start of an implementation which is reduced over time. As we have seen above, in some peer assessment studies, students are provided with criteria or checklists by the teacher; while in others, students and teachers together agree the criteria to be used. In yet other cases, the students identify their own criteria. We see an example of fading in Fineman's (1981) study of peer teaching and peer assessment of student-run sessions. In this study, third-year students identified their own criteria relevant to judging the quality of a presentation, as Fineman (1981: 84) argued that it seemed 'inconsistent with the spirit and purpose of self determination' for criteria to be supplied by teachers.

While it is possible to argue that this degree of autonomy might not be appropriate for beginner students who require more modelling and scaffolding, it seems entirely appropriate for learners in their final year of study to take responsibility for these selections. In Fineman's study, peer, self- and lecturer ratings of presentations were made and 'a remarkably close correspondence' (Fineman, 1981: 87) between lecturer and peer ratings found. In this way, the reflection necessary for autonomous learning is 'enhanced by the use of various techniques for reproducing or "replaying" the performances of both expert and novice for comparison' (Collins *et al.*, 1991: 10). The close correspondence between teacher and peer assessment Fineman found suggests that the students had successfully internalised the standards by which their performance was to be judged and identified criteria appropriate to this task. The students also seemed satisfied with the exercise, as their evaluations of the course overall and the peer assessment component were positive.

Fading of support is matched by the kind of increasing student autonomy described by Brew (1999). Her typology of self- and peer assessment practices derives from the three 'knowledge interests' outlined by Habermas (1987): technical, communicative and emancipatory knowledge. She argued that the ability to assess oneself and one's peers in each of these three areas is essential for the development of autonomous independent professional judgement. In the context of peer or self-assessment, the first of these involves students checking their knowledge, skills or competency against a set of criteria or competency statements. At the next level, students are involved in discussing and negotiating criteria before applying these standards to their own or each other's work. When self- or peer assessment has an emancipatory component, Brew (1999) argued that, in the context of assessment of competencies, students should question and critique the competencies themselves.

Of course, there is more to peer assessment than simply following an 'apprenticeship rulebook'. Our view is that giving students opportunities for taking responsibility in identifying and engaging with criteria, planning their own learning, practising articulating their knowledge to each other, giving feedback and making informed judgements is essential for the development of enduring assessment competence and lifelong learning.

Are there forms of peer assessment to avoid?

Increased peer involvement in a learner's education does not mean that the experience is always improved for participants, though this does seem to happen frequently. It can also be argued that assessment more generally, and indeed some forms of peer assessment, can undermine trust and communicate a distorted view of the place of peers in learning and, thus, be detrimental to learning beyond higher education. As we argue in Chapter 11, even in successful academics, experiences of assessment can leave a residue of hurt and resentment. And learning with and from others also involves an affective element that can affect the quality of learning (McCormick and Pressley, 1997). In addition, some examples of peer involvement, as we shall see, do not seem to be designed to encourage skills and attitudes that have lasting value.

What features of peer assessment might be detrimental to future learning? Conceptions of assessment generally are subject to change. Serafini (2000) discerned 'assessment as measurement' to be the first of three paradigms, followed by 'assessment as procedure' and 'assessment as enquiry'. Birenbaum and Dochy (1996: xiii) saw this shift as being from the 'culture of testing' to a 'culture of assessment'. Peer assessment conducted within the framework of traditional assessment as measurement does not have the power to enable students to benefit from their involvement. Measurement stresses norm-referenced standardised testing and objectivity, standardisation and reliability. Some early peer assessment studies provided no modelling or scaffolding, but still required students to rate their own performance or that of their peers. Although students may do this, they complete the exercise with little or no enhancement of their understanding of standards or criteria. They are no better equipped at the end of the exercise than they were at the beginning. There is no 'value added'.

Although grades and marks are more frequently associated with certification than with learning, current peer assessment studies often involve the awarding of marks. While I am not arguing that marks have no part to play in peer assessment – indeed, many of my own studies have involved this practice – I believe that peer assessment's strength lies in its potential to enhance learning. The act of awarding a grade is of itself meaningless if the learner has no opportunity to learn about standards, or to use the grade as a judgement of knowledge or skills acquisition and a way-station to autonomous peer or self-assessment.

Another current practice involving peer assessment in the context of group working is the analysis of teamworking and group dynamics in order to provide formative feedback to peers. While this practice has obvious benefits, it also has the potential to impair learning. For example, it may undermine co-operation itself. It seems we cannot escape the tension between co-operation and competition that permeates education. This tension is not a new phenomenon: as long ago as the 1930s, May and Doob (1937: 81) observed that, while ideals of cooperation were emphasised in society, the basic structure of the system was competitive. They concluded that education has the power to 'promote' or 'disrupt' both competition and co-operation, pointing to the traditional examination, the bulwark of the assessment as measurement paradigm, as 'a destroyer of cooperation'. However, it can also be argued that future learning requires the ability both to work harmoniously and productively with one's peers and to identify and use criteria and apply standards to one's own work and that of others. Employers claim to value an individual's ability to work as a team member. However, it is also likely that, while they prefer co-operation within the company, they are likely to welcome competition with those outside it. Thus, future learning requires that learners acquire the ability to balance these two conflicting modes of working.

Peer assessment to support future learning

Thus, I see it as beneficial to promote peer involvement in assessment where particular characteristics are present. These include features which:

- are designed to enhance learning;
- require learners to take responsibility for their actions;
- encourage a reflective approach to learning;
- require students to identify and apply standards and criteria;
- provide some degree of modelling and/or scaffolding;
- involve learners in judging their performance or that of their peers – developing and using Sadler's (1989 and 2005) evaluative expertise, providing, seeking and utilising feedback;
- allow learners to practise peer and self-assessment skills in a variety of contexts;
- allow fading of support so that learners may move nearer towards assessment autonomy.

Conclusion

Peers have an important role to play in all our lives, be it in the kindergarten, university, workplace or social club. Through interaction, we learn and develop. I have argued that peer involvement in assessment during formal education has the potential to encourage learning and develop assessment skills that will last a lifetime. Drawing on the work of others (e.g., Kvale, 2006; Collins *et al.*, 1991), I have explored some of the ways in which formal higher education and apprenticeship learning resemble each other, and applied some characteristics of apprenticeship learning to the design of peer assessment schemes likely to promote learner assessment autonomy.

References

Alverno College (2001) *Quick Facts for Educators*, Milwaukee, WI: Alverno College.

Anderson, J.B. and Frieberg, H.J. (1995) Using self-assessment as a reflective tool to enhance the student teaching experience, *Teacher Education Quarterly*, 22 (Winter): 77–91.

Bangert, A.W. (1995) Peer assessment: an instructional strategy for effectively implementing performance-based assessments, Doctor of Education dissertation, University of South Dakota.

Beaman, R. (1998) The unquiet ... even loud, andragogy! Alternative assessments for adult learners, *Innovative Higher Education*, 23, 1: 47–59.

Birenbaum, M. (1996) Assessment 2000: towards a pluralistic approach to assessment, in M. Birenbaum and F. Dochy (eds) *Alternatives in Assessment of Achievements, Learning Processes and Prior Knowledge*, Boston, MA: Kluwer Academic.

Birenbaum, M. and Dochy, F. (eds) (1996) *Alternatives in Assessment of Achievements, Learning Processes and Prior Knowledge*, Boston, MA: Kluwer Academic.

Boud, D. and Middleton, H. (2003) Learning from others at work: communities of practice and informal learning, *Journal of Workplace Learning*, 15, 5: 194–202.

Boud, D., Cohen, R. and Sampson, J. (2001) *Peer Learning in Higher Education*, London: Kogan Page.

Brennan, J., Johnstone, B., Little, B., Shah, T. and Woodley, A. (2001) *The Employment of UK Graduates: Comparisons with Europe and Japan*, Bristol: Higher Education Funding Council for England (available at: www.hefce.ac.uk/Pubs/hefce/2001/01_38. htm [accessed 15 May 2006]).

Brew, A. (1999) Toward autonomous assessment: using self-assessment and peer assessment, in S. Brown and A. Glasner (eds) *Assessment Matters in Higher Education: Choosing and Using Diverse Approaches*, Buckingham and Philadelphia, PA: Society for Research into Higher Education and Open University Press.

Brown, J.S., Collins, A. and Duguid, P. (1989) Situated cognition and the culture of learning, *Educational Researcher*, 18, 1: 32–42.

Bruner, J. (1960) *The Process of Education*, Cambridge, MA: Harvard University Press.

Catterall, M. (1995) Peer learning research in marketing, in S. Griffiths, K. Houston and A. Lazenbatt (eds) *Enhancing Student Learning through Peer Tutoring in Higher Education*, Jordanstown: University of Ulster, Educational Development Unit.

Challis, M. (1999) AMEE Medical education guide no. 11 (revised): portfolio-based learning and assessment in medical education, *Medical Teacher*, 21, 4: 370–386.

Cohen, R. and Sampson, J. (2001) Implementing and managing peer learning, in D. Boud, R. Cohen and J. Sampson (eds) *Peer Learning in Higher Education*, London: Kogan Page.

Collins, A., Brown, J.S. and Holum, A. (1991) Cognitive apprenticeship: making thinking visible, *American Educator*, 6, 11: 38–46.

Co-operative Learning Center (2005) (available at: http://www.co-operation.org/ [accessed 22 May 2006]).

Cowan, J. (1988) Struggling with self-assessment, in D. Boud (ed.) *Developing Student Autonomy in Learning*, 2nd edn, London: Kogan Page.

Dewey, J. (1897) My pedagogic creed, *School Journal*, 54, 3: 77–80 (available at: http://www.infed.org/archives/e-texts/e-dew-pc.htm [accessed 4 November 2005]).

Dochy, F. (2001) A new assessment era: different needs, new challenges, *Research Dialogue in Learning and Instruction*, 2: 11–20.

Dochy, F., Segers, M. and Sluijsmans, D. (1999) The use of self-, peer and co-assessment in higher education: a review, *Studies in Higher Education*, 24, 3: 331–349.

Ewers, T. and Searby, M. (1997) Peer assessment in music, *New Academic*, 6, 2: 5–7.

Falchikov, N. (1986) Product comparisons and process benefits of collaborative self and peer group assessments, *Assessment and Evaluation in Higher Education*, 11, 2: 146–166.

—— (1994) Learning from peer feedback marking: student and teacher perspectives, in H.C. Foote, C.J. Howe, A. Anderson, A.K. Tolmie and D.A. Warden (eds) *Group and Interactive Learning*, Southampton and Boston: Computational Mechanics Publications.

—— (1995a) Improving feedback to and from students, in P. Knight (ed.) *Towards Better Learning: Assessment for Learning in Higher Education*, London: Kogan Page.

—— (1995b) Peer feedback marking: developing peer assessment, *Innovations in Education and Training International*, 32, 2: 175–187.

—— (2001) *Learning Together: Peer Tutoring in Higher Education*, London and New York: RoutledgeFalmer.

—— (2005) *Improving Assessment through Student Involvement*, London and New York: RoutledgeFalmer.

Fineman, S. (1981) Reflections on peer teaching and peer assessment – an undergraduate experience, *Assessment and Evaluation in Higher Education*, 6, 1: 82–93.

Freeman, M. (1995) Peer assessment by groups of group work, *Assessment and Evaluation in Higher Education*, 20, 3: 289–300.

Gillam, A., Callaway, S. and Wikoff, K.H. (1994) The role of authority and the authority of roles in peer writing tutorials, *Journal of Teaching Writing*, 12, 2: 161–198.

Goldschmid, B. and Goldschmid, M.L. (1976) Peer teaching in higher education: a review, *Higher Education*, 5: 9–33.

Greer, L. (2001) Does changing the method of assessment of a module improve the performance of a student?, *Assessment and Evaluation in Higher Education*, 26, 2: 127–138.

Habermas, J. (1987) *Knowledge and Human Interests*, trans. J. Shapiro, London: Polity Press.

Harvey, L., Moon, S., Geall, V. and Bower, R. (1997) *Graduates' Work: Organisational Change and Students' Attributes*, Birmingham: Centre for Research into Quality.

Hawkins, P. and Winter, J. (1995) *Future Graduate Skills in the 21st Century*, London: Association of Graduate Recruiters.

Heron, J. (1988) Assessment revisited, in D. Boud (ed.) *Developing Student Autonomy in Learning*, 2nd edn, London: Kogan Page.

Higher Education Academy (HEA) (2005) (available at: http://www.heacademy.ac.uk/869.htm [accessed 13 May 2005]).

Hughes, I.E. and Large, B.J. (1993) Staff and peer-group assessment of oral communication skills, *Studies in Higher Education*, 18, 3: 379–385.

Hunter, D. and Russ, M. (1996) Peer assessment in performance studies, *British Journal of Music Education*, 13: 67–78.

Kelmar, J. (1992) Peer assessment: a study of graduate students, paper presented at the Forum on Higher Education Teaching and Learning – the Challenge Conference, the Teaching and Learning Group, Curtin University of Technology, Perth, 12–13 February.

Kvale, S. (2006) A workplace perspective on school assessment, Workplace Learning SIG American Educational Research Association Conference, San Francisco, April.

Lapham, A. and Webster, R. (1999) Peer assessment of undergraduate seminar presentations: motivations, reflection and future directions, in S. Brown and A. Glasner (eds) *Assessment Matters in Higher Education: Choosing and Using Diverse Approaches*, Buckingham and Philadelphia, PA: Society for Research into Higher Education and Open University Press.

Lave, J. (ed.) (1999) *Everyday Cognition: Its Development in Social Context*, Lincoln, NE: iUniverse Inc.

Lave, J. and Wenger, E. (1991) *Situated Learning: Legitimate Peripheral Participation*, Cambridge: Cambridge University Press.

McCormick, C.B. and Pressley, M. (1997) *Educational Psychology: Learning, Instruction, Assessment*, New York: Longman.

McDowell, L. (1995) The impact of innovative assessment on student learning, *Innovations in Education and Training International*, 32, 4: 302–313.

Magin, D. (1993) Should student peer ratings be used as part of summative assessment?, *Higher Education Research and Development*, 16: 537–542.

—— (2001) Reciprocity as a source of bias in multiple peer assessment of group work, *Studies in Higher Education*, 26, 1: 53–63.

Mathews, B.P. (1994) Assessing individual contributions: experience of peer evaluation in major group projects, *British Journal of Educational Technology*, 25, 1: 19–28.

May, Mark A. and Doob, L.W. (1937) *Competition and cooperation*, Bulletin No. 25, April, New York: Social Science Research Council.

Newstead, S.E. and Dennis, I. (1994) Examiners examined: the reliability of exam marking in psychology, *Psychologist*, 7, 5: 216–219.

Nightingale, P., Te Wiata, I., Toohey, S., Ryan, G., Hughes, C. and Magin, D. (1996) *Assessing Learning in Universities*, Sydney: University of New South Wales Press.

Orsmond, P., Merry, S. and Reiling, K. (1996) The importance of marking criteria in the use of peer assessment, *Assessment and Evaluation in Higher Education*, 21, 3: 239–250.

Piaget, J. and Inhelder, B. (1966) *The Psychology of the Child*, London: Routledge & Kegan Paul.

Price, J. and Cutler, H. (1995) The development of skills through peer-assessment, in A. Edwards and P. Knight (eds) *Assessing Competence in Higher Education*, London: Kogan Page in association with the Staff and Educational Development Association.

Sadler, D.R. (1989) Formative assessment and the design of instructional systems, *Instructional Science*, 18: 119–144.

—— (2005) Interpretation of criteria-based assessment and grading in higher education, *Assessment and Evaluation in Higher Education*, 30, 2: 175–194.

Serafini, F. (2000) Three paradigms of assessment: measurement, procedure, and enquiry, *Reading Teacher*, 54: 384–393 (available at: http://www.frankserafini.com/PubArticles/ThreeParadigms.htm).

Sivan, A. (2000) The implementation of peer assessment: an action research approach, *Assessment in Education*, 7, 2: 193–213.

Sluijsmans, D.M.A., Moerkerke, G., van Merriënboer, J.G. and Dochy, F.J.R.C. (2001) Peer assessment in problem based learning, *Studies in Educational Evaluation*, 27: 153–173.

Starr, B.C. (1991) Linking students and classes: strategies for improving learning and thinking, *Community/Junior College*, 15, 4: 427–438.

Topping, K. (1998) Peer assessment between students in colleges and universities, *Review of Educational Research*, 68, 3: 249–276.

Trevitt, C. and Pettigrove, M. (1995) Towards autonomous criterion-referenced assessment and self-assessment: a case study, paper presented at the European Association for Research on Learning and Instruction Electronic Conference (accessed through EARLI–AE discussion list).

Vygotsky, L. (1978) *Mind in Society*, Cambridge, MA: Harvard University Press.

Wenger, E. (1999) *Communities of Practice: Learning, Meaning, and Identity*, Cambridge: Cambridge University Press.

Zakrzewski, S. and Bull, J. (1998) The mass implementation and evaluation of computer-based assessments, *Assessment and Evaluation in Higher Education*, 23, 2: 141–152.

Chapter 11

Assessment and emotion

The impact of being assessed

Nancy Falchikov and David Boud

Assessment has traditionally been treated in the literature as a technical activity that involves measurement with little impact on those assessed. This chapter challenges this assumption and suggests that the unintended consequences of assessment are substantial. We identify some literature that might be useful in investigating the role of emotion in learning and assessment, but acknowledge that, surprisingly, it is a greatly under-researched area. We make a contribution of our own through the examination of a set of students' autobiographical stories about the experience of being assessed. We suggest that, while the ways in which assessment is experienced are diverse, the experience of being assessed is inter- preted as both positive and negative in its impact. In some cases the interaction between the learner and the assessment event is so negative that it has an emotional impact that lasts many years and affects career choices, inhibits new learning and changes behaviour towards one's own students in subsequent teaching situations. We suggest that the emotional experience of being assessed is complex and is a function of the relationship between the expectations and dispositions of a learner, relationships between learners and other people, the judgements made about learners and the ways in which judgements are made.

We see this as an important area for investigation, given that assessment is not experienced as a cool and rational process. Emotional responses are part of everyone's experience of being assessed. For some time, it has been claimed that assessment in general, and examinations in particular, can be very stressful. Indeed, this argument has been used as a justification for moving away from testing. It can also be argued that emotional responses have the power to undermine the validity of assessment processes that apparently have face validity. There is also some evidence that emotions may differentially influence individual learners or groups of learners. For example, gender can affect experience of emotion. While the tradi- tional view that women are more emotional than men has been challenged, research has indicated that powerful emotions such as anger, disdain and contempt which indicate a dominant position over others may be 'complementary to traditional male gender roles' (Fischer, 1998: 87). Similarly, Fischer also argued that, for women, expression of powerless emotions such as sadness, fear, disappointment and insecurity is more consonant with the traditional gender view and, therefore, acceptable to many people. In this way, emotional effects may contribute to systematic disadvantage.

Inspecting the literature suggests that there has been a recent upsurge of interest in the effects of emotions, and papers on the subject of emotions, assessment and learning have begun to appear in educational journals. For example, in 2002, Schutz and Lanehart introduced a special issue of *Educational Psychologist* devoted to reporting current work by participants in the 1998 symposium The Role of Emotions in Students' Learning and Achievement, organised by the American Educational Research Association, which took place in San Diego. Up to this point, they claimed, study of emotions in education had been largely limited to research into test anxiety and attribution theory. In 1999, Pressick-Kilborn and Walker explored aspects of student *interest* in their learning, looking back to the work of Dewey (1913), who recognised interest as 'a dynamic, active state based on real objects and the pleasure associated with them' (Pressick-Kilborn and Walker, 1999: 1). Boekaerts (1999) also saw feelings as playing an important part in 'self-regulated learning'.

Recent years have seen a further increase in interest in the role of emotion in learning. Schutz and Lanehart (2002) pointed out that five symposia on the topic of emotions in education had taken place since the 1998 San Diego meeting. Further examples of studies of emotions and affect have appeared in the literature. Gielo-Perczak and Karwowski (2003) noted a shift in emphasis in research into human performance from information processing to frameworks based on affordances, emotions and intuition. More recently, two journals produced special issues on the topic of emotions and learning (*Learning and Instruction*, 15; and *Management Learning*, 36, 3). The special issue of *Learning and Instruction* explored a variety of topics, including interest-based learning (e.g., Krapp, 2005; Ainley *et al.*, 2005), and the sources of emotional and motivational experiences (e.g., Järvenoja and Järvelä, 2005). It also included an evaluation of the Emotional and Cognitive Aspects of Learning (ECOLE) approach, which uses teaching strategies to enhance emotions and achievement (Glaser-Zikuda *et al.*, 2005). The *Management Learning* issue looked at emotion in the context of management learning.

Before we begin to explore further the relationship between assessment and emotion, let us look briefly at how emotions may affect learning more generally.

What is known about how emotions affect learning?

Antonacopoulou and Gabriel (2001) argued that, although it is recognised that emotion is one of the factors that affect learning, our understanding of how this happens is limited. However, psychological theory may aid our understanding of the process. For example, LeDoux (1998) tells us that 'conditioned fear', a condition first elicited by Pavlov in his famous dogs, results from pairings of conditioned and unconditioned stimuli. In the case of assessment, for example, feelings of distress, inadequacy, unfairness or similar negative emotions can come to be associated with assessment experiences. Such conditioned fear is very long lasting. 'The passing of time is not enough to get rid of it' (LeDoux, 1998: 145), though extinction (reduction in likelihood of experiencing negative emotion) can occur if assessment occurs repeatedly without the unpleasant emotions. In conditioned fear, the context becomes part of the conditioned stimulus. Piaget (1981) also recognised the importance of emotion and saw it as providing motivation for cognitive processes. He saw feelings of success or failure as having the potential to assist or restrict learning. Empirical support for this came from studies of adult learning by Snell (1988).

Learning involves a challenge in that it calls into question valued ideas and beliefs. It has the power to cause considerable discomfort. Psychoanalytic approaches have also been applied to the study of emotion and leaning. Antonacopoulou and Gabriel (2001: 439) argued that, when taking a psychoanalytic approach, learning involves 'psychological work' which entails 'accepting and tolerating the anxieties associated with all learning'. As we are aware, such anxieties can be triggered by experiences of failure, disappointment and threat (e.g., that caused by uncertainty, dependency and vulnerability).

What are sources of emotions?

Researchers are now beginning to identify the range and sources of emotions in education, where 'range' refers to the many different types of emotion experienced by human beings and 'source' to the variety of stimuli to emotions. The search for sources of emotions led Pekrun *et al.* (2002) to argue that research has been biased towards negative emotions, often associated with aspects of assessment. Not all emotions are negative, however, and Pekrun *et al.* reported qualitative studies that found a rich diversity of emotions in academic settings. Although anxiety was the most frequently reported emotion, the numbers of negative and positive emotions were found to be similar. One might be forgiven for thinking that negative emotion is exclusively associated with examinations. However, Pekrun *et al.* also noted that anxiety was mentioned in relation simply to being in class or studying at home as well as in the context of taking exams. None the less, some 'suicidal ideation' was mentioned in the context of failing academic exams. Thus, assessment seems to play an important part in the development of negative emotion.

Effects of emotions

Unsurprisingly, negative emotion can have undesirable consequences. For example, field research has shown that test anxiety can reduce working memory which then leads to impaired performance at difficult or complex tasks that draw on such resources (e.g., Hembree, 1988). Pekrun *et al.*'s (2002) research found that anger and anxiety had significant and detrimental effects on study interest and effort, though the correlation was greater for anger. Anger and anxiety were also significantly correlated with irrelevant thinking, and to a comparable degree.

Similarly, both emotions were negatively correlated with the deep processing activities of elaboration and rehearsal. In other words, anger and anxiety were found to affect learning adversely. The emotions were also significantly positively correlated with external regulation and negatively with self-regulation, which could act to bring about feelings of powerlessness. Thus, cognitive processing can be impaired when strong emotions such as anxiety and anger are present. Other effects of a more personal and long-lasting nature are also evident, as we shall see in the autobiographical accounts of being assessed below.

Not all emotion experienced in the academic setting is negative, and some emotions can enhance the learning experience. Krapp (2005: 382), for example, argued the commonsense view that the quality of emotional experiences impacts on the direction of 'motivational development', including an individual's interest. In other words, interest may be created or enhanced by positive emotional experiences rather than negative ones. Positive mood has also been found to facilitate holistic thinking and problem-solving, while negative mood may enhance more focused, detail-oriented and analytic modes of information processing (Pekrun *et al.*, 2002).

Thus, while we can discern an upsurge in general interest in the effects of emotions on learning, the relationship between assessment in higher education and emotion seems underinvestigated and undertheorised. We shall now look at some autobiographical accounts of the experiences of being assessed, analysing them using two theoretical frameworks.

Autobiographical accounts of experiences of being assessed

The accounts used were prepared by part-time students enrolled in an independent study unit designed to give them a taste of working on an ongoing research project conducted by David Boud as part of a master's course in adult education. All students were volunteers between thirty and fifty years of age who had agreed that their work in the unit could be used for research purposes. They were currently involved in teaching and training roles in vocational education and training and in the higher education sectors. Students undertook two assignments. One was to write a short autobiographical essay on their personal experience of being assessed during their careers as learners; the second and major part, not used here, involved an analysis of assessment tasks. Care was taken to ensure that students were not led to focus on either negative or positive experiences. In their first assignment they were encouraged to write rich and detailed accounts of their experience eschewing analysis and drawing out their feelings about the events described. Assignments were not graded. We use this material as a set of rich resources to generate ways of thinking about emotion and assessment that might be fruitful for further investigation, not to suggest transferable conclusions from them.

We found the work of Krapp (2005) useful in carrying out our analysis of these accounts. He argued that humans have three essential needs to ensure well-being and psychological growth: competence, autonomy and relatedness. He reported that subjects who were asked about their feelings during a recent period of learning activities referred spontaneously to experiences relating to these three needs. Interview data also found that interviewees used this same system, in that, averaging two data sets, 74 per cent of learners interviewed referred to competence, 66 per cent to social relatedness and 38 per cent to autonomy.

Another useful framework for looking at personal histories of assessment comes from Efklides and Volet's (2005) editorial for a special issue of *Learning and Instruction*. In it, the editors argued that emotional experiences during learning might be conceptualised as being multiple, situated and dynamic. The term 'multiple' requires that we take into account both feelings and emotions, both of which are present throughout the learning process. For example, within the field of education, metacognitive *feelings* monitor cognitive processing, whereas *emotions* control action that leads to engagement with, or suspension from, learning. Experiences may be said to be 'situated' in that they are triggered by person and task characteristics, as well as by the context and ongoing evaluation of the learning process and outcome. Experiences may have effects that are immediate and direct or long term and latent. They may thus be considered 'dynamic'.

We inspected the autobiographical accounts of personal experiences of assessment and looked for evidence of both positive and negative emotions resulting from the experiences and for signs of the persistent nature of the emotion. In addition, we analysed the accounts using the frameworks of both Krapp's three essential needs and Efklides and Volet's three characteristics of emotional experiences during learning. As is illustrated below, Krapp's three needs emerge from all transcripts, to a greater or lesser degree. We also found numerous examples of the dynamic and situated nature of assessment experiences. We shall look at positive and negative experiences separately.

Positive experiences

We found little evidence of positive assessment experiences, though one student included an insightful account of 'a positive educational and emotional assessment process . . . which had a significant positive effect on my learning'. This account included examples of autonomy, competence and relatedness as well as illustrations of experiences that were situated and dynamic. Positive examples of competence were scattered throughout the account. The author reported a feeling of competence that led to her looking forward to meeting new challenges. She experienced the assessment exercise (a mini-research project) as making her feel 'knowledgeable' about her chosen topic, 'confident, fit and ready to start again'. She received a good grade for the work and concluded that the good assessment result and positive comments had had the effect of 'encouraging me to feel that I am in a position of some authority on this matter . . . and that I have the skills and ability to inquire further'. Furthermore, she reported that the sense of great achievement and pleasure, the feelings of being 'highly satisfied and highly contented', lasted for several months. She saw the experience as partly responsible for her decision to continue with further postgraduate study and reported thinking frequently about the subjects and topics studied in the three years since the experience.

Here we have an example of the long-lasting effects of positive assessment and feedback. The account illustrates well that, when interest is triggered, learners are likely to engage further (see Ainley *et al.*, 2005). Krapp (2005) asserted that interest development would occur only if both cognitive-rational and emotional feedback are experienced in a positive way. In other words, a task must be experienced as personally important or meaningful, and emotional feedback experienced during engagement with the task as positive. This seems to have been the case with this learner. The author identified the authenticity of the assessment task as important. She also saw practical experience as an aid to learning.

She clearly enjoyed the autonomy the project afforded her, appreciating that the course was largely self-directed. She described the 'process of "discovery"' as 'very appealing'. She also expressed satisfaction that she herself had collected the data with which she was working; that they were her own. Relatedness featured in the account as the author acknowledged the importance of working relationships in both work and study contexts. She also speculated that good marks and understanding of the subject represent an 'earned "legitimacy" in the area'. This comment brings to mind Tinto's (1997) assertion that learning communities with a collaborative pedagogy can help 'validate' a student's presence on campus and encourage persistence and retention. Here we also encounter examples of Pressick-Kilborn and Walker's (1999) elements of interest: identification and absorption.

Negative experiences

The essays contained many examples of bad experiences, described in vivid and immediate language and often in great detail.

Krapp's (2005) three needs are particularly prominent in one student's account of her negative experience of assessment. Her task was to make observations on patients as part of her professional training. Competence and relatedness were particularly evident themes, although, as the experience was traumatic for the student, in very negative forms. She reported feeling 'nervous and unsure' before commencing the assessment exercise and 'useless and worthless' during the procedure. She reported blaming herself for what was happening and seeing herself as 'the problem'. Afterwards, she reported that, although she felt that more could have been done to help her, 'At that stage of my life I did not have the skills and experience of pursuing my rights.' These feelings and emotions were intimately associated with issues of relatedness – or lack of it. Staff members were experienced as 'unsupportive' and lacking interest in nursing students. The experienced professional allocated to the student was 'not interested in involving me in the day-to-day activities taking place'. Similarly, her facilitator was seen as unsupportive. She remembers his exact words of criticism, her feeling that she was neither welcomed nor her assistance needed: 'I felt I was just getting in the way' and was 'not part of the team'. Autonomy also featured in the account, again in negative form. During the process of observation she stated, 'I felt I was being treated as a child.' Similarly, in retrospect, she saw that her inability to seek advice or help stemmed from earlier experiences as a student when 'I was taught not to question the teacher, nor to voice my opinion, but to do what was asked of me whether I agreed or not.'

Another account, this time of sitting a traditional exam, focused more on the physiological effects experienced. Although having a supportive family, this learner approached the task 'nervous and lacking self-belief'. She was fully aware of the importance of the exam and of gaining good marks, as the exam was the sole determinant of her performance on the course. On opening the paper, the learner's mind blanked. She reported that her 'breathing was really fast and [that she] was on the verge of tears'. Other physiological responses to stress included: 'words failing to make any sense'; '[I] started panicking'; 'My mind just stopped functioning'.

The traditional exam was the focus of another account. This learner looked back to his examinations in year 10 of school, conducting a spirited critique of traditional assessment. He resented that the whole year was 'wholly directed at passing the school certificate exams'. Lack of autonomy was disliked. Student opinion was reported as 'an expression of frustration at knowing we had little or no choices in the process or the outcome'. The process was described as a 'brain dump' creating 'pointless learning', with little information retained after the exam. The learner reported being aware of lack of real understanding and as resenting this, too. The scoring and normalisation across the state gave rise to further resentment. His account contains a passionate attack on statistical normalisation in general and the bell curve in particular. Unlike the learner in the previous account, this student did not experience stress or any physiological symptoms before, during or after the examination. He reported that he did well in exams, as they 'posed no particular anxiety to me then'. He later grew to 'disdain' them, and developed anxiety towards traditional assessment. His feelings and emotions at the time were of anger and frustration. Other effects were also reported: the author believed the experience of traditional assessment led to the development of a competitive attitude to fellow students. He commented: 'I was no longer striving to succeed. I was striving to win.' In the longer term, the author believed the experiences to be partly responsible for his 'cynical attitude towards any "official system"' and his 'irrational bias' and distrust of all statistical methods. Clinical psychology was later added to his list of 'things to be distrusted', because of its reliance on statistics. In choosing a future career, the learner eschewed anything involving quantitative methods, choosing to study anthropology, which involved qualitative approaches.

A further account illustrated that, while an incident of assessment had had a major role in the academic and personal development of the author, it may have been acting as a trigger to a more fundamental reason for initial failure – an underlying state of severe lack of self-confidence. Again, Krapp's themes of competence, relatedness and autonomy are to be found in statements. After an early career characterised by academic success, the author failed a core subject of the degree course she was studying. The incident had consequences that stretched well beyond that point in time. The author eventually dropped out and subsequently failed to get back into the system due, in her mind, to this one failure. Twenty-five years later, still without a first degree, she ended up, through her professional accomplishments, employed as an academic at an old university and enrolled in a masters degree at another, and still harbouring strong feelings about her earlier failure.

The author writes of her perception of her own lack of confidence and competence: '[I was] terrified that I would be called upon to contribute to the class. I hid at home and eventually stopped coming to class.' Even after a successful semester, she remained totally lacking in confidence in her capacity to continue and she formally discontinued her studies again. Two decades later, 'the old devastation blew back in . . . confirming my inadequacy'. This account is testimony to the long-lasting effects of a bad assessment experience endured by a vulnerable young learner. Even after a series of academic successes and several awards for excellence, she remained harmed by the original experience. 'None of this compensated for the failure fifteen years earlier,' she reflected. During the writing of the account, the author reported being filled with sadness at the emotional upheaval she had endured which 'overwhelmed my sense of self-worth and impacted on career and study choices for twenty-five years'.

The account also contains a passionate critique of traditional assessment, as an 'arbitrary process' which occasionally 'seemed to be at the assessor's whim'. Her experiences 'confirmed my feeling that the process of assessment, and the subsequent personal judgement that occurred when someone awarded a grade, was secret, mysterious and altogether out of my control and understanding'. She now appreciates the value of assessment procedures that are demystified, open and fair and is at pains to ensure her own students receive good advice and support. She also reports having great empathy with students who 'may be struggling with "life" while they deal with assessment'.

In her closing remarks, she acknowledged the 'emotional catharsis' of reflecting on and writing about the events, yet added that, 'as I write, lurking in the shadows is this persistent thought – will this essay be good enough?' She reflected on the strangeness of a situation in which the act of writing about assessment becomes embroiled in the emotions of being assessed, 'even with the distance of time and context'. Powerful emotions, indeed!

Commentary and interpretation

These autobiographical accounts amply illustrate the link between emotions and assessment and provide some support for the frameworks described by both Krapp (2005) and Efklides and Volet (2005). The three essential requirements for well-being and psychological growth – competence, autonomy and relatedness – outlined by Krapp are clearly present in the accounts. Similarly, they also contain examples of Efklides and Volet's conceptualisation of emotional experiences during learning as being multiple, situated and dynamic. Reactions to assessment are multiple: both feelings and emotions are described, as well as some extreme physical symptoms. We found evidence that experiences are 'situated', being triggered by person and task characteristics, as well as by the context and ongoing evaluation of the learning process and outcome. The concept 'dynamic' is also illustrated in the accounts, in that authors describe experiences that give rise to effects that are immediate and direct or long term and latent.

Although the accounts were relatively few in number, we can perhaps draw some tentative conclusions. Our data are testimony to the belief that assessment experiences can be long lasting and influential on personal and academic development. Account after account refers to particular assessment experiences and their lingering effects echoing through time and exerting a continuing influence on personal and professional development, and in most cases on the assessment practices of the author. This seems to be particularly marked for negative experiences. Assessment appeared to be intimately connected to identity. Experiences were taken personally; they were not shrugged off but became part of how these people saw themselves as learners and subsequently as teachers.

We find many examples of the importance of autonomy to learners. However, as Krapp (2005) noted, not all learners are prepared for full autonomy. As he predicted, we find that learners desire and enjoy freedom of action only when they believe themselves to be capable of learning and carrying out the tasks involved.

Although women predominantly wrote the accounts, there may be a hint of gender difference in relation to reactions to some aspects of assessment, examinations in particular. We support our tentative observations by reference to the body of research that points to the existence of stereotypical 'gendered emotional meaning systems'. As we noted above, such systems entail powerful emotions such as anger, disdain and contempt being associated with male experience, and powerless emotions such as sadness, fear and insecurity with female experience (e.g., Fischer, 1998). We found examples of these dramatic differences within the autobiographical accounts.

Miller and Parlett (1974: 49) stated that many students were 'resolutely instrumental', particularly when faced with traditional examinations. They noted that even cue-seekers were sometimes forced to sacrifice intrinsic interest for extrinsic reward when faced with the 'artificial' situation of what they termed 'the examination game'. We see a clear example of this type of behaviour in the account written by a male author who described a wasted year spent preparing for an examination and the development of a competitive attitude towards fellow students. The reward became the winning rather than the learning and understanding. Although there are those who claim that girls are socialised to be less assertive than boys (for a summary of some recent work, see Assor *et al.*, 2005), Ryan and Deci (2000) maintain that controlling behaviours are no less harmful for girls than boys. As we have illustrated in our analysis of autobiographical accounts of experiences of assessment, the traditional examination and its associated lack of student control provided a negative experience for females and males alike.

However, the effects for the two genders were quite different, as predicted by knowledge of research into gendered emotional meaning systems. Females experienced anxiety and stress while males experienced anger. Thus, we would concur with Ryan and Deci.

Several accounts found traditional assessment wanting. As Miller and Parlett (1974: 45) discovered, there appears to be 'a curious mixture of bureaucratic and personalized assessment in operation, accompanied by indecision about what is fair' in examiner marking. This situation seems to have continued, in some corners at least, as the same view was echoed in some autobiographical accounts. As we saw above, one author viewed marking as an 'arbitrary process' that 'seemed to be at the assessor's whim'. We know that teacher marking is notoriously unreliable (e.g., Newstead and Dennis, 1994), so such student opinion may be well founded.

A positive finding of the analysis of accounts was that all of the authors seem to have learned from their experiences, be they good or bad, and now provide their own students with good support and guidance to make assessment meaningful and supportive of learning. Of course, this may be a function of the self-selected nature of the group, as it is extremely unlikely that students would volunteer for a special unit on assessment unless they had come to some resolution about their own assessment issues. For those with negative personal experiences, the provision for their own students includes aspects they noted to be lacking in their own education. A particularly marked aspect is the emphasis such learners now place on openness, demystification of assessment and good relationships between teachers and learners.

Conclusion

From our reading of the autobiographical accounts, we observe that the ways in which assessment is experienced is a function of what the person assessed brings to the event and the event itself. As Gabriel and Griffiths (2002) noted, emotions can be positive or negative, depending on how individuals interpret them. Particularly important are the judgements made by significant others. Negative emotional impact, while not a simple and direct response to negative or inappropriate judgements from others, can be influenced by what assessors say or write and by how the feedback is expressed. The more that is known about the learner, their expectations and dispositions, the greater the likelihood of feedback and judgements, particularly of a negative kind, being received well.

The autobiographical accounts also illustrated, as Pekrun et al. (2002) argued, that simplistic conceptions linking negative emotions with bad effects and positive emotions with good outcomes should be avoided, since positive emotions are sometimes detrimental and some negative emotions can be beneficial. Similarly, Gabriel and Griffiths (2002) noted that while extreme anxiety disables learning, some degree of anxiety is necessary for learning. For some learners, in the absence of anxiety, learning is seen as unnecessary.

What lessons may be learned from our analytic exercise? We argue that, to be helpful to learning and learner development, teachers should prepare themselves to give feedback of an appropriate kind attuned to the learner. In the same way, learners should be helped to prepare themselves for receiving and coping with judgements by others through understanding the assessment regime to which they are subject. In this way, they will come to recognise that failure to respond well to judgements is not necessarily a personal failing, but a consequence of the interaction between their experience and a normally fixed system that may be interpreted idiosyncratically by others. A big problem occurs when one party (the teacher) objectifies all their judgements, and the other party (the student) subjectifies all theirs. Another 'solution', of course, is to include students themselves in the process. Future learning depends on individuals developing self-assessment skills and autonomous learners making their own judgements.

Acknowledgements

We would like to thank the following for their contributions to this chapter: Sonal Bhalla, Matthew Britt, Ros Carter, Mary-Anne Choueifati, Teena Clerke, Colin Tegg.

References

Ainley, M., Corrigan, M. and Richardson, N. (2005) Students, tasks and emotions: identifying the contribution of emotions to students' reading of popular culture and popular science texts, *Learning and Instruction*, 15: 433–447.

Antonacopoulou, E.P. and Gabriel, Y. (2001) Emotion, learning and organisational change, *Journal of Organisational Change Management*, 14, 5: 435–451.

Assor, A., Kaplan, H., Kanat-Maymon, Y. and Roth, G. (2005) Directly controlling teacher behaviors as predictors of poor motivation and engagement in girls and boys: the role of anger and anxiety, *Learning and Instruction*, 15: 397–413.

Boekaerts, M. (1999) Self-regulated learning: where we are today, *International Journal of Educational Research*, 31: 445–457.

Dewey, J. (1913) *Interest and Effort in Education*, Cambridge, MA: Riverside Press.

Efklides, A. and Volet, S. (2005) Emotional experiences during learning: multiple, situated and dynamic, *Learning and Instruction*, 15: 377–380.

Fischer, A. (1998) Emotion, in K. Trew and J. Kremer (eds) *Gender and Psychology*, London: Arnold.

Gabriel, Y. and Griffiths, D.S. (2002) Emotion, learning and organizing, *Learning Organization*, 9, 5: 214–221.

Gielo-Perczak, K. and Karwowski, W. (2003) Ecological models of human performance based on affordance, emotion and intuition, *Ergonomics*, 46, 1: 310–326.

Gläser-Zikuda, M., Fuß, S., Laukenmann, M., Metz, K. and Randler, C. (2005) Promoting students' emotions and achievement – instructional design and evaluation of the ECOLE-approach, *Learning and Instruction*, 15, 5: 481–495.

Hembree, R. (1988) Correlates, causes, effects and treatment of test anxiety, *Review of Educational Research*, 58: 47–77.

Järvenoja, H. and Järvelä, S. (2005) How students describe the sources of their emotional and motivational experiences during the learning process: a qualitative approach, *Learning and Instruction*, 15: 465–480.

Krapp, A. (2005) Basic needs and the development of interest and intrinsic motivational orientations, *Learning and Instruction*, 15: 381–395.

LeDoux, J. (1998) *The Emotional Brain*, London: Phoenix.

Miller, C.M.L. and Parlett, M. (1974) *Up to the Mark: A Study of the Examination Game*, London: Society for Research into Higher Education.

Newstead, S.E. and Dennis, I. (1994) Examiners examined: the reliability of exam marking in psychology, *Psychologist*, 7, 5: 216–219.

Pekrun, R., Goetz, T., Titz, W. and Perry, R.P. (2002) Academic emotions in students' self-regulated learning and achievement: a program of qualitative and quantitative research, *Educational Psychologist*, 37, 2: 91–105.

Piaget, J. (1981 [1954]) *Intelligence and Affectivity: Their Relationship during Child Development*, Palo Alto, CA: Annual Review.

Pressick-Kilborn, K.J. and Walker, R.A. (1999) Exploring conceptualisations of students' interest in learning: the need for a sociocultural theory, paper presented at the Annual Conference of the Australian Association for Research in Education/New Zealand Association for Research in Education, Melbourne, 29 November–2 December.

Ryan, R.M. and Deci, E.L. (2000) Self-determination theory and the facilitation of intrinsic motivation, social development and well-being, *American Psychologist*, 55, 1: 68–78.

Schutz, P.A. and Lanehart, S.L. (2002) Introduction: emotions in education, *Educational Psychologist*, 37, 2: 67–68.

Snell, R. (1988) The emotional cost of managerial learning at work, *Management Education and Development*, 19, 4: 322–340.

Tinto, V. (1997) Classrooms as communities: exploring the educational character of student persistence, *Journal of Higher Education*, 68, 6: 599–623.

Part 4

The practice of
assessment

Chapter 12

Writing about practice for future learning

Peter Kandlbinder

There is a widely held belief in the value of learning through practice. Employers in particular place skills and industry experience above academic knowledge. They often argue that graduates without a period of work experience lack practical skills, such as communication skills, the ability to work in a team, flexibility of thinking and ethical training, which they see as essential for successful future participation in work. Unfortunately, there has been a decline in the ability of many professional courses to provide students with work experience. As such, students are finding it increasingly difficult to learn to apply experience-based knowledge to problem situations they will need for their future learning at work. Frustrated by the difficulty in finding placements, a lack of clear learning outcomes from work experience and the different expectations among students, lecturers and employers, many lecturers committed to equipping students to learn in work situations are searching for alternative forms of practice-based learning by which students can develop insights into themselves as professionals.

This search for alternative forms of practice-based learning has changed how student performance is being assessed. An area of growing experimentation in assessment of practice in universities is known collectively as 'practice-based assignments'. These are an emerging genre of written assessment in which students are required to write about practice rather than perform practical skills. The goal of setting assignments that involve writing about practice is to extend and supplement students' experience and motivate them to discover the skills essential for successful participation in some future, but as yet unknown, workplace. This kind of assignment requires students to demonstrate their performance as professionals by explaining to their lecturer how they would act in a particular situation. It is different from other forms of reflective writing, like the diaries, logs and journals that commonly record experiences of field trips, practicums and internships. While diaries or journals are rarely ever viewed by anyone other than the author, practice-based assignments are written with an assessor in mind and therefore need to conform to academic conventions of argument, logic and justification.

As with any new form of assessment, there is a lack of good models to follow when attempting tasks that involve writing about practice. Students, in particular, experience problems because the distinctive elements of practice-based assignments are not well understood. In this chapter I will explore whether our current experiences in practice-based assessment can clarify the confusion about the intended learning outcomes in these assessment tasks. I take as my starting point a research study conducted at the University of Technology, Sydney (UTS), which provides insights into the current assessment practices of lecturers analysing student writing about professional practice. Using the evidence provided by this study, I will argue that the limitations of writing about practice can be overcome by recognising that these assignments are more about reason than about practice. I will use the perspectives provided by these lecturers to describe how a conceptual understanding of practical reasoning can clarify the purpose of practice-based assignments and the criteria used to mark them. It is this attention to practical reasoning that can turn writing about practice into a powerful, long-term learning experience that supports students' future learning as professionals.

Practice-based assessment in higher education

There are a wide variety of methods used to assess practice in higher education. Brown (1999) describes some of the more common methods, which fall into three main approaches to practice-based assessment. The most familiar method of assessing practice is by direct observation of student performance which might be recorded in checklists, logs, diaries or journals. Second, students might provide a collection of evidence of their performance in a portfolio which demonstrates their competence in some area. Third, students might be asked to write about their experiences of practice in projects and case studies.

Each of these methods of assessing practice has its limitations. Underlying many of the methods is the assumption that students will perform a task that will be observed by a teacher. A major barrier in the use of either direct observation or portfolio is an expectation that evidence of practice will come from the workplace. Due to the difficulties of organising field-based practice, an increasingly popular alternative to workplace learning has become the simulated workplace. These are learning environments designed for students to experience the complexity of a work setting without having to enter an actual place of work. Simulated workplaces adopt varying degrees of realism within a classroom environment to provide students with a comparable experience of workplace problem-solving. Realism is generated in one of two ways: either by replicating the setting in which professionals operate or in replicating the kind of activity in which professionals are engaged.

The kind of problem-solving that would have the most immediate relevance to students' learning is one that has a high level of fidelity with the practices students expect to undertake soon after graduation. For example, a capstone project in marketing has an external client commission the whole class to produce a report on the company's marketing strategy. Students work in co-operative teams that mirror responsibilities in the field to perform a series of staged activities to create the final assignment that is presented to the client. Only those assignments that meet the required standard identified by the lecturer are permitted to progress to the next stage. Having a client other than the lecturer commission the work provides a greater level of realism and immediacy to the task, even through the activities largely take place in a fairly traditional classroom setting.

The alternative approach to simulated work experiences is to concentrate on discrete skills that are recognised as important for future professional practice and develop those skills prior to entering the workplace. For example, creativity has been identified as a skill that is at the heart of effective nursing (Good, 2002). As creativity involves risk-taking it can be a difficult skill to perform and assess during clinical practice (Kinnaird, 2004). The approach to developing nurse creativity adopted by the Faculty of Nursing is to make it a compulsory criterion in the assessment of one of the students' three assessment tasks in one of their second-year subjects. Students are provided with a hypothetical scenario to which they need to respond in a creative way. Assessment of the final assignment judges the student's level of creativity and the appropriateness of the activities for the workplace, but again the learning takes place solely in a classroom setting.

Simulated experiences such as these have a major advantage for assessing practice: the activities are performed under controlled conditions where they can be diagnosed in detail and if necessary repeated until performed successfully. Even where it is possible to observe students performing in professional settings it is not possible to assess students' performance in a complete range of situations. The range of potential contexts is simply too large to cover all contingencies and all assessment therefore has an 'inference of transferability' (Winter and Maisch, 1996). That is, a small sample of the student's overall performance is taken to represent their more general abilities (Brown et al., 1997). There is, therefore, still a need for alternatives to direct observation and portfolios which are time-consuming to assess and often poorly executed (McMartin et al., 2000).

The alternative for assessing practice identified by some lecturers has been to combine simulated work experience with writing about practice. The two examples of practice-based assignments described above have educators setting written assignments based on students' practical experiences in simulated work situations. The lecturers ask students to write about practice because they perceive that there is too little opportunity for students to undertake authentic practice before going into the workplace. Lecturers provide case-study material from real workplaces as a substitute to authentic practice which they can no longer offer their students. The purpose of the case-study material is to stimulate students to think about the ideas they encounter in their classes and consider their implications should they ever find themselves working in similar positions in a future workplace. The lecturers want the students to analyse the workplace through the examples they provided so that the students can determine what aspects are going to influence their decisions after they have graduated.

Representing a professional way of knowing

Assessment tasks involving students writing about practice in simulated work experience aim for equal standing with authentic practice. Alternative assessment types, like essays, already exist to examine students' propositional knowledge. As such, practice-based assignments typically draw on primary sources of data derived from real practice situations, often collected from case studies, projects or practice journals by students or lecturers. The assessment of the students' abilities to perform in real situations is then inferred through their engagement in an activity described in their writing (Gipps, 1994). In other words, practice-based assignments are a second-order form of performance assessment that analyses a student-crafted piece of writing about practice. They complement observations of performance by making the cognitive aspects of practice visible and thereby a consideration in the overall assessment of the student's abilities.

The cognitive component of practical knowledge that can be demonstrated through writing about practice is the student's use of practical reason. This is reasoning that is directed towards future actions which attempts to answer the question of what one should do (Bratman, 1987). Acting professionally is widely recognised as requiring more than the acquisition of a large body of technical or theoretical knowledge (Bereiter and Scardamalia, 1993; Eraut, 1994; Schön, 1983). Professionals operate in complex situations which have multiple solutions to problems, usually without the benefit of an obvious best choice. Rarely do professionals encounter discrete problems in practice and meaningful solutions have to be derived from the situatedness of the problem in a specific context. A sign of professional maturity is a shift away from decisions that are arbitrated by an external authority to one in which individuals provide their own justification for decisions (Dreyfus and Dreyfus, 1986). Perry (1999) found that students who have developed an ability to examine the issues and develop their own opinion could deal with the increased complexity of professional decision-making because they make decisions that have reasons to support them.

In addition to technical proficiency, professionals must demonstrate their capacity for a particular kind of reasoning about which actions are appropriate for a particular work situation. That is, for students to be considered to be able to act professionally in the future they need to demonstrate the ability to employ practical reason whenever they are required to select one alternative over another. Choices are professional when they serve both this goal and the moral imperative of considering the impact each alternative may have on those involved as best as the situation allows (Galotti, 2002). Clearly, this writing about practice is not performance assessment in the usual sense. Consequently, written assignments are incapable of testing the hands-on aspects of professional practice. However, writing can provide insight into students' reasoning and thought processes behind their judgements.

Redefining practice-based assignments to support future learning

When questioned on what they attend to when marking practice-based assignments, lecturers who assessed students' writing about practice agreed that they wanted students to demonstrate a commitment to professional values as they recounted their experiences of practice. Teachers would attempt to comprehend this commitment to professional actions by looking for examples where students' arguments did not match their impression of what a professional would do in a similar situation. Hence, along with intellectual and practical skills considered, the foundation of most professional education, a component of what it means to act like a professional is providing defensible reasons for action. However, some students' experiences of practice-based assignments made them feel underprepared for practice by highlighting that they have too little hands-on experience of common work situations. As such, practice-based assignments need to ensure that they do not undermine the students' long-term capacity to assess their own learning by emphasising the importance of technical skill and instead contribute to the students' cognitive ability to make good professional decisions by focusing on their reasons for their actions.

In this section, I want to counter some of the confusion that can arise from using practice-based assignments by drawing out some of the implications a focus on professional reasoning, outlined in the previous section, has for developing performance criteria for judging the quality of writing about practice. Many of the commonly used criteria for assessing written work, such as the quality of the ideas and evidence used, the development and organisation of the argument, plus the students' ability to express themselves, still apply to practice-based assignments. In addition, students must convince the marker of the rightness of their decision. With this in mind, practice-based assignments that support learning for the future must have the students demonstrate that they did not rely on an external authority in choosing what to do but were able to make their own decisions based on sound reasoning. The criteria outlined below take into account three elements lecturers who use practice-based assignments at UTS indicated were essential for high-quality student responses. They are: engaging productively with context associated with professional practice; choosing appropriate problem-solving processes; and justifying those choices.

The first criterion needed to judge students' professional performance through practice-based assignments, an ability to engage productively with context associated with the professional practice, is determined through the selection of details by which students wish to highlight their capacities as professionals. As Winter and Maisch (1996) argue, it is impossible for students to represent all aspects of the practice context, and authors of ethnographic texts are acutely aware that the observer determines what is observed (Angrosino and Mays de Perez, 2003). When writing about practice, students are being asked to tell their own stories of events and experiences that shaped their development in a professional way of thinking.

Through this narrative, students are expected to demonstrate an internalisation of professional values by describing their observations in a way that conforms to a recognisable professional identity. Dominice (2000) describes this as different from autobiography in diaries and journals in that it is commissioned by the teacher as a kind of small-scale explanatory inquiry. He calls this form of writing 'educational biography' (Dominice, 2000: 1), in which adults undertake a search for subjective meanings and developmental processes in learning. In an educational biography, the student is the subject of their own story, providing insight into what it means to become the subject of their learning situation. The voice used to represent them-selves in their text, particularly as demonstrated through the description of the features of the context and terminology used to describe these features, becomes the first part of the students' claim of professional credentials to the assessor.

The second aspect of writing about practice is choosing appropriate problem-solving processes for the situation. This demonstrates the students' ability to interpret the conditions of practice and attend to key aspects of the practice context. Lecturers indicated in interviews that students were expected to get involved in the situation, paying attention to its salient aspects. They are required to try out different approaches that go beyond the first solution that occurs to them, choosing and working with an idea until it is deemed appropriate for the situation. The students' ability to choose appropriate problem-solving processes will be based on qualities such as recognition of the problem and potential solutions, seeing implications, elaborating and extending ideas and the self-directed evaluation of the ideas. The student's description of the problem-solving processes employed needs to recognise that the conditions under which practice occur are not static (Chaiklin and Lave, 1993) and explain how the response to the context of practice was formed through an interaction between their prior experience and the prac-ticalities of the situation.

The final criterion for judging the quality of practice-based assignments relates to the justification for why the decisions made were correct. The task for students is to produce a persuasive argument for their course of action whose true outcome can never be known by the assessor. In this regard, students will draw upon a range of rhetorical devices that make practice-based assignments different from other forms of reflective writing. They will need to use persuasive language that convinces their lecturer that they understood why this was the best course of action available. In turn the assignment will be judged on the logic of the students' argument and how believably they presented their case.

Learning to act professionally for the longer term

Students admit that they learn to think differently as a result of writing about their practice. By attempting to demonstrate that they no longer need to rely on an external authority for their decisions they open up old patterns of thinking to self-analysis and begin to internalise the professional values associated with professional practice. For students to write convincingly about practice, they need to assess and weigh the practical reasons for their actions relative to the situation in which they find themselves, and ideally come to a well-supported answer about the desirability of certain actions from a professional's point of view. It is debatable whether well-formulated practical reasons will in themselves give rise to desirable actions and in the end it is only when students test their learning in an actual workplace that they will know whether writing about practice taught them to judge the value of their work and therefore contributed to their future learning.

Even though practice-based assignments do not take place directly in the workplace, lecturers interviewed about their decision to have students write about practice were convinced of their importance to students gaining hands-on work-based experience and actively relating these experiences to their academic programme. While this appears to be contradictory, when one acknowledges the cognitive dimension of practice it is possible to see how a simulated workplace does provide an opportunity for students to gain an appreciation of the influence context has on workplace decisions which is necessary for successful participation in future work. As such, well-designed practice-based assignments can play an important part in how lecturers change the way students think about themselves as professionals while they are still at university, and in the process prepare them for their future learning in the workplace.

Students show that they can make appropriate professional choices by using the kind of practical reasoning that is particularly valued in professions. University teachers who want to contribute to longer-term learning of their students through practice-based assignments need to recognise that, as students recount the reasons why their choices of problem-solving processes were the right decisions for the context, they reveal a commitment to professional values of making the best decisions for the circumstances. By writing about their practice they can display an ability to engage productively with the context, choose appropriate problem-solving processes and justify those choices as professionals do. As a result, writing about practice can provide a valuable strategy for ensuring that students possess the practical reasoning skills needed for professional learning in the long term.

Acknowledgement

I would like to thank Associate Professor Alison Lee for the assistance she provided in reviewing earlier drafts of this chapter.

References

Angrosino, M. and Mays de Perez, K. (2003) Rethinking observation: from method to context, in N. Denzin and Y. Lincoln (eds) *Collecting and Interpreting Qualitative Materials*, Thousand Oaks, CA: Sage.

Bereiter, C. and Scardamalia, M. (1993) *Surpassing Ourselves: An Inquiry into the Nature and Implications of Expertise*, Chicago, IL: Open Court.

Bratman, M. (1987) *Intention, Plans, and Practical Reason*, Cambridge, MA: Harvard University Press.

Brown, G., Bull, J. and Pendlebury, M. (1997) *Assessing Student Learning in Higher Education*, London: Routledge.

Brown, S. (1999) Assessing practice, in S. Brown and A. Glasner (eds) *Assessment Matters in Higher Education: Choosing and Using Diverse Approaches*, Buckingham: Society for Research into Higher Education and Open University Press.

Chaiklin, S. and Lave, J. (eds) (1993) *Understanding Practice*, Cambridge: Cambridge University Press.

Dominice, P. (2000) *Learning from Our Lives: Using Educational Biographies with Adults*, San Francisco: Jossey-Bass.

Dreyfus, H.L. and Dreyfus, S. (1986) *Mind over Machine*, New York: Free Press.

Eraut, M. (1994) *Developing Professional Knowledge and Competence*, London and Washington, DC: Falmer Press.

Galotti, K.M. (2002) *Making Decisions that Matter: How People Face Important Life Choices*, Mahwah, NJ: Erlbaum.

Gipps, C. (1994) *Beyond Testing: Towards a Theory of Educational Assessment*, London: Falmer Press.

Good, B. (2002) Creativity: our lifeblood, *Creative Nursing*, 8, 4: 3–4.

Kinnaird, L. (2004) Creativity at the bedside, *Creative Nursing*, 9, 4: 3–4.

McMartin, F., McKenna, A. and Youssefi, K. (2000) Scenario assignments as assessment tools for undergraduate engineering education, *IEEE Transactions on Education*, 43, 2: 111–119.

Perry, W.G. (1999) *Forms of Intellectual and Ethical Development in the College Years: A Scheme*, 2nd edn, San Francisco: Jossey-Bass.

Schön, D.A. (1983) *The Reflective Practitioner: How Professionals Think in Action*, New York: Basic Books.

Winter, R. and Maisch, M. (1996) *Professional Competence and Higher Education: The ASSET Programme*, London: Falmer Press.

Chapter 13

The contribution of sustainable assessment to teachers' continuing professional development

Margaret Kirkwood

This chapter begins by examining why assessment for lifelong learning must underpin the improvement of teachers' professional performances. Teachers must perform their professional roles within existing communities of practice, in which learning is 'socially constructed, participative, embedded and necessarily contextualised' (Boud and Falchikov, 2006: 408). Continuing professional development courses should equip teachers, as members of their practice communities, with the necessary self-assessment skills to reach informed judgements about their own performances, which improvements are necessary, and how to enact them. The development of the chapter illustrates a means of achieving this through combining, in course planning and delivery, three assessment purposes – formative, summative and sustainable. Sustainable assessment injects a longer-term perspective and thus implies a shift in emphasis or focus as opposed to an increased burden of assessment or the 'invention' of new techniques. The manner in which this is done is intended to be seamless and persuasive to participants, and to take full cognisance of the nature of their professional learning.

The Chartered Teacher Programme in Scotland provides an ideal context for exploring important issues and implications which arise when assessment for lifelong learning is made a central feature of continuing professional development courses, since the chartered teacher is expected to be committed to change, development and the improvement of professional performance (Kirk *et al.*, 2003). The Standard for Chartered Teacher is part of a new framework of professional standards for teachers (Scottish Executive Education Department, 2002). It was designed to strengthen their professional role and to raise the quality and standard of school education. It was seen as a way of recognising successful classroom practice which would serve to retain experienced teachers in the classroom rather than have them seek promotion. Consultation on how teachers should achieve chartered teacher status produced clear support for a modular programme leading to the award of a master's degree (Kirk *et al.*, 2003). A nationally co-ordinated study was conducted to pilot four 'core' modules and seven 'option' modules. The illustration in this chapter relates to one of the option modules, *Learning to Think and Thinking to Learn*.

The standard has four components: professional values and personal commitments; professional knowledge and understanding; professional and personal attributes; and professional action associated with accomplished teaching. These should be viewed as interdependent (Kirk, 2004: 12):

> the possession of knowledge without the capacity to effect professional actions of various kinds is pointless; professional action that is not informed by relevant knowledge is haphazard; and knowledge or skills that are not subjected to self-criticism constitute a recipe for professional complacency and ineffectiveness.

A key focus for teachers' self-assessments arises from the need continually to justify their professional practice within a swiftly changing educational context. There has been an increase in the pace and scale of new initiatives stemming from the National Priorities in Education which were formulated shortly after political devolution in Scotland, including integrated community schools, education for citizenship, social inclusion, raising attainment, lifelong learning and a new emphasis on teachers' continuing professional development (see Humes (2005) for a critique of the discourse surrounding these initiatives). Humes argues that teachers should not readily accept the dominant political discourse; rather, they should be prepared to critique ideas and think creatively about longer-term solutions, coming up with 'big ideas' and helping to inform thinking on alternative policy proposals. The standard embraces this philosophy; it is suggested that teachers might undertake critical evaluations of official educational documents, research reports, articles or books in relation to the current educational debates, and engage with others in the critical discussion of educational policy and practice.

Campbell *et al.* (2003) identify how the use and conduct of research by teachers have developed within a profession strongly influenced by policy, wherein an important and close link between research and classroom practice is suggested by frequent references to teaching aspiring to be an 'evidence based profession'. The standard proposes that aspiring chartered teachers should engage in professional inquiry and action research, reflect critically on research evidence and modify practice as appropriate, test whether a particular theoretical perspective applies in practice and interpret changes to education policy and practice and contribute and respond to such changes.

The above requirements extend beyond academic learning to encompass effective participation within the practice community and the systematic and sustained improvement of professional action guided by informed judgement. This has several important implications for course design. Course teams must ensure that the content of modules 'connects' to participants' professional lives and is accessible to them, while also reflecting the centrality of key theories and perspectives in the learning domain (Perkins and Blythe, 1994). They must ensure also that learning, teaching and assessment strategies are coherent and fit for purpose to support the development of understanding and critical reflection, effective participation, the improvement of professional action and the underpinning capacity to assess one's own performance in an ongoing manner.

Since teachers perform their duties within a professional milieu, their assessments of their own performances must reflect the complexity of situations in which they must put their prior learning to use and accrue new learning. In order to equip participants with the abilities to assess their own performances in a manner which takes full account of external influences and to enact effective solutions to complex problems, it is necessary for course teams to adopt teaching and assessment strategies which support the development of metacognition in all its dimensions. By this is meant the active monitoring of one's thinking and consequent regulation and orchestration of cognitive processes. Metacognition is likely to be called into play in situations that stimulate a lot of careful, highly conscious thinking, such as in novel situations where every major step you take requires planning beforehand and evaluation afterwards (Flavell, 1976).

There are important considerations beyond those of identifying the aspects of professional practice on which teachers' self-assessments can most usefully focus, or considering the implications for the design of educational programmes. Unless the prevailing climate in our universities – as the key players in award-bearing continuing professional development for teachers – is receptive to adopting a longer-term perspective when considering assessment purposes, it is unlikely that assessment for lifelong learning will become embedded into institutional policies and practices. One must also assess whether any resulting shifts in practice are manageable in terms of resource demands, particularly in relation to workload in schools (of participants and peers supporting them) and for tutor teams.

The option module: *Learning to Think and Thinking to Learn*

Content, pedagogy and learning outcomes

The design of the option module that features in this chapter has been strongly influenced by the above considerations. It is intended for teachers from across all school sectors and all subject areas. Its content is based on the pedagogical themes of developing pupils' cognitive and metacognitive skills, promoting active learning and deep understanding and attending to the emotional and social dimensions of thinking and pupils' willingness to learn.

A constructivist learning philosophy underpins the module, in relation to participants' own learning and that of their pupils. Thus the module activities promote critical reflection, active inquiry and deep approaches to learning (Biggs, 2003). An important way in which this is manifested is through prompting participants to put new knowledge to the test in the classroom, which requires them to adopt systematic strategies: for example, identifying appropriate sources of feedback and gathering and analysing evidence. Thus their self-assessment skills are called into play through the requirement to reach sound judgements on the efficacy of teaching approaches and the advancement of their own learning. The learning outcomes (see below) are indicative of the broad range and nature of module activities, which require authentic productions and collaboration with peers, both important aspects of effective participation within a community of practice (see Boud and Falchikov, 2006).

Participants are encouraged to draw out the parallels between the module content and how they themselves are learning and being assessed on the module (for example, some form of learning log is maintained by most participants as an aid to metacognitive reflection). Tutor modelling is one of the key pedagogical approaches. When modelling, the tutor demonstrates a particular strategy while also making explicit his or her reasoning. For example, why this strategy and not another? Why applied or modified in this specific way? Through these processes participants can gain valuable insights into the purposes and structure of module activities and assessment tasks.

Each learning outcome is cross-referenced to the relevant competence(s) in the Chartered Teacher Standard. The learning outcomes refer to the effective demonstration of:

- a critical understanding of current approaches and research;
- a broad range of professional skills and personal attributes, including communicating effectively, adopting a problem-solving approach, being creative and imaginative, having an open attitude to change and being systematic;

and the capacities to:

- reflect critically on and evaluate classroom and school practice;
- articulate a personal, independent and critical stance in relation to contrasting perspectives on relevant educational issues, policies and developments;
- inform teaching by personal reflection, discussion, relevant reading and research;
- effect further progress in pupils' learning and create a positive learning climate;
- contribute to enhancing the quality of the educational experience provided by the school; and
- document carefully and review learning over the duration of the module.

The learning outcomes are broadly conceived and thus emphasise the importance of *context* by way of recognising that participants will need to develop unique solutions suited to their own teaching circumstances and the learning requirements of their pupils. They promote *reflexivity* by placing an emphasis on metacognitive processes (such as reviewing learning), and by requiring participants to take account of contrasting perspectives on issues. However, it is not assumed that the learning outcomes can be objectively assessed without the need for any prior interpretation (Hussey and Smith, 2002). Thus, ample opportunities must be provided for engaging with standards and criteria and problem analysis (Boud and Falchikov, 2006).

Assessing for longer-term learning

The assessment regime

Within the assessment regime, formative, summative and sustainable assessment purposes are combined. Formative feedback is intended to shape the development and direction of participants' endeavours towards accomplishing summative tasks, in addition to aiding learning. Summative tasks involve authentic productions and working with peers. Sustainable assessment should support participants to make continuous improvements to their professional performances, and thus it demands an explicit focus being placed on the development of self-assessment skills.

The assessment regime engages participants in activities which reflect the socially situated nature of their professional learning (Boud and Falchikov, 2006). Participants examine standards and criteria, and engage in problem analysis. The issue of how one judges standards is complex since it can take years of experience to accumulate sufficient knowledge to underpin reliable judgement. Participants are encouraged actively to seek out reliable sources of feedback in order to form their judgement. Elements of module activities and assessment tasks are not fully determined in advance. Participants must therefore consider, and may seek advice on, how to pursue them in ways that will be most beneficial to their own learning and that of their pupils, and through this process develop skills in problem analysis and confidence in their own judgement. Transparency of knowledge of assessment processes is promoted through dialogue and tutor modelling. The summative tasks are intended to support a range of ways of portraying achievements, all of which are valid in terms of everyday activities within a community of practice, although within the practice community they may take on a less formal appearance. Thus the module emphasises a range of skills designed to assist participants to act autonomously and make independent judgements, thus contributing towards sustainable assessment goals. The sections below expand on these features.

Summative tasks

Summative tasks involve participants in producing a portfolio and doing a brief oral and written presentation on their classroom research. The portfolio should contain a varied compilation of evidence clearly demonstrating the participants' active and reflective engagement in relevant activities (as indicated above), leading to successful classroom applications and wider impact in the school. It is intended to foster a systematic approach to documenting one's learning and professional practice, and to serve as a prompt for ongoing reflection and self-appraisal of one's performance. The research should relate to the application of theory in the classroom setting. It is intended to provide an opportunity for participants to apply critical analysis and the techniques of systematic inquiry, and to foster a research perspective on classroom practice. Both tasks are contextualised in the workplace and cumulative in nature, providing ample opportunities for student choice and student interaction.

Engagement with standards and analysis of task requirements

Participants are required to make a personal judgement about the extent to which the evidence they include in their portfolios and accounts of their research demonstrates achievement of the learning outcomes. Thus, the responsibility for weighing up the nature and extent of any enhancements to professional performance resides initially with the student. He or she must gather the evidence (using action research) and sift it in order to reach an informed judgement, guided by advice on the general requirements for assessment evidence within the Chartered Teacher Programme (General Teaching Council for Scotland, 2004) and feedback from peers and tutors. However, the final judgement is made by tutors, and in this important respect there is a deviation from the principle that the student's own judgement should prevail. This is one of the most common areas of tension when self-assessment is linked to summative assessment and certification (Tan, 2004), since it could be argued that it disempowers students by giving tutors the final say. However, in comparison with a system in which, for example, students are directly observed by tutors in performance of their classroom roles and graded, the requirement for students to bring forward convincing evidence and arguments for external scrutiny themselves (as a researcher would do when submitting a research paper to a journal) is surely not so disempowering. In professional life, and particularly in today's climate of performativity, one's performance is regularly appraised by others.

An important consideration is preparing participants for summative assessments by building their understanding of the learning outcomes and assessment criteria. This is not a one-way process, since it also extends the tutor team's understanding of how the learning outcomes and assessment criteria might play out across varied teaching contexts. In order to assist participants to weigh up what would be suitable to include as their evidence of having met the assessment criteria, contrasting exemplars of work are presented, such as an extended, reflective response to reading which might be contrasted with a highlighter pen marked over some passages on an article with scribbled notes in the margin. Also, written prompts are inserted into module materials, such as those referring to a guided reading:

> Share your views with other participants on the questions which most interest you using the online forum. Consider whether you will include a developed response in your portfolio, and which learning outcome(s) it will demonstrate.

Or:

1. Use the online forum to share your idea for a generative topic with the group.
2. Create an opportunity to teach your topic and evaluate it. Follow the guidance.

The task of organising the portfolio and making judgements about whether the evidence it contains meets the assessment requirements overall is supported through the suggestion to participants that they should build a 'contents map', for which an exemplar is provided. (Table 13.1 provides an illustration of a typical entry.)

Table 13.1 Illustration of typical entries in the portfolio

Location of item	Title	Brief description	Learning outcomes	Source of item	Enclosures
Section 1	Thinking activity and learning logs.	Classroom application of a thinking skills activity with an S3 geography class.	(a), (b), (c), (f), (h – 4)	O.S. map. Textbook. Learning logs (my own).	Lesson materials. Sample of pupils' work and learning logs. Colleague's observations. My commentary on the lesson – evaluation and personal reflection.

Formative processes – feedback

Another important consideration is providing opportunities for participants to reflect on feedback from peers and tutors as part of a developmental process in learning. Since receiving and discussing feedback face-to-face makes demands on one's emotional reserves and may become confrontational unless managed carefully (Mutch, 2003), the creation of a supportive learning climate is vital.

Early in the module, participants peer-critique work they are considering including as assessment evidence, such as plans for lessons designed to implement a particular theoretical framework or their views on articles or policy reports they have read. They receive from tutors individual 'forward looking' formative feedback on enclosures for their portfolios (see Box 13.1), and feedback addressed collectively to the group.

An issue for tutors is the tone of feedback. Should it be authoritative, or in the style of giving a personal response to what has been read, a reflecting back to the student, such as: 'It seems to me that what you are attempting to demonstrate/ explain is . . .'? Costa and Kallick (2004) refer to dispositions for giving and receiving feedback to improve work, highlighting the importance of being a 'good

Sample portfolio enclosures: formative feedback

Learning outcome (a): The level of analysis in your responses to the questions indicates a developing understanding of the key issues. Remember that you can add other thoughts, perhaps in relation to your own attempts to teach problem solving or on Pauline's workshop . . .

Learning outcome (c): It is good that you have gathered and presented some evidence from the children . . . You didn't really comment on the quality of their work. Consider using the Lesson Record since it will prompt you to consider a range of evaluation questions.

Box 13.1 Extract of tutor feedback

listener': for example, 'I have made some comments about your work. Tell me how you understand my comments.'

Similar processes are put in train for the research dimension. It is felt by the tutor team to be important that participants build a general understanding of educational research inquiry methods, in accordance with the views of Campbell *et al.* (2003: 4):

> Teachers need to know about the basics of good research, whether or not they ever conduct their own research. They need to be able to analyse critically the research evidence that they read as part of their professional role, and to judge its findings and conclusions from a well-informed point of view.

This is not tackled in the conventional, decontextualised manner through study of textbooks on research methods or methods tutorials. Instead, in groups, participants re-examine several of the articles and reports they have read during the module in order to identify and appraise the particular research design that each incorporates. This provides the backdrop to a systematic planning process for the participants' own research, which is supported by a set of prompts covering the stages of preparation and planning, implementation, evaluation and dissemination. Participants critique their research plans in groups, and later grade three exemplars of research reports by former participants (obtained with written permission guaranteeing anonymity).

These measures may, however, be viewed by some participants or tutors as over-directive. They are especially targeted at participants who are unfamiliar with self- and peer assessment, or with portfolio assessment or doing and presenting classroom-based research, since the written assignment is a more common format on taught courses for teachers. Where participants are more experienced in these matters, they will need and be offered less support.

The case-study evidence

The case-study evidence derives from careful analysis of summative performances and the views of participants in the pilot study (see Kirkwood and MacKay (2003) for the full evaluation). The situated nature of participants' learning and its future orientation are very evident. Participants have directed their attention towards applying theoretical knowledge and congruent learning and teaching strategies, gleaned through their studies, to classroom practice, and involving school colleagues and pupils in this process. Beyond this, however, and of particular relevance to the sustainable assessment focus, are the specific or more general references to the skills and tools that are needed to accomplish this. Thus, for example, we find: 'I have to be more critical in my self-evaluation'; 'I did not have the necessary plans made. I did not appreciate the impact the course would have in the whole school'; 'We are given the tools to take matters further'. The ability of participants to appropriate assessment activities to their own ends is conveyed: 'The presentation has given me a ready-made package that I can edit or develop as my knowledge increases, that is there to share with interested colleagues.'

There follows more specific information on the participants and selected evidence to amplify the above observations.

Background on the participants and final assessment outcomes

This first cohort of nineteen participants on the pilot study was formed to reflect the overall gender balance (80 per cent female) and to contain a randomly selected proportion of applicants from different sectors (i.e., nursery, primary, secondary and special needs). Reasons for studying the module were varied: personal interest in the topic, wanting to develop as a teacher and wanting to develop pupils' skills were most frequently cited. Only three participants mentioned a desire to become a chartered teacher. Four withdrew during the module for personal reasons, three opted out of formal assessment, and, of the remaining twelve, eleven passed the module.

Selection of evidence from assessed work, questionnaires and focus-group interviews

Participants' portfolios and research accounts contained rich and varied evidence of successful attempts to embed new pedagogical approaches into their own teaching, successful collaborations with school colleagues, reflective diaries, critiques of published articles and reports, and screenshots of their online discussions with other course participants. Participants included many short vignettes of 'shifts in practice' or made statements to that effect, such as:

> Do you think this is relevant to the world about us? . . . Very often they [your pupils] think of how it's relevant in a way that you haven't, which is totally

surprising and delightful. And I think I'm very careful to always make it clear it is a culture of there's no failure, you're better to have a go at it, it really doesn't matter [if you get it wrong]. That's why we're here, to learn.

My pupils are being challenged to think all the time now.

I always did evaluate my teaching systematically but my teaching is now more varied and experimental and therefore I have to be more critical in my self-evaluation.

Participants discussed the impact on their own pupils' learning and the wider impact of the module: 'Several other members of staff have commented on the thinking abilities of my class recently, including my headteacher.'

Participants illustrated how their ideas on learning were shaped and influenced through wider reading and discussion: 'While I agree with most of [David] Perkins' arguments, I think that it may be advantageous to teach the thinking skills separately and subsequently apply them in separate disciplines.'

Participants indicated how their own perspective on teaching had altered significantly: 'Teachers have not been allowed to think in the present climate and this module gave the confidence to use the skills and experience I have gained over the years to promote better thinking and learning in my class'; 'Taken me down a "different" route – which I find much more satisfying'.

Opinions on how the module was assessed were favourable. When assessing their own performance: 'It was a great help to have specific outcomes to work to'; 'I wasn't used to doing this but it was very useful'; 'A lot of time and effort required, but nothing intrinsically difficult'; and 'Time consuming but a worthwhile exercise as [it] provided knowledge of the system being used to assess the CT modules'. On the choice of summative instruments: 'Arduous, but the best method'; 'needed to do justice to the amount of work that I had done'; and 'both are vital to assess the module'. On portfolios: '[A] very useful tool, in gaining understanding of how my learning has developed through trying out and recording of practical activities coupled with responding to research articles.' On their research: 'My class really benefited from the intervention'; '[It] encouraged me to think through in detail, and summarise the most salient aspects of the course to share with colleagues'; and 'The presentations were particularly useful in encapsulating the range of methods used by colleagues to make thinking visible'.

Participants explained the different ways in which they were attempting to embed new approaches more widely into their workplace settings. One participant working in the Hospital Education and Home Tuition Service said: 'Discussed informally, with a clinical psychologist, art therapist and teaching colleague, the possibility of developing a special interest group, based on a philosophical approach to learning . . . Produced a number of graphical organisers on disc, available for the use of other staff members, as well as myself. These will be extended and modified.'

Issues and implications

Careful consideration of the case-study evidence has led to the following issues and implications being identified. (The discussion takes account of the wider institutional context of the university.)

Additional demands on participants and tutors

Boud (2000) asserts that assessments must do 'double duty', serving formative and summative purposes simultaneously, for the practical reason that higher education tutors (and students) cannot devote time and attention to each separately. Timely and effective formative feedback during the module should in principle lead to more productive learning and ultimately to fewer headaches for participants and assessors with respect to the quality of the summative evidence that eventually comes forward. It makes sense to design an assessment regime in which performances are cumulative and shaped over time, enabling formative feedback to be enacted during study.

Some participants have commented on the arduous and time-consuming nature of assessments. Apart from time spent implementing new approaches in the classroom, most of this work was done in the participants' own time. Both assessment tasks required participants to begin preparations early and to add cumulatively to the evidence, whereas with more traditional, essay-format assignments some participants leave preparations until the end. Furthermore, the explicit emphasis on developing self-assessment skills meant that assessment was foregrounded.

In the light of favourable comments from participants about the intrinsic worth of the assessments, a sensible resolution to this issue would be to create a double module while leaving the assessment demands unaltered. An alternative would be to assess either participants' portfolios or research accounts formatively using a combination of self-, peer and tutor assessment, thus shifting some of the assessment burden from tutors and reducing the summative assessment demands on participants.

In general, it would seem to be desirable to make gradual, incremental shifts in instructional strategies resulting from the injection of a third assessment purpose, and to monitor their impact on student learning and tutor and student workload closely.

Barriers encountered in the workplace and recommendations for good practice

A minority of participants encountered barriers to implementing new approaches. Some discovered there was limited scope for new developments in their school, resulting from a prescribed and content-packed syllabus and teaching plan and/or a school development plan which was dictated by national and local priorities and which could not easily accommodate any additional developments. Others experienced a lack of individual autonomy, resistance from certain colleagues, or little practical support for their research because the school management or colleagues were too busy to provide it: 'My head[teacher] was completing a portfolio . . . My colleague was on the other CT module. This limited the support which I could normally expect from my colleagues.'

The creation of more favourable circumstances in schools for teachers to develop their practice creatively and to make use of the self-assessment skills they have practised during their studies is important for sustainability. Increased participation of field professionals in module and course accreditation and review procedures, and in delivery, could enable the implications of sustainable assessment practices to be worked through in partnership with academics.

A related issue is how sustainable participants' self-assessment skills will prove to be in subsequent modules. This raises important course-related issues such as whether subsequent modules afford sufficient opportunities for participants to practise these skills and to enact feedback. The need for course-wide planning is evident.

Combining and reconciling different assessment purposes

The development of the abilities to inform one's teaching through reading and research and to justify professional practice has been supported by a broad range of pedagogical and assessment strategies, as outlined above. In particular, participants responded well to being encouraged to play an active role in shaping the assessment processes and assessing their own progress in learning throughout the module. An important consideration has been striking a balance between supporting participants and encouraging them to be independent, and guiding participants and encouraging them to be creative and to use their own ideas. Tutors emphasised that participants would need to generate imaginative solutions clearly targeted at their own pupils' learning needs, requiring participants to modify ideas and approaches. They presented contrasting examples of approaches. As a result, participants became more willing to experiment and take risks.

The potentially sustainable nature of the abilities and artefacts which participants have developed through taking part in the module is both apparent to and valued by them. This longer-term perspective appears to have had a motivating influence on most participants.

The boundary between pedagogical strategies and assessment strategies has become blurred as an inevitable consequence of the increased focus on formative and sustainable assessment, both of which foreground learning purposes. A clear implication is the need for researchers who are interested primarily in assessment questions to work more closely with those whose main leaning is towards pedagogical questions.

Scope for innovation in course design and flexibility for tutor teams and participants

This was a new module within a new course and national programme, offering fresh possibilities in terms of course design and delivery. In different circumstances, it may be much harder to inject a third assessment purpose, sustainable assessment, into an existing course or programme, where one might anticipate resistance from those staff and participants who are comfortable with the status quo.

While, overall, it can be concluded that sustainable assessment can indeed contribute towards preparing teachers to meet future challenges and enabling them to improve their professional practice, and that it is not incompatible with the current model of teachers' continuing professional development in Scotland, this cannot be stated as a general conclusion that would apply in all circumstances to all teachers. The standard offers a seemingly appropriate set of learning targets and considerable flexibility in how these can be overtaken, thus presenting fewer restrictions to course teams and offering more scope for participants to plan their own learning than might be the case if a different set of professional standards had to be addressed.

The university practice of specifying learning outcomes in course documentation in advance (which has become the common practice in UK universities) does create some restrictions; provision cannot be readily tailored for particular cohorts and participants cannot negotiate different learning targets. Thus, in this important respect the idea of building learner agency could not be explored to its fullest extent.

Conclusion

This chapter has argued that self-assessment must underpin the improvement of teachers' professional performance, and therefore continuing professional development courses must be designed with sustainable assessment at their core. It has highlighted a range of learning, teaching and assessment strategies which were successfully combined in the delivery of a postgraduate module for experienced teachers in order to meet this objective. Arising from this are a number of important issues which extend beyond the boundaries of the design of individual postgraduate modules. The socially situated character of teachers' learning, which is typically embedded in everyday tasks and contexts (Boud and Falchikov, 2006), demands that attention be given to forming closer partnerships between academics and field professionals in order to create better support for participants' learning. A planned, systematic and sustained approach to building self-assessment skills for lifelong learning must be adopted to effect the desired improvements in teachers' professional actions. Teachers themselves have a vital role to play in formulating and shaping the approach. Pedagogical and assessment strategies should no longer be considered in isolation by course teams or researchers.

References

Biggs, J. (2003) *Teaching for Quality Learning at University*, Maidenhead: Open University Press.

Boud, D. (2000) Sustainable assessment: rethinking assessment for the learning society, *Studies in Continuing Education*, 22, 2: 151–167.

Boud, D. and Falchikov, N. (2006) Aligning assessment with long-term learning, *Assessment and Evaluation in Higher Education*, 31, 4: 399–413.

Campbell, A., Freedman, E., Boulter, C. and Kirkwood, M. (2003) *Issues and Principles in Educational Research for Teachers*, Southwell: BERA.

Costa, A.L. and Kallick, B. (2004) *Assessment Strategies for Self-Directed Learning*, Thousand Oaks, CA: Corwin Press.

Flavell, J.H. (1976) Metacognitive aspects of problem solving, in L.B. Resnick (ed.) *The Nature of Intelligence*, Hillsdale, NJ: Erlbaum.

General Teaching Council for Scotland (2004) *Achieving the Standard for Chartered Teacher: Guidance for Schools* (available at: www.gtcs.org.uk/cpd [accessed 6 September 2004]).

Humes, W. (2005) The discourse of community in educational policy, *Education in the North*, 12: 6–13.

Hussey, T. and Smith, P. (2002) The trouble with learning outcomes, *Active Learning in Higher Education*, 3, 3: 220–233.

Kirk, G. (2004) The chartered teacher: a challenge to the profession in Scotland, *Education in the North*, 11: 10–17.

Kirk, G., Beveridge, W. and Smith, I. (2003) *Policy and Practice in Education: The Chartered Teacher*, Edinburgh: Dunedin Academic Press.

Kirkwood, M. and MacKay, E. (2003) *Evaluation of Learning to Think and Thinking to Learn: A Pilot Study of an Option Module for the Scottish Chartered Teacher Programme*, Glasgow: University of Strathclyde Faculty of Education.

Mutch, A. (2003) Exploring the practice of feedback to students, *Active Learning in Higher Education*, 4, 1: 24–38.

Perkins, D. and Blythe, T. (1994) Putting understanding up front, *Educational Leadership*, 51, 5: 4–7.

Scottish Executive Education Department (2002) *The Standard for Chartered Teacher* (available at: www.teachinginscotland.com [accessed 6 September 2004]).

Tan, K.H.K. (2004) Does student self-assessment empower or discipline students?, *Assessment and Evaluation in Higher Education*, 29, 6: 651–662.

Chapter 14

Developing assessment for informing judgement

David Boud and Nancy Falchikov

At the start of this book, we proposed that a new discourse of assessment in higher education is required and that it should focus on the key organising idea of informing judgement. We suggested that there is a need for a way of discussing assessment that draws attention to its educational features rather than its regulatory ones. The notion of informing judgement is not just a rhetorical intervention into debates about teaching, learning and assessment but an idea that aims to change current assessment practice to give a sharper educational focus. However, it is not sufficient to focus on the ways we talk about assessment alone. New sets of practices and ways of organising assessment need to be developed in order to enact this way of thinking. The kinds of assessment activity in which staff and students engage will need to shift in emphasis.

The prominence we give to judgement is echoed throughout the book. Barnett (Chapter 3), for example, views judgement as a central feature of academic life. He argues that 'judgemental space' characterises higher education, and is the price, or the value, of participating in academic life. He argues persuasively that we may achieve what he terms 'authentic being' through judgement, and sees assessment as necessary to help students enter into academic life by ensuring they have met standards. Students, he asserts, need to develop a capacity to 'live well with questioning'. In a case-study account of continuing professional development for experienced teachers, Kirkwood (Chapter 13) also stresses the importance of informed judgement, a process learned and practised through many activities, such as problem analysis, gathering evidence, seeking and selecting feedback. She acknowledges that the art of making judgements is complex, as it can take years of experience to accumulate enough knowledge to underpin reliable judgement.

Current assessment practice comes under criticism in many chapters. Kvale (Chapter 5), in discussing socio-political issues in assessment, both highlights the contradictions present in the practice and suggests reasons why beneficial innovative practices are not more widely used. He identifies some educational consequences of the knowledge economy and explores what he deems to be the role of traditional education in discouraging lifelong learning, calling for a focus on 'life-wide and lifelong learning'. Barnett (Chapter 3) similarly critiques current assessment practices, asking whether assessment actually discourages the development of appropriate qualities in our students. In Chapter 11 we discussed the impact of unintended consequences of being assessed, focusing particularly on emotional effects. Ecclestone (Chapter 4) reminded us of the importance of the context in which learning and assessment take place, discussing different 'assessment identities' and 'assessment careers' and their impact on achievement.

Some contributors have provided suggestions about how we may start to work to achieve our goals for better assessment practice, and several have taken Biggs's (2003) appeal for constructive alignment as a stimulus to their own discussions. Kvale (Chapter 5), for example, concurs with Dochy and his colleagues (Chapter 7) in believing that the alignment of assessment, learning and instruction is one of the most important issues in educational innovation in recent years. Dochy *et al.* themselves discussed constructive alignment in terms of 'assessment engineering', while Barnett (Chapter 3) discussed alignment at the level of the individual learner, arguing that we want students to align themselves with their own claims. He also submitted that we need a 'curriculum for authentic becoming' in which 'the power of summative assessments to humiliate and subject students might be vanquished'.

Knight (Chapter 6) investigated the relationship between what he termed 'warranting', or certifying achievement, and future learning. While acknowledging the unintended consequences of current warranting practices, he maintained that warranting is a professional necessity. However, he proposed a 'new account of warranting' in which experts continue to judge 'mundane' achievements as now, but also test evidence supplied by students to support their claims regarding complex achievements. In addition, he recommended that the quality of the learning environment rather than the achievements themselves might better fall under official scrutiny. Hounsell (Chapter 8) argued that feedback, presently accorded a Cinderella status within higher education, should be seen as an invaluable end in itself, beyond as well as within the university. He emphasised the importance of 'congruence' between feedback and learning outcomes. In Chapter 3, Barnett argued that higher education is a matter of the development of human qualities and dispositions, of modes of being, as well as of knowledge, understanding and skills. He asserted that standards are inherent in the fields and practices in which students are engaged and that there can be no escape from those standards or from being judged according to them. He pointed to the tension between the journey towards 'increasing authenticity' and adherence to standards, between increasing singularity and increasing collectivity.

Several chapters documented recent innovations in assessment that have a part to play in our venture to rethink assessment for future learning. Some contributors looked at the involvement of students in assessment. Falchikov (Chapter 10) presented an account of the role peers have in learning and assessment in higher education. Tan (Chapter 9) investigated the role of self-assessment in promoting lifelong learning through the development of skills 'to conduct and evaluate learning, self-direction and responsibility for learning'. Other contributors focused on the assessment tasks themselves. Portfolios came under scrutiny in a consideration of the contribution of sustainable assessment to teachers' continuing professional development by Kirkwood (Chapter 13), while Kandlbinder (Chapter 12) presented an account of practice-oriented assessment in higher education.

In this concluding chapter, we bring together many ideas discussed throughout the book. We raise questions about what a focus on informing judgement implies and propose a framework for thinking about how assessment practices can be established across entire programmes to build capacity for students to become judges of their own learning. The chapter focuses on what we identify as key elements in the process of creating opportunities for developing evaluative expertise. It starts by reviewing the arguments we have used about the need for aligning assessment with longer-term learning and what these imply for the intermediate steps needed to produce this outcome. It goes on to identify the key elements and illustrates these with respect to a range of current assessment activities. Next, it discusses a framework for the selection of tasks to guide the development of learners' capacity to make increasingly sophisticated judgements. These need to be applied over a wide range of subject matter and at different levels of a course. We argue that it is necessary to view assessment practices throughout a programme as a whole if capacities for effective judgement are to be systematically developed.

Ways of thinking about assessment practices

In earlier writing we have identified both everyday assessment practices and ways of thinking about these practices that stimulate the development of learning for the longer term (Boud and Falchikov, 2005 and 2006; Falchikov and Boud, forthcoming). Here we draw on and reframe some of these ideas, but for the sake of clarity of exposition do not separately reference ourselves.

In thinking about building students' evaluative capacity it is necessary to consider both the assessment components of courses and teaching and learning activities. While these have been conventionally separated, they must be viewed together if students are to learn about assessment and if assessment is to support their learning. So while we might emphasise assessment tasks, these tasks may not be ones undertaken for purposes of generating marks and grades; they may be located within the space of lectures and tutorials. Similarly, what occurs in teaching includes the modelling of making judgements and making explicit how ideas from the literature have influenced judgements being made now. Students hopefully see experienced practitioners – their lecturers – thinking through the problems and issues that confront them in the subject and explaining them in ways that reveal those features it is necessary to attend to if the subject is to be understood and practised well. We have placed great value on transparency, in terms of making explicit procedures, standards and criteria. Transparency not only invites analysis of task structure and purpose but fosters consideration of the epistemology of learning embedded in tasks; that is, the nature of what is needed to appreciate and execute the tasks.

Building evaluative capacity involves not only exposure to models but opportunities for practice. Making judgements is an engaging act; it is not sufficient to 'know about' making judgements and be able to answer questions about how other people do it. Like any other form of practice, it is a skilful activity that is embodied and involves more than the intellect (Dreyfus and Dreyfus, 2005). Students need to desire to make good judgements not only because they themselves will be judged on this, but because it is a part of becoming an accomplished and effective professional. This can mean that it is easier to embed processes and activities to promote developing judgement into programmes that have an obvious point of external reference than into those that do not. Access to the world of practice enables students to see that the tasks in which they are involved have standards that go beyond what they might otherwise see as arbitrary requirements of the course and that, if they aspire to be practitioners, they must appropriate these standards for themselves and develop ways of ensuring that their judgements meet them.

In most areas, practice is not something that can take place in isolation as a purely individual act. It is socially constructed and often occurs in settings with other people, including practitioners and clients (Schwandt, 2005). This leads to a further important consideration: the role of peers in developing judgement. In some ways the role of teachers is akin to that of clients: they 'commission' the work that students do and give final approval through marking and grading. Peers take the surrogate role of other practitioners who, in most professional settings, are involved in being consulted during the process of formation and offer their views about the work as it unfolds. Their comments are vital in the initial expressing and testing of ideas and of refining judgement about what is involved in any given task. That this occurs informally should not lead us to underestimate the importance of this aspect of the activity. We have emphasised the importance of students working with their peers for a number of other reasons (Falchikov, 2005; Boud *et al.*, 2001). Working with peers involves students necessarily expressing what they know and this fosters the linking of new knowledge to what is already known. Learning with peers also encourages the judging of progression towards goals (testing new knowledge) as well as self-monitoring and reflexivity.

We have advocated that assessment practices involve what we have termed 'authentic' representations and productions. This means that students can gain experience in distinguishing tasks from often distracting contextual features and relevant cues from the complexity of the settings in which tasks are embedded. This may involve learners creating their own assessment tasks and it provides them with opportunities to appropriate assessment activities to their own ends. Activities used in authentic assessment include the use of 'real-life' tasks, exhibitions, interviews, journals, observations, oral presentations, performances, portfolios and patchwork texts and simulations. Dierick and Dochy (2001) argue that students rate assignments such as projects, group exercises and peer assessment as meaningful because they are authentic.

We see value in students engaging with communities of practice and with the ways in which knowledge is represented. In workplaces, learning is a part of participating in work, not something that is acquired and represented as a possession of the learner (Sfard, 1998). It is a part of everyday activities and is an adjunct to, and necessary part of, almost everything that we do. In other words, assessment can be usefully conceptualised in terms of participation in practice (see Lave and Wenger, 1991). Rømer (2002), in developing Lave and Wenger's work, argues that once learning has occurred, the learner is able to participate more competently or more fully in the communities of practice that occur within a profession. However, students are not always clear about the community of practice, and therefore the community of judgement, with which they should be identifying. Community activities are not necessarily clear and the pathways from peripheral to full participation are often obscure.

While feedback is an essential component of the process of developing assessment autonomy (see Chapter 8), feedback in itself is not sufficient. Indeed, feedback that focuses students' attention on the idiosyncratic requirements of a given teacher may inhibit the development of judgement. When teachers act as surrogates for the variety of sources of feedback that may be found in a given community of judgement and are seen by students as acting in this way, feedback can be extremely valuable. We have been particularly impressed by one of Sadler's observations about feedback: that is, there has to be evidence that information on their work provided to students has been subsequently utilised, otherwise it is impossible to conclude that feedback has occurred (Sadler, 1989). Too often information is provided to students without the feedback loop being completed. It is therefore impossible to tell if it has been worthwhile. Informed judgement also requires the testing of what has been learned through resort to evidence (e.g., Osborne and Wittrock, 1983; Jonassen et al., 1999). Feedback may come from many places: peers, teachers, practitioners, clients and so on.

We have identified many higher education assessment practices that provide learners with beneficial learning experiences. Some provide learners with experiences in identifying critical aspects of problems and issues along with requisite knowledge to address them (e.g., Angelo and Cross, 1993). Others give them opportunities to identify, develop and engage with criteria and standards. A common example of this is often associated with self- and peer assessment (e.g., Chapters 10 and 9; Falchikov 2005: ch. 5). Peer learning and peer assessment are good examples of practices that involve other people in a learner's development. They involve learners in giving and receiving feedback from a variety of sources: self, peers, teachers, employers and other parties external to the educational institution (Boud et al., 1999 and 2001: Falchikov, 2001). They also help the development of other skills, such as listening and diplomacy.

As it stands, the corpus of work discussed above presents a smorgasbord of good ideas, any one of which might be found in any current course. However, a greater degree of consistency within the activities experienced by students is needed to have a major impact on their development. Therefore, the individual elements need to be combined. Biggs (2003) has discussed this as 'constructive alignment' and has, like many others before him, advocated the design of fully integrated programmes in which teaching methodologies, learning outcomes and assessment strategies all work in harmony. However, it is necessary to look beyond the immediate context of higher education that Biggs has emphasised: alignment with future needs is also required.

A scheme for developing assessment skills for future learning

How can some of these ideas be combined to produce fully integrated programmes? Simply incorporating attractive features into any given course unit is unlikely in itself to satisfy the requirement for students to build judgement capacity over time. Also, we do not believe that an assessment skill developed in the context of one subject area necessarily transfers to others. The standards and criteria to be applied in any given type of work need to be understood in their own terms. For example, what constitutes good scholarly writing in one subject discipline is not necessarily identical to that for another. The development of evaluative expertise therefore needs to occur throughout a programme of study and across the different subject areas and learning outcomes expected for it. We propose a scheme for thinking about the organising of tasks to promote the development of students' ability to make increasingly sophisticated judgements about learning. The aim of this scheme is to emphasise the importance of building evaluative expertise across courses and programmes and ensuring it is integrated throughout. While the elements of this scheme may be seen as stages, the nature of the development involved means that judgement capability does not build linearly but through cycling through different tasks and returning to previous tasks when confronted with new domains of learning. While we are cautious about claims for the transferability of skills, we believe that by having sufficiently future-oriented activities in a variety of contexts, the chances of building judgement will be enhanced.

The key elements of this scheme are as follows:

1. Identifying self as an active learner.
2. Identifying own level of knowledge and the gaps in this; finding ways of moving from what is known to what it is desirable to know.
3. Practising testing and judging.
4. Developing judgement skills over time.
5. Embodying reflexivity and commitment.

These elements are set out in Figure 14.1. Note that they are represented as overlapping each other in a regular fashion. While there may be a tendency towards the order as shown, it is rarely as neat and progressive as this! Some elements may deviate from the suggested order and others may permeate the developmental process. For example, what we have labelled as element 5 (embodying reflexivity and commitment) must be present at some level throughout the process of developing independent assessment skills, and, similarly, practising testing and

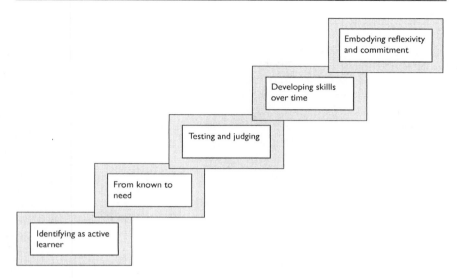

Figure 14.1 Elements of informed judgement

judging (element 3) are required throughout. In our scheme, unless students see themselves in the role of 'learner', they are unlikely to be concerned with knowledge or lack of it. Unless knowledge is valued and unless they have the desire to move from the known to the unknown, or to improve their own skill level, there is no need for them to test and judge themselves. Therefore, a minimum level of engagement must be present for judgement to develop.

Steps towards promoting students' informed judgement

Element 1: Identifying oneself as an active learner

Before students can begin to take responsibility for testing and judging themselves and their own performance, they need to see themselves first as learners and second as active learners. It might seem odd to imply that students might not see themselves as learners, but there are situations in which those whom external parties might identify as learners do not view themselves in this role. In the workplace, as we have observed, this may present a problem, and many people learning at work do not identify with this role and may even reject it (Boud and Solomon, 2001 and 2003). However, in our role as teachers, we can encourage students to see themselves as learners and legitimate this role by valuing their engagement with learning tasks. Depending on their prior learning careers, however, students may not see the need to be *active* learners. This can occur when they have been tightly coached in school with respect to closely specified curricula or have been sufficiently able to cruise through earlier assessment tasks without giving them their full attention. If they see learning as a task of engaging with what is put before them, they may not develop the disposition to be judges of their learning outside the narrowly defined realm of packaged material. An important part of university courses is to have tasks and learning activities constructed so as to render learning, and the need for learning beyond the given, visible, as we have discussed earlier (see Shulman, 2000; Hounsell, 1987).

It is possible to design authentic representations and productions with which learners can more readily identify as relevant for their anticipated future practice (see Torrance, 1995; Goldfinch *et al.*, 1999). These can emphasise the importance of context and encourage learners to recognise that solutions vary according to context by designing learning and assessment tasks which are themselves varied and located in a diversity of settings. Most importantly, students should be treated in all interactions as active players without whose involvement in organising their own learning nothing will occur.

Element 2: Identifying one's own level of knowledge and the gaps in this

Any kind of judgement requires that learners be able to discern variation and identify key features of concepts being learned (see Bowden and Marton, 1998). Practice in discernment is therefore one of the features of developing judgement. Learners need to find ways of moving from what they know to what they deem desirable to know. This apparently simple statement involves a complex set of developments: learners need to assess their level of knowledge; they need to understand what they are aiming to achieve in terms of longer-term goals and then address the question of how this may be achieved. Sadler (1989 and 1998), among others, as mentioned previously, has advocated that learners develop evaluative expertise, and currently students may be found assessing their own learning or that of their peers (see Chapters 9 and 10). In the workplace, one's supervisor or colleagues can supply pointers. In either context, we recognise that judgement does not come fully formed and that staging is needed to develop expertise.

Learners need to find ways of building from what they know to what they don't know. We value the work of Vygotsky and the neo-Vygotskians (Vygotsky, 1978; Bliss *et al.*, 1996; Hogan and Pressley, 1997) on scaffolding of knowledge in this context. We can only hope to help students develop capacity for judgements if we know where they are starting from and help them build from there (as Ecclestone argued in Chapter 4). If we are not conscious of the extent to which students are able to form their own judgements, then we cannot devise strategies to move them further. We can encourage learning by scaffolding knowledge by means of teaching approach (e.g., Pata *et al.*, 2005) or by making the role of students within course units clear and coherent (e.g., Seidel *et al.*, 2005).

Vygotsky's concept of the zone of proximal development (ZPD), created 'as a metaphor to assist in explaining the way in which social and participatory learning takes place', is often invoked by those concerned to improve student learning. Vygotsky defined the ZPD as the difference between a learner's 'actual development level as determined by independent problem-solving' and the level of 'potential development as determined through problem-solving under adult guidance or in collaboration with more capable peers' (Vygotsky, 1978: 86). Creation of a ZPD through negotiation between a more advanced partner and the learner characterises many 'new' assessment schemes, rather than a 'one-way' process of scaffolding. Kvale (Chapter 5 and 2006) advocates the application of the principles of apprenticeship learning to this end. According to Collins *et al.* (1991), in traditional apprenticeships, the expert shows the apprentice how to do a task. The apprentice observes and then practises the skills. The master gradually turns over more and more responsibility to the apprentice, who is eventually able to carry out the task independently.

Element 3: Practising testing and judging

Testing and judging involves application of research and analytic skills, as well as application of standards and criteria and resort to evidence (e.g., Ramaprasad, 1983; Butler and Winne, 1995; Boud, 1995). These applications form the next stage in the developmental journey towards lasting assessment expertise. Testing and judging activities form a step towards active participation in one's own learning, helping to develop active learners and learner agency. In terms of preparation for a lifetime of self-assessment, particularly beneficial to learners is the act of choosing and applying appropriate assessment activities and evaluative tasks to one's own work (e.g., Woodward, 1998; Winter, 2003).

Feedback from a variety of sources is crucial to the development of evaluative expertise (see Chapter 8), whether in the workplace or the higher education classroom. Standards and criteria provide a 'baseline' against which the learner can measure his or her own achievements, and practice applying these to educational processes or products has been advocated widely as a means of encouraging learner engagement (e.g., Dierick and Dochy, 2001). Peers constitute another rich source of information in the search for feedback (e.g., Falchikov, 2001 and 2005).

Element 4: Developing these skills over time

Learners need to practise and develop skills of testing and judging, but they also need to develop confidence in their judgements and acknowledge compromise of judgements by surrounding circumstances (see Kahnemann *et al.*, 1982). Courses can help in this respect by designing tasks to encourage students to be confident of what they know or do not know (see Ewers and Searby, 1997). Similarly, elements of tasks should not be fully determined so as to provide opportunities for learners to take the initiative and consider risk (e.g., Beck, 1992; Giddens, 1991). Desirable assessment practice focuses on producing rather than reproducing knowledge and fostering systematic inquiry. Independent assessors need opportunities for taking the initiative in order to develop both their ability to consider risk and confidence in their own judgements. Learning and assessment should be integrated over time and courses.

Element 5: Embodying reflexivity and commitment

As we have already argued, fostering awareness of personal and professional practice begins as soon as learners begin the process of judgement – as the first element of our scheme when students commit to the role of learner. However, awareness and reflexivity are likely to become refined and to develop with continued practice. In fact, it can be argued that this step can never be completed, as learning is not a finite activity.

Developing the skill of being an informed judge of one's own learning is not simply cognitive. Like all expertise, it requires conscious volition, and it is embodied in the person of the learner. It is not the kind of skill that once acquired can be called on at will in every new circumstance. It is a form of what Aristotle discussed as 'practical wisdom', or phronesis. In terms of Dreyfus and Dreyfus's (2005) views about developing expertise, practical wisdom forms the stage beyond *expertise* and *mastery* and is about developing the style of the culture of experts that involves how the student 'encounters himself or herself, other people, and things' (Dreyfus 2001: 47). It provides a background that makes further learning possible: that is, 'the general ability to do the appropriate thing, at the appropriate time, in the appropriate way' (Dreyfus, 2001: 48). It is impossible to operationalise this in ways that might occur for other elements because it is always embodied.

The five elements that make up our scheme for helping develop informed judgements are further elaborated in Table 14.1. The elements depict ways of thinking about everyday teaching and learning or assessment practices that emphasise preparation for learning that is socially constructed, participative, embedded and necessarily contextualised. In the central column, 'What tasks may be involved?', we list some ways in which development within and towards stages may be encouraged.

Implications for the design of programmes

While each of these features of assessment discussed above can play a part in helping learners develop informed judgement, individual initiatives cannot achieve this end on their own. A major barrier to the implementation of these ideas is the fragmentation of the curriculum in higher education, especially of assessment. This has led to the detailed design and execution of assessment tasks often being considered only by the person responsible for each unit of study and seldom, unless seen as obviously deviant or unfair, being subject to review. A more systematic approach is necessary if skills in judgement are to be built over time and across the curriculum. The major implication of this approach is the need for integration of various kinds. There are three main aspects to this.

Integration of assessment with teaching and learning

Teaching acts help inform students' judgements, and assessment activities are also *de facto* learning tasks, whatever else they may be. This implies a need to move from the (often inappropriate) separation between teaching and learning activities, on the one hand, and assessment activities, on the other. For example, inclusion of modelling of good practice and discussion of criteria and standards of good work become legitimate parts of teaching and learning activities, and assessment tasks that are learning activities in their own right become legitimate assessment activities.

Integration across different course units

As we have suggested earlier, responsibility for the development of assessment for informing judgement cannot solely reside in a single course unit or even group of units. It is a notion that crosses every programme. Therefore, a holistic view of assessment needs to be taken in which the contributions of each unit of study to the whole are considered. Our experience suggests that students are already aware of this need. A major challenge of this view is to establish the desire to work across course units and to find ways for those responsible for each to co-operate in co-ordination. This is a major challenge to traditional approaches to course organisation that is already being prompted by new quality-assurance procedures. It is necessary to go beyond the monitoring and taking account of student satisfaction across courses to focus on integration of activities, particularly assessment. The concerns that students often express about assessment overload and the coincidence of multiple assessment tasks in different units provide the opening for a deeper engagement with the integration of developing judgements we discuss here.

Knowledge and skill are aggregated into bodies of knowledge, disciplines and areas of professional practice. As we have noted, development of judgement in one sub-area does not necessarily transfer into others. In other words, in spite of there being generic skills and expertise common to any undergraduate programme, becoming a graduate in a given area involves acquiring the knowledge and skills that go with the knowledge groupings associated with the degree programme and developing the capacity to make judgements associated with it. However, all programmes are collections of particular subject-matter that form a starting point for developing expertise in a given domain. Major examples across programmes, with the notable exception of Alverno College (Mentkowski and associates, 2000), are still relatively uncommon.

Table 14.1 What are the aspects of learning that constitute or lead to informed judgements?

Element	What tasks may be involved?	Examples of sources
1. Identifying self as active learner	Construct tasks and learning activities to be transparent and render learning visible Invite analysis of task structure and purpose Foster consideration of the epistemology of learning embedded in tasks Introduce tasks in ways that draw attention to how they are constructed Design authentic representations and productions Identify and use communities of practice to assist in developing criteria for good work and peer feedback Construct tasks to reflect forms of activity in professional practice commensurate with level of skill possessed (i.e., ensure high level of authenticity) Focus on tasks that involve producing rather than reproducing knowledge (foster systematic inquiry) Implement participatory and active approaches; build learner agency and construct active learners Involve learners in creating aspects of assessment tasks Provide opportunities for learners to appropriate assessment activities to their own ends (e.g., portfolio construction, patchwork text)	Collins et al., 1991 Shulman, 2000 Torrance, 1995 Brew, 2006 Woodward, 1998; Winter, 2003
2. Moving from what is known to what needs to be known	Recognise that judgement does not come fully formed and that staging is needed to develop expertise. Scaffold knowledge and assessment expertise Foster engagement with standards and criteria and problem analysis Involve peers and others Emphasise importance of context Locate issues in a context that must be taken into account Identify aspects of context that must be considered Decide on what aspects of work require feedback from others in the context	Vygotsky 1978; Bliss et al., 1996; Hogan and Pressley, 1997; Dochy, 2001 Dierick and Dochy, 2001 Falchikov, 2001 Lave and Wenger, 1991; Wenger, 1998

Category	Description	Reference
	Locate knowledge in local practice (situated learning and communities of practice)	
	Work collaboratively with practitioners and other parties external to the educational institution	Goldfinch et al., 1999
	Involve engagement with communities of practice and ways in which their knowledge is represented	
	Encourage discernment of variation: key features of concepts being learned	Bowden and Marton, 1998
3. Practice in testing and judging	Apply research and analytical skills; resort to evidence	Boud, 1995
	Practise self-assessment	Ramaprasad, 1983; Butler and Winne, 1995; Falchikov, 1996;
	Widen and utilise types and sources of evidence of learning	Black and Wiliam, 1998;
	Encourage seeking of feedback from many sources, including practice settings, literature and research	Sadler, 1998; Hounsell, 2003; Kahnemann et al., 1982
4. Developing assessment skills over time	Consider risk and confidence of judgement	
	Provide scope for taking initiative (e.g., always taking the safe option is not encouraged)	Ewers and Searby, 1997
	Do not fully determine elements of task	
	Design tasks to encourage students to be confident of what they know and do not know	
	Integrate learning over time and courses through joint planning of assessment across modules	
5. Embodying reflexivity and commitment	Foster awareness of personal and professional practice	Edwards et al., 2002
	Establish a teaching and learning climate that fosters reflexivity	
	Involve portrayal of outcomes for different purposes	
	Leave students better equipped to complete future tasks	
	Involve portrayal of achievements to others (e.g., portfolio or patchwork text construction)	

Integration by students

No matter how well designed the course, or how co-operative those responsible for each unit, ultimately students are responsible for undertaking their own integration of the varieties of experience they encounter. There are clear signs that they recognise this need. Consolidation of learning occurs in modularised programmes through the use of final integrating capstone or keystone units. In these, the task for students is not the learning of new material but the interrelating of material from previous units into coherent forms through integrating essays and project activities. In addition, there are also new forms of assessment that work across course modules. The most developed example of the latter is the idea of patchwork assessment (Winter, 2003). In patchwork assessment, students take a variety of different assessment pieces from different units and weave them into a consolidated form that better represents the totality of their work than any one of the isolated pieces. The metaphor of patchwork illustrates that while, individually, any particular piece of assessment might not be able to be integrated elegantly with any other, when there are sufficient pieces, new patterns can be formed that represent outcomes beyond those represented in any one of the elements. The patchwork text can also make clear the role that context has in setting and assessing the extent to which standards have been met in different contexts (e.g., Rees and Preston, 2003). More common is the increasing use of portfolio approaches both for consolidating learning and for assessment purposes (Klenowski *et al.*, 2006).

What these approaches have in common is the bringing together of evidence of learning from a variety of sources combined with a reflective commentary. Sources may be limited to formal courses, but increasingly the drawing of material from all learning events is becoming more common. The role of these activities is for students to make sense of the often disparate events in which they have taken part for purposes of learning, assessment and practice and to draw from them both portrayals of achievement and indications of how they have been developing their judgement over time.

Conclusion

We now have considerable assessment resources on which to draw to help students develop their capacities for judgement across their courses and beyond. When we combine this with the well-established role of teaching to extend students we have the potential to make a major impact. The challenge is to deploy these resources well and to avoid the inadvertently fragmenting tendencies of many changes to higher education. If courses are seen to promote the development of judgement over time, it is an easier task to project this development into the future. Through practising judgement over a wider and more sophisticated range of activities, students can be equipped for what they need well beyond graduation.

References

Angelo, T.A. and Cross, K.P. (1993) *Classroom Assessment Techniques: A Handbook for College Teachers*, 2nd edn, San Francisco: Jossey-Bass.

Beck, U. (1992) *Risk Society*, London: Sage.

Biggs, J. (2003) *Teaching for Quality Learning at University*, 2nd edn, Buckingham: Society for Research into Higher Education and Open University Press.

Black, P. and Wiliam, D. (1998) Assessment and classroom learning, *Assessment in Education*, 5, 1: 7–74.

Bliss, J., Askew, M. and Macrae, S. (1996) Effective teaching and learning: scaffolding revisited, *Oxford Review of Education*, 22, 1: 37–61.

Boud, D. (1995) *Enhancing Learning through Self-Assessment*, London: Kogan Page.

Boud, D. and Falchikov, N. (2005) Redesigning assessment for learning beyond higher education, *Research and Development in Higher Education*, 28 [special issue ed. A. Brew and C. Asmar]: 34–41.

—— (2006) Aligning assessment with long-term learning, *Assessment and Evaluation in Higher Education*, 31, 4: 399–413.

Boud, D. and Solomon, N. (eds) (2001) *Work-Based Learning: A New Higher Education?*, Buckingham: Society for Research into Higher Education and Open University Press.

—— (2003) 'I don't think I am a learner': acts of naming learners at work, *Journal of Workplace Learning*, 15, 7–8: 326–331.

Boud, D., Cohen, R. and Sampson, J. (1999) Peer learning and assessment, *Assessment and Evaluation in Higher Education*, 24, 4: 413–426.

—— (eds) (2001) *Peer Learning in Higher Education: Learning from and with Each Other*, London: Kogan Page.

Bowden, J. and Marton, F. (1998) *The University of Learning: Beyond Quality and Competence in Higher Education*, London: Kogan Page.

Brew, A. (2006) *Research and Teaching: Beyond the Divide*, London: Palgrave Macmillan.

Butler, D.L. and Winne, P.H. (1995) Feedback and self-regulated learning: a theoretical synthesis, *Review of Educational Research*, 65, 3: 245–281.

Collins, A., Brown, J.S. and Holum, A. (1991) Cognitive apprenticeship: making things visible, *American Educator*, 6, 11: 38–46.

Dierick, S. and Dochy, F. (2001) New lines in edumetrics: new forms of assessment lead to new assessment criteria, *Studies in Educational Evaluation*, 27: 307–330.

Dochy, F. (2001) A new assessment era: different needs, new challenges, *Learning and Instruction*, 10, 1: 11–20.

Dreyfus, H.L. (2001) *On the Internet*, London: Routledge.

Dreyfus, H.L. and Dreyfus, S.E. (2005) Expertise in real world contexts, *Organization Studies*, 26, 5: 779–792.

Edwards, R., Ranson, S. and Strain, M. (2002) Reflexivity: towards a theory of lifelong learning, *International Journal of Lifelong Education*, 21, 6: 525–536.

Ewers, T. and Searby, M. (1997) Peer assessment in music, *New Academic*, 6, 2: 5–7.

Falchikov, N. (1996) Improving learning through critical peer feedback and reflection, *Higher Education Research and Development*, 19: 214–218.

—— (2001) *Learning Together: Peer Tutoring in Higher Education*, London: RoutledgeFalmer.

—— (2005) *Improving Assessment through Student Involvement*, London: RoutledgeFalmer.

Falchikov, N. and Boud, D. (forthcoming) The role of assessment in preparing for lifelong learning: problems and challenges, in A. Havnes, and L. McDowell (eds) *Balancing Dilemmas in Assessment and Learning in Contemporary Education*, New York: Routledge.

Giddens, A. (1991) *Modernity and Self-Identity: Self and Society in the Late Modern Age*, Cambridge: Polity Press.

Goldfinch, J., Laybourn, P., MacLeod, L. and Stewart, S. (1999) Improving groupworking skills in undergraduates through employer involvement, *Assessment and Evaluation in Higher Education*, 24, 1: 41–51.

Hogan, K. and Pressley, M. (1997) *Scaffolding Student Learning: Instructional Approaches and Issues*, Cambridge, MA: Brookline.

Hounsell, D. (1987) Essay writing and the quality of feedback, in J.T.E. Richardson *et al.* (eds) *Student Learning: Research in Education and Cognitive Psychology*, Milton Keynes: Open University Press.

—— (2003) Student feedback, learning and development, in M. Slowey and D. Watson (eds) *Higher Education and the Lifecourse*, Buckingham: Society for Research into Higher Education and Open University Press.

Jonassen, D.H., Peck, K.L. and Wilson, B.G. (1999) *Learning with Technology: A Constructivist Perspective*, Upper Saddle River, NJ: Merrill.

Kahnemann, D., Slovic, P. and Tversky, A. (1982) *Judgement under Uncertainty: Heuristics and Biases*, New York: Cambridge University Press.

Klenowski, V., Askew, S. and Carnell, E. (2006) Portfolios for learning, assessment and professional development in higher education, *Assessment and Evaluation in Higher Education*, 31, 3: 267–286.

Kvale, S. (2006) A workplace perspective on school assessment, paper presented at Workplace Learning SIG, Annual Conference of the American Educational Research Association, San Francisco, April.

Lave, J. and Wenger, E. (1991) *Situated Learning: Legitimate Peripheral Participation*, Cambridge: Cambridge University Press.

Mentkowski, M. and associates (2000) *Learning that Lasts: Integrating Learning, Development and Performance in College and Beyond*, San Francisco: Jossey-Bass.

Osborne, R.J. and Wittrock, M.C. (1983) Learning science: a generative process, *Science Education*, 67, 4: 489–508.

Pata, K., Sarapuu, T. and Lehitenen, E. (2005) Tutor scaffolding styles of dilemma solving in network-based role-play, *Learning and Instruction*, 15: 571–587.

Ramaprasad, A. (1983) On the definition of feedback, *Behavioral Science*, 28: 4–13.

Rees, B. and Preston, J. (2003) The international patchwork: introducing reflexivity into the business curriculum, *Innovations in Education and Teaching International*, 40, 2: 123–132.

Rømer, T.A. (2002) Situated learning and assessment, *Assessment and Evaluation in Higher Education*, 27, 3: 233–241.

Sadler, D.R. (1989) Formative assessment and the design of instructional systems, *Instructional Science*, 18: 119–144.

—— (1998) Formative assessment: revisiting the territory, *Assessment in Education*, 5, 1: 77–84.

Schwandt, T. (2005) On modelling our understanding of the practice fields, *Pedagogy, Culture and Society*, 13, 3: 313–332.

Seidel, T., Rimmele, R. and Prenzel, M. (2005) Clarity and coherence of lesson goals as a scaffold for student learning, *Learning and Instruction*, 15: 539–556.

Sfard, A. (1998) On two metaphors for learning and the dangers of choosing just one, *Educational Researcher*, 27, 2: 4–13.

Shulman, L.S. (2000) Teacher development: roles of domain expertise and pedagogical knowledge, *Journal of Applied Developmental Psychology*, 21, 1: 129–135.

Torrance, H. (ed.) (1995) *Evaluating Authentic Assessment: Problems and Possibilities in New Approaches to Assessment*, Buckingham: Open University Press.

Vygotsky, L.S. (1978) *Mind in Society: The Development of Higher Psychological Processes*, Cambridge, MA: Harvard University Press.

Wenger, E. (1998) *Communities of Practice: Learning, Meaning and Identity*, New York: Cambridge University Press.

Winter, R. (2003) Contextualising the patchwork text: addressing problems of coursework assessment in higher education, *Innovations in Education and Teaching International*, 40, 2: 112–122.

Woodward, H. (1998) Reflective journals and portfolios: learning through assessment, *Assessment and Evaluation in Higher Education*, 23, 4: 415–423.

Index

academic virtues 33
achievement: complex 79, 81, 82, 84; documenting and presenting claims 83; images of failure 44–5; public representation of 81; portrayal of 193
Adelman, C. 75, 85
affective dispositions 132, 134; learning outcomes 88, 138
Ainley, M. 145, 149, 154
Anderson, C. 109, 110
Anderson, J.B. 133, 140
Angelo, T.A. 185, 195
anger 146–7, 150
Angrosino, M. 163, 165
Antonacopoulou, E.P. 145, 146, 154
anxiety 65, 134, 146–7, 150, 153
apprenticeship 59, 129, 130, 135, 137, 189; learning 129–31, 135; model 130
Askew, M. 188, 192, 195
Askew, S. 106, 110, 194, 196
assessment: active student roles in 88; authentic 23, 36, 60, 66, 67, 68, 75, 83, 184; autobiographical accounts of experiences 147–53; backwash effect 21; careers 41, 51–3; censorship and construction of knowledge 63; combining and reconciling different purposes 178; consequences of 19, 21, 76, 144, 146; context of 9, 22, 182; contribution to learning 17; control instrument for economic accountability 69; criteria 16, 51,107, 132, 136, 137, 138, 139, 160, 163, 171, 172, 186, 189, 191, 192, negotiating 120; criterion-referenced 75, 78; culture 44, 47, 51, 88, 138; damaged by experience of 38; developing skills over time 193; discourse of 15–9, 22, 181; dispositions about 43; double duty 7, 41, 177; educational features of 21–3; effects of 89–96; emotion 144–55; engineering 87–100, 182; enquiry 138; excessive 17; fair 49; for accountability 67–9; for authentic being 39; for certification 4, 62–3, 134, 138; for discipline and control 63; for informing judgement, development of 181–97; for learning 18, 64, 67–8, contradictions of 57–71; in apprenticeship training 59–61; for longer-term learning 171–6; for selection 62–3; form of classification 36; high-stakes 4, 103; identities 41, 43–4; implications for design of programmes 190–4; in an age of uncertainty 29–30; in history of higher education 61–2; influences beyond graduation 21; involving students 9, 182; is process of forming a judgement 20; judgement 77–8; low-stakes 103, 107; measurement 139–8; need for 32–4; negative experiences of 149–51; negative student responses 94; norm-referenced 23, 75, 138; personal histories of 148; policy 7; positive experiences 148–9; post-assessment effect 95–6; pre-assessment effect 90, 91; preferences 94; previous experiences of 41; procedure 138; pure-assessment effect 91, 96; purposes 3–5, 57–71; reflection 120; reframing 14–25; responsibility 60; skills for future learning, scheme for developing 186–90; student involvement in 131; sustainable 7, 51–3, 101–13, 115, 123, 125, 167–80, 183; systems 42–3; task ladder of increased responsibility 60; through use 59; ungraded 75; visible 188

Improving Assessment through Student Involvement:
Practical solutions for aiding learning in higher
and further education

Nancy Falchikov
(University of Edinburgh)

The assessment of students is an activity central to the role of any
professional in further and higher education, and is an area that is the subject
of constant innovation and debate. This book provides a scholarly account
of the many facets of assessment, with a particular focus on student
involvement. Peer and self-assessment are powerful assessment tools to add
to the existing tutor-based methods of assessment and feedback, and this
book is a comprehensive guide to the methods and issues involved. Practical
and accessible in style, yet grounded in research and rich in evidence-based
material, *Improving Assessment Through Student Involvement* will be valued
by all FE or HE professionals wanting to enhance both the effectiveness and
quality of their assessment methods.

Hardback ISBN: 978–0–415–30820–5
Paperback ISBN: 978–0–415–30821–2
e-Book ISBN: 978–0–203–22099–3

Learning Together:
Peer tutoring in higher education

Nancy Falchikov
(University of Edinburgh)

The number of students in higher education has expanded dramatically in recent years, but funding has not kept pace with this growth. The result is less contact time for lecturers and their students, and corresponding worries about how the quality of teaching and learning can be improved. Peer tutoring is one method which is growing in popularity, and has already proved successful in a number of countries. This book provides an introduction to the methods and practice of peer tutoring focusing on how to set up schemes and how to cope with common problems. It discusses the theory behind this form of learning and the beneficial effects associated with it. Summaries are included at the end of each chapter.

Hardback ISBN: 978–0–415–18260–7
Paperback ISBN: 978–0–415–18261–4
e-Book ISBN: 978–0–203–45149–6

Peer Learning in Higher Education:
Learning from and with each other

Edited by David Boud, Ruth Cohen and Jane Sampson
(University of Technology, Sydney, Australia)

While peer learning is often used informally by students – and for many can
form an essential part of their HE experience – this book discusses methods
of developing more effective learning through the systematic implementation
of peer learning approaches.

Paperback ISBN: 978–0–7494–3612–4

The Challenge of Problem-based Learning

David Boud and Grahame Feletti

Problem-based learning is a way of constructing and teaching courses using problems as the stimulus and focus for student activity. This edition looks at the topic in the light of changes since the first edition (1991). There are new chapters on the impact of PBL, and inquiry and action learning.

Hardback ISBN: 978–0–7494–2291–2
Paperback ISBN: 978–0–7494–2560–9

Enhancing Learning through Self-assessment

David Boud
(University of Technology, Sydney, Australia)

Self-assessment is increasingly used in higher education as a strategy for
both student learning and assessment. This book examines the full range of
concerns about self-assessment, placing it in the wider context of innovative
teaching and learning practices.

Paperback ISBN: 978–0–7494–1368–2